Extremism, Ancient and Modern

Near Eastern archaeology is generally represented as a succession of empires with little attention paid to the individuals, labelled as terrorists at the time, that brought them down. Their stories, when viewed against the backdrop of current violent extremism in the Middle East, can provide a unique long-term perspective.

Extremism, Ancient and Modern brings long-forgotten pasts to bear on the narratives of radical groups today, recognizing the historical bases and specific cultural contexts for their highly charged ideologies. The author, with expertise in Middle Eastern archaeology and counter-terrorism work, provides a unique viewpoint on a relatively under-researched subject.

This timely volume will interest a wide readership, from undergraduate and graduate students of archaeology, history and politics, to a general audience with an interest in the deep historical narratives of extremism and their impact on today's political climate.

Sandra Scham is Adjunct Associate Professor of Archaeology and Anthropology at the Catholic University of America and a countering violent extremism specialist who works with USAID and the Department of State. She lived in the Middle East for over seven years, teaching and implementing Israeli–Arab exchange and peace-building projects. She is the Co-Editor of the *Journal of Eastern Mediterranean Archaeology and Heritage Studies*, served as Editor of *Near East Archaeology*, published by the American Schools of Oriental Research, and is a contributing editor to *Archaeology* magazine. She has taught courses on archaeology, politics and the heritage of the Middle East at the University of Maryland and Stanford University.

T0413632

Extremism, Ancient and Modern

Insurgency, Terror and Empire
in the Middle East

Sandra Scham

Routledge
Taylor & Francis Group

LONDON AND NEW YORK

First published 2018
by Routledge
2 Park Square, Milton Park, Abingdon, Oxon OX14 4RN

and by Routledge
711 Third Avenue, New York, NY 10017

Routledge is an imprint of the Taylor & Francis Group, an informa business

British Library Cataloguing-in-Publication Data
A catalogue record for this book is available from the British Library

Library of Congress Cataloging-in-Publication Data
A catalog record for this book has been requested

ISBN: 978-0-415-78840-3 (hbk)
ISBN: 978-0-415-78839-7 (pbk)
ISBN: 978-1-315-22532-6 (ebk)

Typeset in Bembo
by Deanta Global Publishing Services, Chennai, India

Contents

Acknowledgment

I wish to acknowledge the invaluable contributions of some very important individuals, not necessarily to this book—in which I do not purport to represent anyone's views except my own—but to my knowledge of the Middle East and its people. Ann Killebrew, without whom I would understand so much less about the Ancient Middle East than I do now, enabled me to experience Turkey, Israel and Palestine in a new way. I am also indebted, more than I can tell, to Ken Holum and Adel Yahya, peace be upon them both. Ken set me on the path of Middle East archaeology and Adel opened my eyes to the meaning of the past in the present.

I dedicate this book to them and to my husband, Paul, and my daughters, Petra and Anat.

Prologue
The Middle East and me

As a junior in high school, I heard Barry Goldwater's famous exposition that "extremism in defense of liberty is no vice" on television which, in that same year, was dubbed a "cool medium" by Marshall McLuhan (MacLuhan 1964).[1] Although it can be argued that television has "heated up" since that time, I watched it with the detachment of a young person who found politics boring. Nevertheless, I do remember that election in general because it was the first one in which my parents could vote. No, they weren't immigrants—we lived in the District of Columbia, capital of the nation—which, before that time, was inexplicably disenfranchised.

I later discovered that the anarchist Karl Hess, who once wrote admiringly about "men who suddenly tire of palaver and reach for the rifle on the wall" (Perlstein 2009: 315), penned this controversial speech. Apparently, it persuaded my father to vote for Goldwater, one of the few who did in that year of a historic election landslide, while my mother preferred Lyndon Johnson. I suppose that, using the same roundabout logic that is now applied by counterterrorism analysts, one might say that would make my father, who clearly responded to this narrative, a supporter of extremism (Hoffman 2006; Smith 1994). Because I witnessed what surely must have been the first time the word entered into the lexicon of modern American politics—in this case as a credo for a Republican nominee, later, the idea of associating extremism with religion seemed unusual. After all, I never thought of Barry Goldwater as religious and later read that he was even suspicious of religion.

After years of lecturing at university, I now understand that millennials have really experienced no other context for it and, despite the fact that President Obama demurred against associating extremism with "any one religion," invariably linked the word with Islam. Unlike those days when an agnostic Jewish-Episcopalian could run on the Republican ticket, now *all* candidates for high public office in the United States have to lay claim to piety, including the current President of the United States, whose life up to that point had been about as profane as one could imagine. He was quick to adopt at least one of the tenets of "old-time religion"—that is, regarding a designated "other" religion as the incarnation of evil. Growing up surrounded by Southern Baptists, I remember that our *bête noire* was Catholicism. Clearly, there was only one choice for Donald Trump. Islamism, a term I have tried scrupulously to avoid in this book since it conveys little beyond rank prejudice, is now back in government parlance.

It will quickly become apparent, if not from the title, then from the first paragraphs of this introduction, that this book, while written by an archaeologist, is not entirely about the ancient past. Further, it is not about the destruction of cultural heritage by extremists—something that should concern all of us but which I will leave to be addressed by others in my field. Rather, this book is about the meaning of cultural heritage, and more particularly, the narratives attached to it, to groups accused of extremist actions and the larger societies in which they live. Most of what I have learned about the Ancient Near Eastern past has been via the modern Middle Eastern present—a present that, for many in the West, unfortunately appears to be one of eternal conflict.

My interest in the earliest narratives that continue to motivate people in the region has been gestating for decades, but I think it would be useful in understanding the premise of this book to explain how I got to this point. The beginning of my involvement with the Middle East was in 1993 when, after years of overt conflagrations and covert contacts, Israeli Prime Minister Yitzhak Rabin and Jordan's King Hussein signed a peace treaty in Washington, DC. While it was the earlier Oslo Accords between Rabin and Yasser Arafat that garnered most of the news coverage, this was the event I had been waiting for.

If I had decided to work in any other region, I would scarcely have taken note of the whole process but a tangential consequence of this accord (to almost anyone else but me) was that, because of it, I could work in Jordan without having to obtain a new passport or omit my experience in Israel from my CV. Taking advantage of the situation as soon as we could, my husband and I landed at Queen Alia Airport in Amman in the summer of 1994, during the interregnum between Oslo I and Oslo II, to scope out sites for my subsequent fieldwork in Jordan. The border agent who looked at the Israeli stamps on our passport was visibly startled and ran to get his superior. The latter simply shrugged—a clear signal that it didn't matter anymore. My license to work there came through without a problem.

Rather than a gradual awakening, my comprehension of the political nature of the past was more of an epiphany—an experience not unknown to many visitors to the Holy Land. Although it was little more than a year after my first visit to Jordan when a "greater land of Israel" ideologue struck down Prime Minister Yitzhak Rabin as he departed a peace rally, it was not this climactic event that sparked a sudden realization of the fact that the past in the Middle East was a minefield. Rather, it came in the form of what was later described as the "Western Wall Tunnel Riots" of 1996. As I packed my bags to begin what became a six-year sojourn, the once and future Prime Minister Benjamin Netanyahu, under cover of night, elected to open an archaeological tunnel under the hill that is now graced by the Muslim Dome of the Rock (the spot from which Mohammed is believed to have ascended to heaven).

Palestinian Muslims, incensed by this intrusion under holy ground, protested vehemently and, for them, tragically. Eighty people were killed. This was the first such event to be described but, unfortunately, not the last. In subsequent years, archaeological excavations of tunnels under the Haram al-Sharif and consequent protests became a regular occurrence (Scham 1998). It was not merely the pretext that archaeology had provided for this surreptitious act that struck me as significant. Rather, it was the fact that the archaeologist responsible for opening the tunnel was described as expressing utter bewilderment over the furor that resulted from his actions. He believed, quite sincerely it seems, that he was simply making an important archaeological site accessible to the public (Ben-David 1996). Even I, political ingénue that I was, could have predicted the adverse consequences from this project but, by all appearances, he was completely oblivious to that possibility.

Despite all of these portents of the chaos to come, when I moved to the Middle East and began my archaeological career, it seemed to me to be an exhilarating time to be there, we were filled with hope. I began to work with several organizations involved in Jewish–Arab cooperation—which is probably just a synonym for consistently protesting actions by the Israeli government, beginning for me with the evacuation of the Jahalin Bedouin from the Judean and Negev Desert lands they had occupied for generations (see Chapter 4, this volume). I had the privilege to work with the late Dr. Adel Yahya, an archaeologist and champion of Palestinian heritage, who devoted his career to, among other things, documenting the oral histories of refugees and other Palestinians in the West Bank and Gaza, reviving traditional crafts and "peace tourism." In the Spring of 2000, we[2] applied for a grant under a United States Department of State program that was set up under the Wye River Accords—which famously produced no viable political outcomes.

Five months later, we received word that we had received the grant just as the Al-Aqsa Intifada was beginning. Two of the principal investigators of the project lived in Jerusalem and the third in Ramallah. In the midst of this turmoil, I had little time to think about whether what I was doing, teaching and supporting Israeli and Palestinian common heritage, was at all beneficial. The question that arose immediately was how we could possibly accomplish cooperative work on archaeological sites when Palestinians could not cross the border and the only way Israelis could go to the West Bank was in uniform, especially working under conditions of bombardments coming from both sides. We made plans initially to meet in Beit Hanina (a Palestinian area where those of us with American passports could go) and, later, we met, as it turned out, in Çatalhöyük and Istanbul in Turkey, Salt Lake City and Los Angeles in the United States and, four years later (finally) in Ramallah, Haifa and Akka/Akko (Scham 2003).

Meanwhile, everyone I knew in both Jerusalem and Palestine had a story of barely escaping destruction. My husband, whose office was at Hebrew University, claimed that because I had made breakfast one day (a rare event) he skipped lunch and was saved from being blown up in the cafeteria, which was across from his office. A friend's migraine had, similarly, saved me from a blast that took place in the café where we were to meet in Jerusalem. Yet, despite the frequent suicide bombings, the tragedy of this situation, as later became known, fell most heavily upon Palestinians who experienced over twice as many deaths. Violent Israeli reprisals in the West Bank, where I had been working on heritage projects accelerated and, while I did not personally know any of the Israelis who were killed or wounded by suicide bombers, I knew that the threat was a daily concern.

More frequently, I heard about the relatives of Palestinians we knew. A colleague whose nephew was gunned down in front of a hotel where we had stayed while working in Ramallah, a friend who quickly had to hang up the phone because she heard that the neighborhood where her sister lived was under attack by the Israeli Defense Forces, another colleague whose brother was killed, made it fairly clear to me that there was a dim future for cooperative projects. We sought the relative "safety" of the United States and returned home in the summer of 2001 and made the decision to stay for good in September.

As anyone reading this could have guessed, we discovered that month, in a dramatic way, that the conflict had followed us home and, in the process, had grown to global proportions. Later, when Osama Bin Laden offered an explanation about the events of 9/11 that after "we witnessed the oppression and tyranny of the American/Israeli coalition against our people in Palestine and Lebanon, it came to my mind" (Al Jazeera English 2004). The historical narratives, both ancient and recent, that we had been working on in the Middle East became the stuff of headlines.

Nevertheless, the media essentially told us nothing about the people who had been labeled as terrorists—their families, their beliefs or even *why* they embraced, in the words of Jameson, "history that hurts" as their cause. In Israel, it is taken as common knowledge that to explain extremist behavior is to justify it and to understand it is to accept it. My hopes that the broadranging multi-cultural society of the United States would be different were undoubtedly naive. If there is one thing that unites people in favor of an overly simplistic proposition it is an act of war. This had become a Manichaean struggle between the "sons of light and the sons of darkness," to borrow a phrase from one of the most famous archaeological finds in the world—the Dead Sea Scrolls (Crawford 2002).

From 2001 to 2002, my year of attempting not to live dangerously, with a newly minted Ph.D., I effectively began my academic career in America. Teaching can be an aggravating or an eye-opening experience—sometimes both at once when you're grading papers that defy all reason. After the events of 9/11, however, my students became more curious about the Middle East because it had become an unavoidable topic in the media. They wanted to know about terrorism and it became apparent to me that my anecdotes about living in Israel and Jordan were not particularly enlightening and, further, as I was teaching archaeology, perhaps not entirely relevant to what we were studying.

Prior to one class, however, I discovered online a particularly cogent insight into how violence connects the past and the present and why we should acknowledge rather than disavow it. In an interview published in 1999, the ever-controversial Camile Paglia complained that

> [t]here's something dangerously solipsistic about our young people. They know less and less about the world around them. They know less and less about history. Of course, that's my generation's influence: We wanted to give them an education that seemed relevant to their lives, but the end result is that their education is specious and empty.

Then she stated something about her students that I already knew from my own experience but had hesitated to bring to the classroom.

> They love learning about the destruction of ancient cultures—that's just the kind of horror they need. Destruction is an important theme of human experience, and they don't get it from their education, which is increasingly happy talk now. If they study the Aztecs, they learn that the Aztecs were a wonderful people, never mind the slaughter and the living hearts being torn out of chests.
>
> (Paglia 1999)

As subsequent discussions revealed, students in my class *had* received what Paglia dismissed in this same interview as a "sanitized" education. While they learn little about the means (mostly violent) to the ends of history, they have become habituated, perhaps by those ever-popular forensic television shows focusing on serial killers, to the idea that horrific violence is fictional, faraway, random, rare and, most of all, the product of severe psychosis or rampant irrational, perhaps even hallucinatory, belief. They would be as shocked by Arendt's observations about Eichmann that "[d]espite all the efforts of the prosecution, everybody could see that this man was not a 'monster,' but it was difficult indeed not to suspect that he was a clown" (Arendt 1964: 55), as people were when it was first published.

Since 2001, I have always asked students whether anything in their education had prepared them for understanding what was happening in the Middle East today. Assuming that they had experienced at least one history course, I wanted to know how much they knew about the fear that people, whether they are considered as freedom fighters or extremists, inflicted upon imperial, and later national, powers over the centuries but I also wanted to know if they had learned about why those people committed the acts. Remembering the relish with which I read about cultures that practiced human sacrifices and the Salem Witch Trials in school, I expected that these would be subjects today's students would also respond to. They do seem to learn about all of these things—but with a calculated dispassion. Similarly, while we anthropologists have long realized that it is possible for us to make a cultural study of even the worst human behaviors, few of us do it either very effectively or with much emotional engagement. Geertz's (1973) "thick description" of the Balinese cock fight from this standpoint, while unsparing in its details, is also a way of distancing himself from his own feelings about the brutality of the scene he is observing. Cultural anthropologists need to create cognitive constructs like this to divorce their emotions from the more appalling aspects of human behavior.

We archaeologists are not similarly challenged because the remnants of the past that we try to extract meaning are curiously silent about the impact of brute force. Even the proclivity of the Assyrians to decorate their palace dining rooms with carved images of flayed bodies does not outrage us. It is all part of that long ago that we have come to love. Assyriologists and Egyptologists seldom cast aspersions on the morality of their subjects. Thus, while artifacts may represent our scholarly connection to past cultures, they are also used to elide for us some of their more unsavory aspects. By this trick of consciousness, Sennacherib becomes far less ruthless than Al-Baghdadi and the symbols of his power far more important than most human lives. Instinctively, some groups accused of extremism know about this hypocrisy. The Taliban regime in Afghanistan may have first come to the world's attention by destroying an archaeological site and the Islamic State continues that tradition by destroying ancient sites in Iraq and Syria. Not only do these sites represent an alien culture to them, they also represent an "in-your-face" declaration to the West that "this is not the only aspect of our cultures that you should care about." Meskell, in examining the concept of "negative heritage," described how one Taliban representative explained the destruction of the Bamiyan Buddhas as a "reaction of rage after a foreign delegation offered money to preserve the ancient works at a time when a million Afghans faced starvation" (Meskell 2002: 563).

These are the crimes that archaeologists remember most, conveniently blotting out the significance of the deaths of over a million people, mainly because we want to love our specimen cultures and our "complex" sites. Because of this, we are reluctant to put our considerable analytical skills to work in investigating repellent human actions. The actions of people claiming fealty to religious leaders, bookended for people in the United States by the Al Qaeda attack of 9/11 and by the rise of the Islamic State around a decade later, have eluded the efforts of historians who characterize these events as caption history. "What Went Wrong?" (Lewis 2002), "Clash of Civilizations" (Huntington 1996), "Jihad Versus McWorld" (Barber 1995) and a more recent entry "The ISIS Apocalypse" (McCants 2015—the author is, interestingly, a student of the Ancient Near East) all suggest that the history of this region has been given a leg up from generalized conceptual threat to a highly organized virtual threat. Despite the fears of terrorist attacks in the West that all of these titles stoke, it is casualties *in* the Middle East rather than those inflicted by people *from* the region, that have mounted. Civilization Clash Autumn may have given way to Arab Spring, but those revolutions devolved, with almost lightning speed, into winter. Even as countries in the Middle East and North Africa brought down old regimes—new autocrats, or grueling civil war, rose up to replace them. American and European "negotiators" are again engaged in dividing up the Middle East to achieve "peace and stability" without consulting any of the people who will be most affected.

The impulse to explain the still repeating pattern of empire-insurgency-new empire in the Middle East by referencing its ancient past is hard to ignore. In reading the newspapers, I am immediately struck by the extent to which events in the modern world contain vestiges of the ancient one. Suicide bombers who speak of the Biblical Samson as a model, the anthem of a so-called terrorist group that declares "we are the children of the Medes," the enticing prospect of restoring the glory that was Al-Andalus and the need to re-establish an Israelite frontier for which little or no evidence exists are real connections to a world that existed long before the appearance of any modern nation-state.

The antagonism between the desert and the sown that probably developed in prehistory persists today in Egyptian and Israeli attitudes toward the Bedouin. The denigration of mountain dwellers by lowlanders, beginning with the Sumerians of the Bronze Age, is another theme that finds expression in the treatment of the Kurds by several nation states in the Middle East. The dread of invasion by "sea peoples" alternately characterized as refugees and aggressors, seen in the annals of New Kingdom Egypt, is being acted out today against Palestinians and Syrians. International ignorance about Yemen, with its history of fiercely independent northern tribal groups, has resulted in a gross mischaracterization of the grievances that brought the Huthis to rebel against their central government. The ancestors of those same groups successfully defied the authority of Christian overlords in the Arabian Peninsula in the sixth and seventh centuries. Jewish radicalism, which has grown exponentially since we left Israel, is a direct product of narratives of ancient Jewish nationhood stretching back for three millennia that have formed the core ideology for Israel's claims to all of the land held by their ancient ancestors.

The selection of these groups for the analyses presented here is a highly idiosyncratic one. All the modern groups discussed are those that I have had some direct or indirect experience of through living in, or visiting, the countries from which they came. The ancient groups are those that I have studied in connection with a decades-long career in Middle Eastern archaeology. It is my premise that there are lesser known and acknowledged cultures and civilizations that influence today's resistance movements than the oft-cited examples. In this age of searching for genealogies, both biological and historical, some of the connections made in these pages will strike many as tenuous. These are invented traditions in many cases, but the links are representative of "real virtuality" where the message *is* the message (Castells 1996: 368).

Now it is not just academics who are interested in the representations of the past in the present. Under the mistaken notion that history repeats rather than echoes, Western governments have taken an interest in historical narratives or, as the United States Military phrases it, "insurgent archetypes" (Joint Chiefs of Staff 2013: 5). As an anthropologist working in international development with a long-standing interest in historical narratives, I have worked for the U.S. Department of State on countering violent extremism and found it to be merely a growth industry with a unique self-perpetuating business model. This unlikely pairing of my expertise on the ancient past with projects that deal with what seems to be the most immediate issue of the twenty-first century was also a singularly frustrating experience. The "why" of violent action seldom surfaced in these investigations, which concentrated on "radicalization models." Performing deep cultural research is clearly not a priority of counter-terrorism analysts.

Whether Western governments want to know about the past or the present of violent extremism, the latter is, like any historical phenomenon, partially the product of narratives. Although these narratives may be based upon bygone glories, another less celebrated but, nevertheless, powerful element in this mythic past is marginalization that is centuries, perhaps even millennia, old. The relationship between Middle Eastern archaeology (or Ancient Near Eastern archaeology) and modern events is a close one. Imperial domination has been the mainstay of curricula on this subject for decade. Even currently used textbooks (Richard 2012; Sasson 1995; Gates 2011; Cline 2013) reference the imperial periods in discussing the past of the region. Critical perspectives such as the volumes edited by Pollock and Bernbeck (2004) and Meskell (1995), as well as Silberman's many articles and books (2001, 2007, 1997, etc.) seldom reach classrooms or are simply sampled as auxiliary texts to the more traditional surveys. This book will not be likely to change that situation, as it is not a chronological presentation of the region.

This book examines the deep historical narratives of extremism in the Middle East through the approach of critical discourse analysis within the framework of White's (1984; 2009a) views on narratives and Galtung's theories on structural and cultural violence (Galtung 1990), combined with auto-ethnography. For the purposes of this discussion, both White and Galtung have flaws. Galtung's work is powerful but simplistic and White, despite the fact that his *Metahistory* (1973) has been hailed as the most influential book on the philosophy of history published in the twentieth century four decades later, is consistently disregarded by historians (Pihlainen 2017). I have seen both Galtung's and White's work used by archaeologists (Bernbeck 2008; Hodder 1993) in the past twenty years, however, and this has stimulated me to rethink what both could contribute to the archaeology of narratives.

Galtung, in one sense, seems an unusual choice for this discussion. His views of structural violence, while interesting, do not seem to me to lead anywhere beyond the usual "catalogue of grievances" approach to looking at extremism—but his lesser known work on cultural violence is actually of great use in this regard. As Deitler has noted, archaeology provides the "symbolic hardware" for many constructions of the past (Dietler 1994: 597) and symbols of cultural violence are burdened with intense emotions in the Middle Eastern past and present.

With White, there seems to be no need to discuss how his work relates to narrativity—he has written great a deal about it and, while no one could describe his work as absolutely clear on any subject, it is considerably more transparent on this topic than it is on many others. I find his interest in narrative poetic structures to be a good starting point for my own examination of narratives. This literary approach is part of what critics of postmodern historians dislike most about White's work, but it has great appeal to me for two reasons: (1) I studied poetry before I studied archaeology—and before I realized that poetry is more evocative of the past than history; and (2) while the Middle East has had a number of great historians, chiefly in the medieval period, the story of its peoples in antiquity has been best told in the poetry of the Bedouin, the Ancient Egyptians, the Babylonians, the poets of Islamic and pre-Islamic Arabia and, last but not least, the Bible. As readers will note in the following chapters, I make frequent use of this poetry to capsulize the narratives discussed. In the world of literary theory, White may have become dated (Letzler 2012), but archaeologists are often the last to arrive at the party and seem to have been slowly discovering him (Lesure 2015).

Another argument for employing White's work is that, despite the sometimes off-putting discursive nature of *Metahistory,* he is a categorizer and neatly (perhaps too neatly) pulls in the threads of theoretical literature on narrative to form a more patterned approach. This, in fact, may be his primary appeal to archaeologists who are, as is probably evident, very much given (still) to ordering things into groups. I have embraced White's notion of emplotment, in particular, in classifying the narratives in this book because narratives have become an obsession for analysts of extremism. Here, I realize, I am indebted to Ricoeur (1990), who visualized all narratives as emplotted (Ahumada 2015) and, going even further back, to Vico (Paul 2011). White's categorization (again the classificatory obsession) of emplotments has been brought much to my mind as I have perused the counter-terrorism and counter-insurgency literature on narratives and ideology that does not very convincingly connect the two. It is my contention here that examining the romantic aspects of resistance or the tragedy of martyrdom and marginalization, within this connecting framework, can provide a greater understanding of these narratives.

Most of all, I appreciate the fact that it is White's view of narratives that has provided the opening for a discussion of the narratives of disenfranchised peoples. Much of his moral discourse on this subject has been shaped by Benjamin's work (Benjamin 1940, trans. 2005) on the "anonymous and the neglected of history," as White describes it, and the "critique of professional historiography's identification with history's 'victors,' interest primarily in the actions of great men, and association with centers of power and patronage" (White 2009b). Since this book is, most of all, an exploration of the narratives of the disenfranchised as represented in inscriptions, newspaper articles, speeches and other texts, it must examine the cultures of inequality and power. As a side issue, but one of some importance today, Chapters 1 and 2 discuss the treatment of narratives (and the limitations thereof) in counter-terrorism literature and what this research might gain from a broader perspective on narrativity. Finally, in this book, I explore all of these through the medium of material culture. So, in a sense, what is intended here is a kind of forensic examination of extremism in the past as an analogy for the present.

The argument that concentrating on conflict in the archaeological and historical record of the Middle East is a distortion of its past has some validity. It is a stereotype that glosses over centuries of peaceful co-existence. I do agree with Paglia's words that "[d]estruction is an important theme of human experience," (Paglia 1999) but, of course, that is not intended to provide a carte blanche for making it the only theme of anyone's history. Partly, this focus on extremism is due to the nature of Ancient Near Eastern texts. The texts (including the Biblical ones) are the bullies that must be reckoned with in Middle East archaeology for they remain the basis for determining how a site is named, how it is reported, how it is to be excavated and what happens to it after excavation. Nonetheless, much as I would like to blame all of these things for my concentration on violence, I can see that, looking back, I have had an uncommonly strong interest in conflict throughout my life. I am not, however, interested in conventional war but rather in those unexpected political attacks committed by groups of outraged individuals that are always characterized as "senseless violence." It is my belief that there may not be a logic but there is always a sense.

The Middle East is, undeniably, a region where humankind flourished, innovated, philosophized and pushed civilization forward. It is also a region that has, since prehistory, been the main stage for multiple historical re-enactments of extremism, resistance and imperialism. It is a puerile, but nonetheless true, observation that violent upheaval and human invention are not strangers to each other so perhaps it is some comfort, after all, to view alarming events through the lens of the *longue durée* (Braudel 2009). With that said, I should with candor note that the "universalist" extremist messaging about the Islamic caliphates that has captured so much attention in recent years is largely omitted from this discussion.

I have also purposely omitted any discussion of extremist online would-be warriors in the West, most of whom are remarkably ignorant of their heritage, who have been recruited to lay down their lives for … whatever. One might note an absence of exponents of the Christian religion among these narratives. While there have certainly been Christian extremists in the Middle East, primarily among the Crusaders, Christianity is, as many have been sad to note, no longer represented by significant numbers of people in Middle Eastern countries. Western Christian fundamentalists who want to fight for every inch of the Holy Land "down to the last Israeli," as a colleague of mine used to say, are also not the kind of people I am interested in here as others have discussed them in great detail (see Gorenberg 2002). They certainly have quite a say in the politics of the region but they are not native to it.

Archaeologists essentially get their knowledge from fieldwork—from being on site to find answers. Therefore, the militant movements I am primarily interested in are the rooted ones[3]—both in and of the land where they began and where they will doubtless end in one fashion or another. The peoples, both ancient and modern, described here have one thing in common—and it is not religious ideology. Rather, these are movements spawned in the wake of a moment of insight of "being conscious of themselves as prisoners in their own land" (Said 1994: 214). Thus, it is most of all the sense that, even though they have been made to feel like strangers, they can look out upon the places where their putative ancestors lived and still think, *"this* is ours."

Notes

1 MacLuhan was possibly one of the most influential public intellectuals of the sixties and seventies and a "founding father" of media studies.
2 The official grantees were the University of Haifa and the Palestinian Association for Cultural Exchange. The principal investigators in addition to myself were Ann Killebrew, Professor of Classics and Mediterranean Studies, Pennsylvania State University and the late Adel Yahya, Director of the Palestinian Association for Cultural Exchange.
3 In a sense this is the flip side of what Kwame Appiah has called "rooted cosmopolitan-ism" (Appiah 1997, 2005).

Bibliography

Ahumada, M. 2015. Framing Moral Sensitivity as Perception in *Developing Moral Sensitivity* (D. Mower and W. Robison, eds.), pp. 113–130. London and New York: Routledge.

Al Jazeera English. 2004. Full Text of Bin Laden Speech. Retrieved from: www.aljazeera.com/archive/2004/11/200849163336457223.html.

Appiah, K. 1997. Cosmopolitan Patriots. *Critical Inquiry* 23/3: 617–639.

Appiah, K. 2005. *The Ethics of Identity: A Rooted Cosmopolitan.* Princeton NJ: Princeton University Press.

Arendt, H. 1964. *Eichmann in Jerusalem: A Report on the Banality of Evil.* New York: The Viking Press.

Barber, B. 1995. *Jihad Versus McWorld: How Globalism and Tribalism Are Reshaping the World.* New York: New York Times Book.

Ben-David, C. 1996. Archaeologists Lament Government's Handling of Tunnel Furor. *Jerusalem Report* 7/12: 16.

Benjamin, W. 1940. *On the Concept of History.* Trans. 2005 by Dennis Redmond. Retrieved from: www.marxists.org/reference/archive/benjamin/1940/history.htm.

Bernbeck, R. 2008. Structural Violence in Archaeology. *Archaeologies* 4/3: 390–412.

Braudel, R. 2009. *History and the Social Sciences: The Longue Durée,* trans. by Immanuel Wallerstein. *Review* 32/2: 171–203.

Castells, M. 1996. *The Rise of the Network Society: The Information Age: Economy, Society, and Culture, Volume I.* Oxford: Blackwell Publishers.

Cline, E. 2013. *Biblical Archaeology: A Very Short Introduction.* Oxford: Oxford University Press.

Crawford, S. 2002. The Dead Sea Scrolls: Retrospective and Prospective. *Near Eastern Archaeology* 65/1: 81–86.

Dietler, M. 1994. 'Our Ancestors the Gauls:' Archaeology, Ethnic Nationalism, and the Manipulation of Celtic Identity in Modern Europe. *American Anthropologist* 96/3: 584–605.

Galtung, J. 1990. Cultural Violence. *Journal of Peace Research* 27/3: 291–305.

Gates, C. *Ancient Cities: The Archaeology of Urban Life in the Ancient Near East and Egypt, Greece and Rome* (2nd Ed.). London: Routledge.

Geertz, C. 1973. *The Interpretation of Cultures: Selected Essays.* New York: Basic Books.

Gorenberg, G. 2002. *The End of Days: Fundamentalism and the Struggle for the Temple Mount.* Oxford: Oxford University Press.

Hodder, I. 1993. The Narrative and Rhetoric of Material Culture Sequences. *World Archaeology* 25/2: 268–282.

Hoffman, B. 2006. *Inside Terrorism.* New York: Columbia University Press.

Huntington, S. 1996. The *Clash of Civilizations? The Debate.* New York: Simon and Schuster.

Joint Chiefs of Staff. 2013. *Counterinsurgency.* Retrieved from: www.dtic.mil/doctrine/new_pubs/jp3_24.pdf.

Lesure, R. 2015. Emplotment as Epic in Archaeological Writing: The Site Monograph as Narrative. *Norwegian Archaeological Review* 48/2: 57–74.

Letzler, D. 2012. Review of American Postmodernist Fiction and the Past, by Theophilus Savvas (2011). *Orbit: A Journal of American Literature* 1/2.

Lewis B. 2002. *What Went Wrong? Western Impact and Middle Eastern Response.* Oxford: Oxford University Press.

MacLuhan, M. 1964. *Understanding Media: The Extensions of Man.* New York: Signet Books.

McCants, W. 2015. *The ISIS Apocalypse: The History, Strategy, and Doomsday Vision of the Islamic State.* New York: MacMillan Press.

Meskell, L. 1995. *Archaeology Under Fire: Nationalism, Politics and Heritage in the Eastern Mediterranean and Middle East.* London: Routledge.

Meskell, L. 2002. Negative Heritage and Past Mastering in Archaeology. *Anthropological Quarterly* 75/3: 557–574.

Paglia, C. 1999. Why School? Interview with Ingrid Sischy. Retrieved from: www.geocities.ws/covermeinjoy/nadasurf2.htm.

Paul, H. 2011. *Hayden White.* London: Polity Press.

Perlstein, R. 2009. *Before the Storm: Barry Goldwater and the Unmaking of the American Consensus.* New York: Nation Books.

Pihlainen, K. 2017. *The Work of History: Hayden White and the Politics of Narrative Construction.* Routledge Approaches to History. London: Routledge.

Pollock, S. and R. Bernbeck (eds.). 2004. *Archaeologies of the Middle East: Critical Perspectives.* Hoboken: Wiley-Blackwell.

Richard, S. (ed.). 2012. *Near Eastern Archaeology: A Reader.* Winona Lake, IN: Eisenbrauns.

Ricoeur, P. 1990. *Time and Narrative, Volume 1.* Chicago, IL: University of Chicago Press.

Robins, G. 2015. Gender and Sexuality in *A Companion to Ancient Egyptian Art* (M. Hartwig, ed.), pp. 120–140. London: Wiley-Blackwell.

Said, E. 1994. *Culture and Imperialism.* New York: Vintage Books.

Sasson, J. M. ed. (1995). *Civilizations of the Ancient Near East.* Vols. 1–4. New York: Scribner.

Scham, S. 1998. Mediating Nationalism in Archaeology. *American Anthropologist* 100/2: 301–308.

Scham, S. and A. Yahya 2003. Heritage and Reconciliation. *Journal of Social Archaeology* 3/3: 399–416.

Silberman, N. 1982. *Digging for God and Country: Archaeology, Exploration, and the Secret Struggle for the Holy Land, 1799–1917.* Sheffield: Sheffield Academic Press.

Silberman, N. 1997. *The Archaeology of Israel: Constructing the Present, Interpreting the Past.* New York: Alfred A. Knopf.

Silberman, N. 2001. If I Forget Thee, O Jerusalem: Archaeology, Religious Commemoration, and Nationalism in a Disputed City, 1801–2001. *Nations and Nationalism* 7/4: 487–504.

Silberman, N. 2007. Two Archaeologies. *Near Eastern Archaeology* 70/1: 10–13.

Smith, B. 1994. *Terrorism in America: Pipe Bombs and Pipe Dreams.* Albany, NY: State University of New York.

Smith, B. 2006. *Terrorism in America: Pipe Bombs and Pipe Dreams.* New York: Columbia University Press.

White, H. 1984. Question of Narrative in Contemporary Historical Theory. *History and Theory* 23/1: 1–33.

White, H. 1973. *Metahistory: The Historical Imagination in Nineteenth-Century Europe.* Baltimore, MD: Johns Hopkins University Press.

White, H. 2009a. *Postmodernism and Historiography.* Special Public Opening Symposium. Kyoto: Ritsumeikan University. Retrieved from: http://www.ritsumei.ac.jp/acd/gr/gsce/news/200901022_repo_0-e.htm.

White, H. 2009b. *The Content of the Form: Narrative Discourse and Historical Representation.* Baltimore, MD: Johns Hopkins University Press.

Wilkinson, T. 2016. *Writings from Ancient Egypt.* London: Penguin Classics.

Section 1

Narrativity, agency and emplotment

1 The Passion will play

Narrativity and resistance

> The compelling aspect of the narrative is not only in its content, but how it is presented (i.e., promoted and publicized) to the target audience, which normally requires ideological leaders. It is consistently reinforced through communication and through propaganda of the deed.
>
> (Joint Chiefs of Staff 2013: 3–24)

> What else could narrative closure consist of than the passage from one moral order to another?
>
> (White 1980: 26)

The Oberammergau Passion Play has descended upon that otherwise peaceful and devout town in Bavaria every ten years with the regularity of a cicada invasion. The only such production to survive at least two attempts by the Catholic Church to eradicate it as anachronistic, the play is both famous and notorious. It was a favorite of Adolf Hitler's in its original, and clearly anti-Semitic, form and it is also considered as a stimulus for any number of historical riots in which Jews were regularly subjected to pillage and slaughter. Recent attempts to tone down the play's more incendiary aspects have received a guarded imprimatur from the leaders of international Jewish organizations who, for understandable reasons, remain suspicious of these productions (Wetmore 2017).

Nevertheless, the production has worldwide fame and perhaps influenced other such productions. In the nineteenth century, for example, Iran adopted a similarly dramatic means to depict the persecution and death of the founder of their state religion. The Passion Play in its present form, does little more than reiterate the synoptic gospels. Yet, it is still considered by many to represent the archetype for Christian narratives of intolerance, a persistent source of Jewish discomfort with European culture, and, lastly, a painful milestone on the way to the founding of the State of Israel, in other words, a "repository of negative memory in the collective imaginary" (Meskell 2002: 558). Judaism, Islam and Christianity, and the legacy of the Holocaust and the Crusades, seem to continually collide and reverberate in the performance of this historical ritual. The drama commemorates miraculous events but persecution is at its heart.

The finite nature of providence, rather than a desire for retribution, is what seems to have continually propelled the progression from celebration to devastation. To be benevolent to us, God must be malevolent to others—a belief that only the Jewish Bible seems, ironically, to confirm. Historically rooted in a competition of religious interests that originated in the Middle East and was transplanted to European soil, the Passion Play is fueled by the same fervor that impelled Crusaders to unsuccessfully try to "take back" a Holy Land they never really knew. And still, the would-be passion players of the Middle East, historically characterized by Western governments as Saracens, extremists, terrorists and insurgents, haunt the stages of conflicts past looking for inspiration, justification or simply a reason to continue the drama. *Die Passion zahlt* [the Passion will pay for it] people like to say in Oberammergau, usually in reference to town expenditures (*Time* 1980), but the passion also exacts payment in return. That payment, for many, constitutes a forfeiture of any hope for rapprochement.

Tangential connections with the Middle East aside, it is not surprising that the Passion Play has come readily to the minds of other scholars in describing archaeology and archaeological sites in the Middle East. Silberman has called the ruins of Masada "an elaborate and persuasive stage scenery for a modern Passion Play of national rebirth" (Silberman 1989: 88). Parsing the term, Hodder has explored two different kinds of engagement with the past, on the one hand, it is "highly commercial and disinterested—the past as play, the Orient as theme park," while, on the other, it is "motivated by specifically highly charged interests." "But," he continues, "passion and play are not opposed in some simple opposition. In the global process, they interact and feed off each other in myriad ways, equally emboldening and undermining the other" (1998: 138).

As archaeologists, our imagination of agency is often that of placing actors willy-nilly on the stage of the past. Hodder's detachment as an interpreter of Catalhöyük, a site that extends far back into unremembered time, is a logical (even necessary) scholarly position, as any individual claims or associations regarding the site compete more in the realm of ownership than ideology. While there is excitement, akin to passion, in his employment of "thick description" (Hodder 1998: 124) in looking at contending perspectives, the emotion is tied to the material culture and not to the agents that created it. Silberman's seemingly unpopulated (or rather depopulated) performance at Masada also suggests a distance between individuals past and present and their historical dramas. Most assuredly, the past in the Middle East is theater; entertaining theater that has great relevance to the religions and cultures of the present, but when the actors rather than the play are the thing, the theater of the past is more open to interpretation than ever before—a prospect that is at once both stimulating and daunting.

Analysts of terrorism in the Middle East also commonly employ the metaphor of the Passion Play. One such writer describes Sayyid Qutb's suffering in prison as representing a "passion play for Islamic Fundamentalists" (Wright 2016: 13). Another counter-terrorism specialist, interviewed by ABC News, describes his work as "a bit part in an international passion play that the whole world was watching" (Ferran 2015). Further, while theatre, as those in the West know it, is not a part of Islamic culture, there is a very near relative to the Passion Play performed by Shi'a every year in the Middle East to commemorate the tragic murder of Husayn ibn Ali, the grandson of Muhammad and his third successor (Lee 2014). The Passion Play encompasses many meanings that bear a strong relationship to the narratives that inform the intransigent positions of Western nation-states and Middle Eastern disenfranchised groups alike.

As indicated by the excerpt at the beginning of this chapter, the United States Military, one of the chief players in this drama, has a strong interest in those narratives—and, most particularly, in developing a compelling counter-narrative to violent extremism (Corman 2011). The mechanism by which this might be accomplished is seldom described and, given the superficial nature of the counter-terrorism analyses it would be based on, it is doubtful that any interested party would benefit from further explication. The advice of the American Military on this subject is succinct, i.e., "[s]ervice forces should receive appropriate cultural awareness training before joining specific COIN operations." Such awareness, should it arise, will, according to the Counterinsurgency Manual, enable the creation of a counterinsurgency message (the "COIN narrative") that "overshadows and counters the insurgents' narrative and propaganda." This narrative, the American Military envisions, has to be "culturally authentic" and has to "appeal to a wider audience, yet must be shaped and adapted to appeal to the cultural perspective of the population" (Joint Chiefs of Staff 2013: I-7). A suitable illustration accompanies this advice showing that the narrative requires "opportunity, motive and means" in order to lead to action—thus suggesting that the narrative can be short-circuited by addressing those three items. The origin of the narrative, according to this diagram, is the reframing of "core grievances" by "leaders" of uncertain origin.

Counter-terrorism and counter-insurgency specialists are particularly fond of the word grievance because it both trivializes the causes of violent extremism and absolves governments of any responsibility to redress them. A grievance is not the same as an injustice. An injustice cries out for correction, at least to Western minds, a grievance may or may not be valid. Further, none of the theorists that have deeply examined narrative formation would recognize the military's flowchart as a roadmap to cultural understanding. Rather, they see narrative as a universal canon of belief arising from a complex tapestry of the past and present in a specific cultural context. Even the functionalist Malinowski characterized the narrative process in suitably lyrical terms as one where "immediate history, semi-historic legend and unmixed myth flow into one another" and "form a continuous sequence" (1954: 126).

A similar notion of putting the real and the imaginary on equal footing in narrativity has also occurred to Hayden White (1980). Narratives mediate and resolve conflicting claims of the real and the imaginary, according to White, and by examining them in that light, "we begin to comprehend both the appeal of narrative and the grounds for refusing it." That appeal rests in both the inherent claim of a truth represented by the narrative and the beliefs of those who accept it as true. Influential narratives do not flow from the minds of grievance synthesizers. Similarly, the mechanistic production of a "culturally authentic counter narrative" will neither overshadow nor short circuit their attraction. Narratives do not have to be objectively true, in fact they almost never are, and therefore cannot be proven false.

Foucault proposes that the term archaeology, which emphasizes ruptures and discontinuities over continuities, traditions and categorizations, is a less restrictive term than "history" with its narrative compulsion (Foucault 1972). For White, the "archaeology of ideas" "forms a fugal counterpoint to the 'history' of ideas; it is the synchronic antithesis of the compulsively diachronic representation of the phases through which formalized consciousness has passed" (White 1978: 239). Narrative, for White, is the means of translating knowing into telling (White 1980) and resolves "the problem of fashioning human experience into a form assimilable to structures of meaning that are generally human rather than culture-specific. We may not be able fully to comprehend specific thought patterns of another culture, but we have relatively less difficulty understanding a story coming from another culture, however exotic that culture may appear to us" (White 1980: 5).

White offers a more persuasive analysis of how narrative replacement can happen. "Moving on" from an old narrative to a new one, he suggests, necessarily involves the establishment of a new moral order. Essentially, White believes that history, as narrative, is still a story with a beginning, middle and end—and, like many stories, it has a moral attached to it—a moral that signals a shifting "by narrative means" of significances, "from one physical or social space to another" (White 1980: 26) rather than an actual ending to real events. White cannot envision a story of the past that does not include some kind of moral judgment. "Could we ever narrativize without moralizing?" (White 1980: 27) he asks, with the implication being that simply applying terms such as "terrorist," "extremist" or "radical" to narratives is a pointless exercise if one truly wants to understand them. Everyone in the culture from which powerful narratives emanate has a stake in authenticating and promulgating them—or rejecting them entirely. In either case, it is their own moral order that is at stake, if one accepts White's pronouncement that "a refusal of narrative indicates an absence or refusal of meaning itself" (White 1980: 6).

In the context of the ancient world, narrativity has had a greater appeal to art historians than to historians and Hayden White's "linguistic turn" has been looked upon as a dangerous curve for those accustomed to more straightforward approaches to the past. But art is not uncomplicated history—nor is it meant to convey a complete story in the absence of explanatory written text. In this respect, Winter (2010) has observed the difficulty in deriving narratives from ancient art because such material culture tends to be "allusive" rather than explicit. She cites the traditional Ancient Near Eastern device of pictorially telling a story only in the culminating scene or solely through reference to things that stand for the concepts being conveyed.

This art is exemplary of Ancient Near Eastern insurgencies that are successful in achieving their ends, specifically the empires of Mesopotamia, Arabia and the Levant, which appeared suddenly and where succession was, to say the least, irregular—in some instances characterized by assassination following assassination and, in others, simply an arbitrarily successful power grab (Knapp 2015). Not surprisingly, many of these narratives contain elements of heroic resistance overpowering corrupt authority. Significantly, they are less characteristic of Ancient Egypt, which has a long history of formalized and central government in spite of many attempts to devolve power to regional entities (Derricourt 2015; Wilkinson 2016).

Reflexivity, that concept that had seemed to have so much relevance when I studied it in my method and theory class, seems a poorly fashioned tool of the trade when one is confronted with another that, in some ways, has consistently challenged and captured the Western imagination. I have no wish to join the long line of Orientalists working in Middle East archaeology who became so enamored of the region that they audaciously took upon themselves an identity constructed from what they believed to be its essence (Scham 2009). But reflexivity in all its aspects is not to be denied as a fitting approach to the burden of two histories (and many more as well) imposed upon those of us who work in the Middle East. The deeper meaning of the term serves to highlight the inescapable fact that generations of anthropological participant-observers have tried to ignore:

> [T]he ethnographer is so thoroughly implicated in the phenomena that he or she documents, that there can be no disengaged observation of a social scene that exists in a "state of nature" independent of the observer's presence. In other words, "the ethnography" is a product of the interaction between the ethnographer and a social world.
>
> (Atkinson 2006: 402)

This is the reflexivity that informs autoethnography.

Although the old school condemns it as "narcissistic and over-indulgent," autoethnography serves an important purpose in challenging the unconscious approach to culture as performance art taken by a number of ethnographers in the past. In the words of one proponent, "autoethnography seeks to describe and systematically analyze personal experience in order to understand cultural experience ... thus, as a method, auto-ethnography is both process and product" (Ellis 2010). Clifford Geertz has to be acknowledged here as the source, if not the progenitor of this view of ethnography is an "interpretive" science. "[T]here are three characteristics of ethnographic description:" he pronounces, "it is interpretive; what it is interpretive of is the flow of social discourse; and the interpreting involved consists in trying to rescue the 'said' of such discourse from its perishing occasions and fix it in perusable terms" (Geertz 1973: 21).

All of this may imply that I will make no pretense of neutrality—an implication that in this instance is accurate. Neutrality is the "stance of heartbreak" as one observer of the Modern Middle East has said (Monk 1999) and while that writer may have thought that he achieved it after much struggling, I haven't even tried. As difficult as it is for me to make a pretense of objectivity in my approach to any of these narratives, it is even more difficult to expurgate from the following chapters the series of experiences that I had while living and working in the Middle East that informed my work far more than any project, class or curriculum. In every sense, I "got schooled" while working in the region and, in particular, in those precise moments where I felt I was most lacking in understanding about what was happening around me.

Another theoretical construct that informs this work, as noted in the introduction, is Galtung's theory of structural and cultural violence. Using the autoethnographic approach right off the bat, I will here have to state my view that it is not without some apprehension about the controversy that has surrounded him in the recent past. This episode, in itself, represents a cautionary tale about the impassioned nature of modern Middle East narratives and the pitfalls that await anyone who seeks to analyze them so it is worth describing some details. Galtung's seminal research was questioned some years back when he provoked an outrage following his public remarks that suggested a possible connection between the terrorist responsible for the massacre of children in Norway in 2011 and the Mossad, while, at the same time, reviving the tired conspiratorial cliché that the true story would never emerge because "Jews control the media." Advising his audience members to peruse the "Protocols of the Elders of Zion" was the clincher and the mainstream reaction was immediate and forceful condemnation (Omer 2013).

He lost grants, was suspended by the World Peace Academy and is still being chided by his fellow scholars in print and online. Other media, in particular, proliferating right wing websites all over the world, have hailed him as a new "alt-right" hero—an "honor" that he surely never expected to earn. What is curious about this whole affair is that Galtung reached these conclusions supposedly after a close study of Anders Breivik, the self-professed defender of "White Christian Europe" who perpetrated the Norwegian massacre. Breivik was also regarded by authorities as a highly dangerous, blatantly paranoid person—a quality not generally sought out as advantageous for a covert operation. In addition, Breivik issued a thousand-page manifesto stating that he modeled his philosophy on Al Qaeda, professing profound admiration for Osama Bin Laden, whom he credits as having established the "most successful revolutionary force in the world" (Pidd 2012).

In any case, it was not a desirable situation for the "father of peace studies" to find himself in but the worldwide reaction on both sides of the political spectrum was telling. In the end, most people came to see the accusation for what it was—a bizarre musing by someone who sees Israel as an enemy of peace. However offensively Galtung expressed his criticism of Zionism, it was not symptomatic of a growing anti-Semitism among peace researchers (Kempf 2012). Fears that European disapproval of Israeli politics would translate into more action-oriented ideologies dissipated somewhat only to be revived again by the "rise" of nationalist politics all over the world in 2016. Europeans and Americans are still preoccupied with the "other" Middle East, in the form of a massive influx of refugees and the irreparable rupture in pan-European identity and the passive globalization that has consequently emerged. Of course, extremists are indeed targeting Jews in Europe and the United States, and also Muslims, and liberals, and school children, and park rangers and LGBT people.

In the wake of all of this confusion, it is unlikely that the default extremism that will emerge and take over will be old-fashioned racist anti-Semitism, although it is certainly a component of a number of radical ideologies— primarily those of white supremacists. What is more likely is that amorphous extremism in the West will grow, expand and contract, to suit individual and collective angst. The right wing in Western politics lays the blame at the door of a passionless liberalism that denies the growing apprehension of White Western Europeans about the crumbling of their world. The left suggests that the failed project of liberalism to truly address inequality is to blame. Perhaps both are equally true—passion and inequality are close companions in the history of violence and most assuredly continue to be today. It is a faction-less marriage of two universal human propensities.

The new reality of extremism reaches across the political spectrum and is partly based upon the fact that Western economies have long been engaged in designating winners and losers in the game of globalization. Galtung suggested as much when he stated, in reaction to the charges of anti-Semitism as well as his new popularity with White Supremacists, that "power is today in the hands of China, Japan, the EU relative to the USA; Germany relative to the EU periphery and the World Bank relative to much of the Third World. Not even the wildest anti-Semite will construct this as a Jewish conspiracy" (Galtung 2012). This statement is a further articulation of Galtung's "structural theory of imperialism," which, employing political science definitions of imperial center and periphery, posited a "periphery of the periphery" that was kept in a constant state of disenfranchisement by a collusion between the center of the center and center of the periphery (Galtung 1971). As an example of one of the three categories of violence discussed by Galtung—direct, structural and cultural imperialism in Galtung's view, is merely "a species in a genus of dominance and power relationships" (Galtung 1971: 81).

Cultural violence is the means by which imperialism maintains order and is represented by "any aspect of a culture that can be used to legitimize violence in its direct or structural form." This concept seems to be uniquely suited to looking at the remnants of the ancient past—particularly those used as symbols for an embattled present. Flags, anthems, military parades, portraits of leaders, inflammatory speeches, posters and other enduring and ubiquitous symbols that remind people of their subjection and inferiority are emblems of cultural violence (Galtung 1990). Insurgents use these kinds of symbols in furtherance of their cause to remind people of other unpleasant realities—the injustices they have suffered. The imperial symbol upside down or defaced, images that glorify workers, representations of guns, bombs and other weaponry are not atypical and, if the insurgency is successful, they can choose to incorporate these symbols into the old imperialist ones, continue to use them or simply create new less incendiary examples. Much of the symbolic material culture that continues to excite archaeologists constitutes expressions of past cultural violence.

In that regard, Silberman has written that archaeology is "linked closely with the rising or falling fortunes of each ethnic group or nation-state." When translated into specific narratives, these symbols of the past, he argues, are "powerful and entirely exclusivist links" between modern nationalist movements and some idealized and ethnically homogeneous "Golden Age" (Silberman 2013: 73). Thus, contemporary groups labeled as terrorist or extremist have drawn upon past rebellions and their symbols, in order to construct narratives that support direct violence aimed at eradicating the cultural violence that has oppressed them. These representations also serve as an argument in the face of claims by nation-states that the actions of these organizations are rampant irrational terrorism based on a nihilistic or apocalyptic world view.

The axiom in counter-terrorism circles is that radical thinking is not the same thing as extremism. While this is certainly true, it does not lead to a better understanding of how ideas deemed to be "radical" by Western nation-states translate into violent actions. Some narratives are more powerful than others. In both Israeli and Palestinian cultures, for example, the sacredness and significance of Jerusalem is a master narrative that often transcends any devotion to religion on either side. This narrative plays an undeniable causal role in conflict dynamics, by ruling out certain political options as either possible or impossible. Once this version of reality becomes a hardened story it can be retold time and again and often employed simply to generate an emotional response. Another formidable aspect of powerful narratives is that they are portable and can be used to create local narratives. Thus, the larger narrative that "West is at war with Islam" becomes far more potent where the target population for it is, quite literally, a target.

Narratives also cannot be devoid of specificity. The perspective that there is a single narrative, promulgated by the proponents of one particular faith, that propels individuals from highly diverse environments toward violence defies decades of accumulated knowledge about the Middle East. The basis for this idea, the eponymous Global Jihad, underlies the ideological, and largely ineffective, tools of the counter-terrorism infrastructure. Widely dispersed attacks perpetrated by Muslims in recent years (although there were more perpetrated by non-Muslims during the same period), the proliferation of radical websites and the unprecedented attacks on the United States by citizens of a nation that, inexplicably, is still a major ally, are frequently cited in the literature as evidence for its existence. Any one of these factors alone would not validate the concept of global religious conflict but, taken together, like those that are used to verify all conspiracy theories, they paint a false but disturbing picture.

In studying the symbols and concepts used in various parts of the world to motivate individuals toward sometimes violent political engagement, I have come to the conclusion, hardly astounding, that the most powerful narratives are local ones. Huthis in Yemen may share some beliefs with their co-religionists in Iran but their long and tortuous path to so-called extremist action was via generations of conflict in their region with governing bodies from the Byzantine Empire forward and three religions have provided the semiotic tools for the cultural violence enacted against them and their ancestors. Thus, the use of religion to legitimize actions has become an integral feature of their historic struggles—not a motivation for them. Similarly, the characterization of Sinai Bedouin rebellions as "Islamist" glosses over millennia of distrust of nomadic people by governing powers, whether colonial or national.

The lived realities of people who continuously return to the explanatory framework of stories to convey vital information about who they are and what they believe are difficult for modern nations to comprehend. In all societies, narratives occupy a central place in psychological and social worlds but this is particularly significant where stories and storytelling are established and respected modes of communication (Stephens and McCallum 1998). Historical narratives are supported by stories and even though every story within a narrative need not have exactly the same characteristics, they relate to one another in a way that creates a unified whole that is greater than the sum of its parts. It is important to point out, with respect to narratives, that they represent a distinct type of shared reasoning that is based upon a very pragmatic world view—that is, a story that is authentic if its audience can deduce positive outcomes from it and can align it with their values (Fisher 1987).

Founded in postcolonial theory, the study of domination and resistance has a particular focus on narratives (Gubrium and Holstein 2001). Resistance is often seen as a by-product of the exercise of agency by those who identify themselves as oppressed, such as people who are living under a regime of severely restricted freedom or, alternatively, occupation by a foreign power (Pile 1997). The double-sided coin of resistance also suggests both something that impedes movement as well as a propelling force toward upheaval. The theme of rejecting a secular, globalized consumerist zeitgeist in favor of a (largely fictitious) medieval past, and employing modern technology while doing so, is a perfect example. Resistance does not always have a combative connotation. Passive resistance is the notable example but there are others such as economic boycotts and peaceful protests. Violent resistance is also similarly difficult to characterize as either good or bad, although the concept of resistance is generally more amenable to arguments about ideological "purity." The famous maxim that "resistance to tyranny is obedience to God," variously attributed to Thomas Jefferson, John Knox and Susan B. Anthony, is one such example, but the conceptual conjoining of militancy and religious devotion can be found in battle cries that have been used to rally the masses throughout history (Scham 2001).

Looking at resistance as a product of festering rage, in most cases justifiable, against the United States and other Western nation-states, the most important question that arises is how certain men and women become susceptible to extremist narratives while others do not. First, the groups themselves are constituted quite differently from the way in which they are usually portrayed in the popular press. Far from being anarchic, they offer to bring order out of chaos. If group members adhere to Islam or Judaism, extremist groups also offer something not ordinarily associated with them—the rule of law. It is, admittedly, an idiosyncratic interpretation of that law, but it stands in opposition to the numerous erratic dictatorships and incompetent governments that have plagued the Middle East since it was divided up for the convenience of Western governments (Fromkin 2009). Not surprisingly, the preponderance of extremist messaging on social media is positive in nature and promises a world of prosperity and fairness.

All of this leads to the uncomfortable conclusion that extremist groups propose to accomplish everything that governments should but, typically in the Middle East, have not. They even offer foundation myths that corroborate their actions and support the historic nature of their rights—to call these radicalization narratives makes little sense. Further, the part that religion plays in this Passion Play is subtext rather than text—an aspect of the play that can be discerned only in its performance. Religion as an integral part of culture is surely a motivating factor but assuming that it is either the most or the only motivating factor is to absolve Western nations of their responsibility for creating the current new world disorder.

One aspect of extremism that I believe this book does not give enough attention to is why so few of the extremist historical narratives involve women leaders and leadership. Although the focus is on groups rather than individuals, to the extent that prominent individuals are mentioned they are, in most cases, male. The notion that women can be extremists is obviously well documented and there are many reported cases in both ancient and modern history. Thus, while the world of extremism is not necessarily a gendered one, there are numerous studies of women who became involved in political violence. These often characterize their decisions to engage in violence as based upon personal circumstances more often than deep ideological conviction (Skaine 2005; Narozhna and Knight 2016; Jayasena 2017). It has been suggested, however, that this is an assumption based upon a lack of evidence.

There are certainly fewer known militant women in both modern and ancient times than there are men. More importantly, women who have left behind social media statements, video testimonials or other written or oral explanations about the factors that encouraged them to take action are even scarcer. Men who have published such statements generally represent their actions using well-worn political rhetoric or slogans rather than discussing psychological or social motivations but this, by no means, suggests that personal circumstances do not enter into their decisions. Interviews with would-be political suicides who have survived indicate that this is, in fact, the case (Rajan 2011). So consequently, as is the case with other disenfranchised populations, there is still a dearth of historical material on women's leadership in insurgent movements today.

There are, nevertheless, a number of narratives about famous women in ancient Middle Eastern history whose legacy has inspired generations of female militants. The Scythian tribal queen, Tomyris, Herodotus tells us, killed no less a personage than Cyrus the Great and then took his head and put it into his own wineskin filled with human blood (Fabre-Serris and Keith 2015). She has become a legendary figure in Central Asia and Turkey where variants of her name are popular. Many centuries before Tomyris, Queen Semiramis ruled Assyria, possibly the most misogynist society in the Ancient Near East, for many years. She tricked her husband's army into following her after his death and led them on to victory. Both women were historical figures, although the stories that have accrued to them are obviously not.

The historical record of Zenobia, the queen who fought Rome, is less shrouded in mystery. Zenobia became a powerful symbol for Syrian Nationalists beginning in the nineteenth century (Sahner 2014). It could be argued that Zenobia was a model for the first recorded woman suicide bomber in modern history, Sana'a Mehaidli, who, in 1985, drove a truck laden with explosives into an Israeli convoy in Lebanon, and for the first PKK (Partiya Karkerên Kurdistanê or Kurdistan Workers' Party) suicide bomber, Zeynep Cinaci (see Chapter 4, this volume), whose name is a derivative of the name Zenobia. Both women left behind written statements explaining their actions, which did not refer to depression, suicidal tendencies or personal tragedy but, rather, to the oppression of their people (Narozhna 2010). Sana'a Mehaidli's death is still marked as a "funeral-wedding" on a regular basis in Lebanon where she is referred to as the "Bride of the South."

In 2003, the first female Palestinian suicide bomber (see Chapter 5, this volume), Wafa Idris, detonated a 22-pound bomb in the center of Jerusalem.

What followed this act was a rash of articles focusing on her depression over being childless, her divorce, her bad relations with her family—in short, virtually everything except political activism. In the months immediately after her death, more women suicide bombers appeared in the West Bank. So, clearly, warrior women past and present have been committing extreme violence in the Middle East for some time. To the extent a relationship between these women and their ancient prototypes is apt will be noted in the following chapters, but that by no means constitutes an adequate treatment of a subject made all the more complicated by our persistent misunderstanding of the topic of women and leadership in Islamic societies.

I was reminded of this a few years ago while I was attending a meeting of the heads of women's organizations in Afghanistan. All of them were women and all wore headscarves, a symbol of subservience to some in Europe and the United States (Laborde 2005); none of them were reluctant to speak in the presence of both men and women whether Afghan or Western. When one non-Afghan participant expressed their support for women's empowerment in Afghanistan there was a vociferous objection from many of them—but not for any reason that would make sense to most Westerners. One of them, a woman who was educated in the West, attempted to explain. "Look around this table," she said. "All of these women are empowered. What we don't have are the resources to make that power felt in this country!" The idea of Western countries devoting time and money to the self-actualization of Afghan women struck them as ludicrous.

I do not really believe that women in any society, given the same opportunity, means and encouragement to do so as men, would hesitate to commit violence. In fact, the notion of women needing empowerment and generally lacking tendencies toward aggression does not have as long a history as some might suspect. This idea became very popular during the Vietnam War protests and was associated with the passive resistance peace movement. Gandhi, patron saint of pacifists, fervently believed that women leaders would make the world less brutal although he was later to be proven wrong by at least one militant woman taking the reins in his own country (Taneja 2005). There were many proponents of non-violence who adopted Gandhi's view in the tumultuous 1960s, among them one of the more original thinkers of that time, Buckminster Fuller. Although most people consider him to have been an architect, Fuller never settled on a single profession. He described himself as "comprehensive anticipatory design scientist" who worked on housing, shelter, transportation, education, energy, environmental protection, alleviating poverty and, last but not least, women's empowerment based on their naturally peaceful inclinations. He once stated that women should rule the world because they would turn government into "public nurturance" (Sieden 2000).

While his feminist views have not stood the test of time, Fuller is responsible for a phrase that keeps cropping up in religious discourse (Cooper 1998; Houston 2015; Isbell and Bill 2015)—which was surely the last place Fuller intended it to go. Basically, the poem was about the deficiencies of Western society, including organized religion. It began "The revolution has come—set on fire from the top, let it burn swiftly" and ended, more memorably, "God, to me, it seems, is a verb not a noun, proper or improper; is the articulation not the art, objective or subjective; is loving, not the abstraction 'love' commanded or entreated; is knowledge dynamic, not legislative code, not proclamation law, not academic dogma, not ecclesiastic canon. Yes, God is a verb, the most active, connoting the vast harmonic reordering of the universe from unleashed chaos of energy" (Fuller 1971: 22). It is clear that what Fuller intended by this poem was the form of anarchy that he became famous for advocating—that without government and other institutions, good would be permitted to triumph over evil—a narrative that White might characterize as "romantically emplotted."

Another deity, at least for historians and archaeologists, that would qualify for predicate status is the Past. "A verbal structure in the form of a narrative prose discourse" is how White (1973: 2) characterizes history, but the lived and living Past really spills over into many other parts of speech as well. As a noun, the Past is a repository of powerful stories and plots locked inside the minds of individuals as securely as the text of a play, performed by the same cast for generations, is locked in the memories of its actors. As a verb, it represents the shifting struggle between the ancient ties of religious and ethnic identity juxtaposed against the natural inclination of people to just get on with the business of living whether they are surrounded by tranquility or violent civil war. As a complete thought, the Past is a landscape of continuous movement and, potentially, has millions of different narratives making ripples in its not so still waters. It was, in fact, the American historian Will Durant who famously described this landscape as a constantly moving "stream with banks." "The stream," he said, "is sometimes filled with blood from people killing, stealing, shouting and doing the things historians usually record, while on the banks, unnoticed, people build homes, make love, raise children, sing songs, write poetry and even whittle statues. The story of civilization," he concluded, "is what happened on the banks" (Durant 1963: 92).

Bibliography

Aderet, O. 2012. Pioneer of Global Peace Studies Hints at Link Between Norway Massacre and Mossad. *Haaretz English*, April 30, 2012. Retrieved from: www.haaretz.com/israel-news/pioneer-of-global-peace-studies-hints-at-link-between-norway-massacre-and-mossad-1.427385.

Atkinson, P. 2006. Rescuing Autoethnography. *Journal of Contemporary Ethnography* 35/4: 400–404.

Cooper, D. 1998. *God Is a Verb: Kabbalah and the Practice of Mystical Judaism*. New York: Riverhead Books.

Corman, S. 2011. Understanding the Role of Narrative in Strategic Extremist Communication in *Countering Violent Extremism: Scientific Methods and Strategies* (L. Fenstermacher and T.

Leventhal, eds.), pp. 36–43. Topical Strategic Multi-Layer Assessment and Air Force Research Laboratory Multi-Disciplinary White Paper in Support of Counter-Terrorism.

Derricourt, R. 2015. *Antiquity Imagined: The Remarkable Legacy of Egypt and the Ancient Near East.* London and New York: I.B. Tauris.

Durant, W. 1963. Interview. *Life Magazine* 5516: 92.

Ellis, C. 2010. *The Ethnographic I: A Methodological Novel about Autoethnography.* Walnut Creek, CA: Altamira.

Fabre-Serris, J. and A. Keith. 2015. Introduction in *Women and War in Antiquity* (J. Fabre-Serris and A. Keith eds.), pp. 1–10. Baltimore, MD: Johns Hopkins University Press.

Ferran, L. 2015. Study: Fighting Terrorism Enriching, But Obsessive "Dark Side" Infects Life. *ABCNews*, January 30, 2015. Retrieved from: http://abcnews.go.com/US/study-fighting-terrorism-enriching-obsessive-dark-side-infects/story?id=28614193.

Fisher, W. 1987. *Human Communication as Narration: Toward a Philosophy of Reason, Value, and Action.* Columbia, SC: University of South Carolina Press.

Foucault, M. 1972. *The Archaeology of Knowledge and the Discourse on Language.* Trans. by A. M. Sheridan Smith. London: Tavistock Publications.

Fromkin, D. 2009. *The Peace to End All Peace: The Fall of the Ottoman Empire and the Creation of the Modern Middle East* (2nd Ed.). New York: Henry Holt and Company.

Fuller, B. 1971. *No More Secondhand God and Other Writings.* Garden City, NJ: Anchor Books.

Galtung, J. 1971. A Structural Theory of Imperialism. *Journal of Peace Research* 8/2: 81–117.

Galtung, J. 1990. Cultural Violence. *Journal of Peace Research* 27/3: 291–305.

Galtung, J. 2012. TRANSCEND International's Statement Concerning the Label of Anti-Semitism Against Johan Galtung. Retrieved from: www.transcend.org/tms/2012/05/transcend-internationals-statement-concerning-the-label-of-anti-semitism-against-johan-galtung/.

Geertz, C. 1973. *The Interpretation of Cultures: Selected Essays.* New York: Basic Books. pp. 3–30.

Gubrium, J. and J. Holstein. 2001. Introduction: Trying Times, Troubled Selves in *Institutional Selves: Troubled Identities in a Postmodern World* (J. F. Gubrium and J. A. Holstein, eds.), pp. 1–20. New York and Oxford: Oxford University Press.

Hodder, I. 1998. The Past as Passion and Play: Çatalhöyük as a Site of Conflict in the Construction of Multiple Pasts in *Archaeology Under Fire: Nationalism, Politics and Heritage in the Eastern Mediterranean and Middle East* (L. Meskell, ed.), pp. 14–139. London: Routledge.

Houston, S. 2015. God is a Verb: "Orange Is the New Black" Dares to Show Faith in a Positive Light. *Salon.com,* July 18, 2015. Retrieved from: www.salon.com/2015/07/18/god_is_a_verb_orange_is_the_new_black_dares_to_show_faith_in_a_positive_light/.

Isbell, J. and J. Bill. 2015. *Finding God in the Verbs: Crafting a Fresh Language of Prayer.* Downers Grove, IL: InterVarsity Press.

Jayasena, K. 2017. *Motivations of Female Suicide Bombers from a Sociological Perspective.* Northridge, CA: California State University Press.

Joint Chiefs of Staff. 2013. *Counterinsurgency Manual.* Retrieved from: www.dtic.mil/doctrine/new_pubs/jp3_24.pdf.

Kempf, W. 2012. Antisemitism and Criticism of Israel: A Methodological Challenge for Peace Research. *Journal for the Study of Antisemitism* 4: 515–532.

Knapp, Andrew. 2015. *Royal Apologetic in the Ancient Near East.* Atlanta, GA: Society for Biblical Literature Press.

Laborde, C. 2005. Female Autonomy, Education and the Hijab. *Critical Review of International Social and Political Philosophy* 9/3: 351–377.

Lee, R. 2014. *Religion and Politics in the Middle East: Identity, Ideology, Institutions and Attitudes.* Boulder, CO: Westview Press.

Malinowski, B. 1954. Myth in Primitive Psychology in *Magic, Science and Religion and Other Essays*, pp. 176–183. Garden City, NY: Doubleday.

Meskell, L. 2002. Negative Heritage and Past Mastering in Archaeology. *Anthropological Quarterly* 75/3: 557–574.

Monk, D. 1999. *An Aesthetic Occupation: The Immediacy of Architecture and the Palestine Conflict.* Durham, NC: Duke University Press.

Narozhna, T. 2010. Between Shadows and Hopes: Discursive Representations of Female Suicide Bombings and the Global Order in *Order and Disorder in the International System* (S. Krishna-Hensel, ed.), pp. 149–170. London: Routledge.

Narozhna, T. and A. Knight. 2016. *Female Suicide Bombings: A Critical Gender Approach.* Toronto: University of Toronto Press.

Omer, A. 2013. *When Peace Is Not Enough: How the Israeli Peace Camp Thinks about Religion, Nationalism and Justice.* Chicago, IL: University of Chicago Press.

Pidd, H. 2012. Remorseless and Baffling, Breivik's Testimony Leaves Norway No Wiser. *The Guardian,* April 17, 2012. Retrieved from: www.theguardian.com/world/2012/apr/17/breivik-court-boasts-killing-utoya.

Pile, S. 1997. Introduction in *Geographies of Resistance* (S. Pile and M. Keith eds.), pp. 1–32. London: Routledge.

Rajan V. 2011. *Women Suicide Bombers: Narratives of Violence.* London: Routledge.

Sahner, C. 2014. *Among the Ruins: Syria Past and Present.* Oxford: Oxford University Press.

Scham, S. 2001. The Archaeology of the Disenfranchised. *Journal of Archaeological Method and Theory* 8/2: 183–213.

Scham, S. 2009. "Time's Wheel Runs Back" Conversations with the Middle Eastern Past in *Cosmopolitan Archaeologies* (L. Meskell ed.), pp. 166–183. Durham, NC: Duke University Press.

Seiden, L. 2000. *Buckminster Fuller's Universe: His Life and Work.* New York: Basic Books.

Silberman, N. 1989. *Between Past and Present: Archaeology, Ideology, and Nationalism in the Modern Middle East.* New York: Alfred E. Knopf.

Silbernan, N. 2013. The Tyranny of the Narrative. *Journal of Eastern Mediterranean Archaeology and Heritage Studies* 1/1: 175–184.

Skaine, R. 2005. *Female Suicide Bomber.* Jefferson, NC: McFarland.

Stephens, J. and R. McCallum. 1998. *Retelling Stories, Framing Culture: Traditional Story and Metanarratives in Children's Literature.* London: Routledge.

Taneja, A. 2005. *Gandhi, Women, and the National Movement, 1920–47.* New Delhi: Har-Anand.

Time. June 9, 1980. Religion: Once More Oberammergau. Retrieved from: http://content.time.com/time/magazine/article/0,9171,952665,00.html.

Wetmore, K. 2017. Introduction: Forty-first in the Twenty-First in *The Oberammergau Passion Play: Essays on the 2010 Performance and the Centuries Long Tradition* (K. Wetmore, ed.), pp. 1–15. Jefferson, NC: McFarland and Co.

Wilkinson, T. 2016. *Writings from Ancient Egypt.* London: Penguin Classics.

Winter, Irene. 2010. *Art in the Ancient Near East: From the Third Millennium B.C.E.* Netherlands: Brill.

White, H. 1973 (reissued 2014). *Metahistory: The Historical Imagination in Nineteenth-Century Europe.* Baltimore, MD: Johns Hopkins University.

White, H. 1978. *Tropics of Discourse: Essays in Cultural Criticism*. Baltimore, MD: Johns Hopkins University.

White, H. 1980. The Value of Narrativity in the Representation of Reality. *Critical Inquiry* 7/1: 5–27.

Wright, L. 2016. *The Terror Years: From Al-Qaeda to the Islamic State*. New York: Alfred A. Knopf.

2 Gunpowder, treason and emplotment

Narrative and agency

Remember! Remember!
The Fifth of November,
Gunpowder, Treason and Plot,
I know of no reason
Why Gunpowder treason
Should ever be forgot!

English Folk Verse (c.1870)

A terrorist is someone who has a bomb, but doesn't have an air force.

(Blum 2011)

Those seventeenth-century extremists, who were the subject of the famous piece of doggerel quoted at the beginning of this chapter, and the individuals that William Blum's ironic statement described as "terrorists" have interesting similarities. In both cases, they had an axe to grind, explosives and a seemingly expendable means of delivering them. On the one hand Blum's words, however, are meant as criticism of the indiscriminate use of missiles and drones by the United States military. Thus on the one hand, the anonymous author of the poem on the Guy Fawkes plot condemns the perfidy of those who threatened the stability of government. On the other hand, Blum attacks violence committed by the government itself. Although very different in their perspectives, and separated by several centuries, the creators of these sentiments inhabited worlds that were technologically distinct from one another—but not morally so. Blum's best-known reader, and another person who was deeply disillusioned by American foreign policy, was Osama Bin Laden (Montgomery 2006)—a fact that probably has not escaped government enemies list compilers. So it should be immediately clear that his was not a popular view though, via the internet, he has been able to promulgate it to millions.

This is certainly something that John Milton, the author of every free expression enthusiast's favorite poem, would envy. *Areopagitica*, that eloquent argument that "though all the winds of doctrine were let loose to play upon the earth, so Truth be in the field, we do injuriously, by licensing and prohibiting, to misdoubt her strength," was, in fact, an attack on Catholicism.

Milton was profoundly affected by the Gunpowder Plot and his epigram on "[p]erfidious Fawkes," contains a charge that is not unlike one that is leveled at today's terrorists. "You were going, obviously, to send them to the courts of high heaven in a sulphurous chariot with wheels of whirling fire" he accuses after querying "[d]o I misjudge, or did you wish to seem merciful in one way and to atone for your crime with a kind of wicked piety?" (Milton 1957: 13). Blum poses quite a different question in his remarks on the similarly traumatic events of September 11, 2001, when he asks "[w]hat if the government, with its omnipresent eyes and ears, discovered the plotting of Mideast terrorists some time before and decided to let it happen — and even enhance the destruction—to make use of it as a justification for its 'War on Terror'?" (Blum 2010).

Guy Fawkes, and presumably the suicide attackers of 9/11, believed that their acts were in defense of religion and therefore no vice, Blum believes that government's opportunism in the face of such attacks is no virtue and Milton believed that religious fanatics were so rampant among Catholics that he would deny them the freedom to speak. Whether history judges you as an unbeliever, religious fanatic, traitor, terrorist, extremist or a freedom fighter, however, has little to do with how you are seen in the immediate aftermath of your actions. What it mostly comes down to is whether you were successful in establishing a new hegemony that enables you to create your own history or, alternatively, whether your story survives historical attempts to repress it and maintains a consistent appeal against the odds. English Catholics gave up their aspirations to see a member of the Roman Church on the throne long ago. Consequently, Guy Fawkes is remembered today mostly as a figure to burn in effigy (Sharpe 2005). Bonnie Prince Charlie dreamed of a united Catholic Europe but earned a place as a heroic figure because of a nineteenth- and twentieth-century resurgence of Scottish nationalism in a country that is now overwhelmingly protestant (and a little assistance from the Scottish poet Robert Burns) (McLynn 2011).

While time may never succeed in rehabilitating the people that Western governments consider terrorists today, it still must be conceded that it is a possibility. Nevertheless, the further one goes back in time, the harder it is to make the case that what is considered terrorism today really ever happened in the distant past. Many scholars would object to discussing Bronze and Iron Age peoples as passionate and violent proponents of ideology or religion. Perhaps adopting Blum's view that "[t]he word 'terrorism' has been so overused in recent years that it's now commonly used simply to stigmatize any individual or group one doesn't like, for almost any kind of behavior involving force. Terrorism is fundamentally propaganda, a very bloody form of propaganda" (Blum 2006: 32) and, of course, in Blum's view, whether individuals commit it or the state matters little. Let us just say that, in defense of the right to self-definition, our ancient prototypes were driven to adopt some extremist tactics and that much of the evidence that we now have concerning the violence of their acts is indeed propaganda.

In this sense, ancient extremism can be seen in the same way as it has been ever since the first inscriptions from the Ancient Near East were translated—as extremist empires subject to attack and overthrow by extremist groups. Somehow this seems to be a fairly modern way of examining ancient phenomena but, curiously, much of what we know about the Middle Eastern past confirms this assumption. Nevertheless, I would be remiss if I give the impression that there is anything in the way of a scholarly consensus that defining ancient cultures as extremist is a traditional way to look at the ancient world. In fact, the only theorists that seem to be interested in delving into deep time for analogies to today's violent extremism are political and military strategists (Chaliand and Blin 2007; Lutz and Lutz 2005) rather than historians or archaeologists.

The odds-on favorites for analysts of extremism with a mind to discuss the ancient past are the Jewish zealots of the first century CE (Anderson and Sloan 2002; Mahan and Griset 2012). Those members of the Judean Tea Party seem to have followed a deceptively familiar trajectory toward radicalism, which may account for their popularity as historical examples among counter-terrorism analysts. They were moderate to begin with but Roman efforts to stamp them out became more excessive and, as a result they, in turn, became more violent—eventually earning the name of *sicarii* (assassins). Josephus characterizes them as a rampaging lawless group bent on destroying all civilization: "These were such men as deceived and deluded the people under pretense of Divine inspiration," he wrote, "but were for procuring innovations and changes of the government" (Josephus et al. 2004: 127). Their final stand at Masada has given them the aura of nationalist freedom fighters in today's Israel, although contemporary accounts from their fellow Jews condemn them as extremists (Brighton 2009; Hoenig 1972). It is not to wonder at their appeal for counter-terrorism analysts (D'Alessio and Stolzenberg 1990; Ross 2011). They have all of the necessary attributes—the fact that they committed suicide (largely a myth strangely embraced, until lately, by the Israel Defense Forces) (Ben-Yehuda 1995); the proclivity to indiscriminately kill innocent civilians; and, last but not least, "irrational" religious beliefs—conveniently espoused by the ancestors of a significant ally of the United States and Europe today. The latter is probably intended to dispel the notion that counter-terrorism studies are inherently Islamophobic.

Without precisely defining what a terrorist, an extremist or an insurgent in cultures far distant from our time looks like, authors who write about them seem content to use the term "terror" in a more general manner instead. They do often give lip service to the use of terror (historically at least) by nation-states and empires but it is clear that their focus is primarily on "extra-legal" activities by "unauthorized" individuals (Richards 2015). A typical summation is, "terrorism, the principal aim of which is to terrorize, is a historically far broader phenomenon than suggested by the term's current usage, which essentially boils it down to the description or analysis of the illegitimate use of violence in terrorist-type activities" (Chaliand and Blin 2007: vii). Aside from employing circular reasoning, Chaliand and Blin quickly pivot to non-state sponsored terrorism opining that "[s]tooping to often pathetic means, terrorism is a way of creating power in the hope of seizing from below that which the state wields from on high" (2007: viii)—making the clear moral equation that the would-be "new boss" is likely to be the "same as the old boss" (Townshend 1971).

To be a terrorist, at least in Western eyes, would appear to require an official categorization as such. Despite the fact that these three terms are used interchangeably, only one at present is an official matter of international law (Saul 2008). Violent extremist is becoming more popular as a term used in discussing "prevention" solutions (perhaps because countering something gives it too much credence) but terrorism is the tried and trusty term preferred by governments. Nevertheless, when it comes to self-definition, one would be highly unlikely to encounter a self-avowed terrorist. Resistance is far and away the most used term, although there seems to be as yet no single word that characterizes participants in such causes. Further, some engaged in resistance may prefer the term insurgent.

Formerly in Iraq, insurgents were seen as rebels or fighters against a ruling or occupying authority until the rise of ISIS.[1] In Afghanistan, because a large part of the insurgency has involved Taliban fighters, the term insurgent has been less used in the West. Are Islamic State fighters insurgents? Possibly, insofar as they are fighting against Western occupying authorities in Iraq and Syria. Are Al Qaeda members insurgents? Perhaps to the extent that their localized affiliates have set their sights on bringing down their own governments. Do both see themselves as insurgents? The requirements of insurgency—unlawful behavior and increasing support for the overthrow of a governing structure suggest that they may.

According to the United States Army Counterinsurgency Manual (2013), probably the most influential non-authoritative source on the phenomenon, insurgent objectives can be generally categorized as "reform, revolution, secession, nullification, and resistance," but, the Manual continues, "These categories are archetypes, and many insurgencies exhibit characteristics of more than one category, often as a result of alliance building" (United States Army Counterinsurgency Manual 2013: II-9). That the military views the insurgent as an archetype is not surprising given its supposed emphasis on "cultural understanding" as a counterinsurgency tactic. During the Iraq War, the *Human Terrain System,* which one participant characterized as "a complex mix of brains and ambition, idealism and greed, idiocy, optimism, and bad judgment" (Gezari 2013: 197) was established to provide the military with an approximation of the perspectives of the local populations (i.e., the "human terrain") in the regions in which they were deployed.

This initiative was deployed in recognition of the fact that one of the weaknesses immediately perceived by erstwhile Middle East experts after the events of 9/11 was the woeful inadequacy of our education system in informing the younger generation about the Arab and Muslim worlds. The geography and history of the region had already fallen off the radar in most middle and high schools in the United States and the number of students who could even locate Iraq on a map was a paltry 13 percent in 2002 (*National Geographic* 2002). Relics of the Cold War, represented as much by the tenacious officials in the higher echelons of the State Department as by the survival of more official policies, had caused a kind of arrested development in recognizing the realities of an inconsistently globalizing, balkanizing and, consequently, chaotic world (Pew Research Center 2001). The entire country had been caught unawares—not by an enemy with stockpiles of nuclear weapons but by a small group of determined zealots wielding box cutters. Leveraging Title VI of the Higher Education Act, another relic of the Cold War emanating from the National Defense Education Act, "Centers and Research Studies" and "Language Institutes," to use the terms of the legislation, were set up at American institutions of higher education everywhere. Internationally, the State Department met the challenge by introducing English language programs for Madrassa students in majority Muslim countries that sought, presumably as a sidebar, to inculcate an appreciation of American values (JBS International 2007). At home, the State Department established Arabic as a "strategic language" and offered grants and scholarships to students interested in pursuing Middle East studies.

The seeming embrace of Islamic culture in the interests of restoring peace and security, despite some ultra-conservative detractors, was probably a good idea at the time. The undoing of good intentions, however, has been the permanent overreaction in the West to any unlawful incident that involves a Muslim. The so-called cultural rapprochement that the American Military is still seeking could have been achieved more readily by employing cultural interpreters. Unfortunately, the latter effort was derailed by violence committed by one individual at Fort Hood in 2009. This act was committed by no less than a major in the Army, and a psychotherapist in the bargain, whose daily involvement with soldiers having post-traumatic stress disorder affected him deeply. Widely seen as exemplifying the imminent danger of sleeper extremists, the resulting backlash against Muslims in the military had a chilling effect on their willingness to serve in it or associate with it. Leading congressional fearmonger Peter King held hearings on the subject, concluding that his committee had "reason to believe that the actual number of radicalized troops is far more than publicly realized or acknowledged" (Goodman 2011). They did not comment several years later when a similar, but less deadly, shooting took place at Fort Hood perpetrated by another frustrated veteran with post-traumatic stress disorder (PTSD), and virtually no ties to Islam.

Asked about security improvements in the wake of continuous shootings at military bases, committed by many more non-Muslims than Muslims, former Defense Secretary Hagel said, "Obviously when we have these kinds of tragedies on our bases, something's not working" (Pickler 2014). What is not working is the continuing idea that these shootings are politically or religiously motivated, an idea that has resulted in increasing resources devoted to ferreting out radicals rather than funding much needed mental health programs both in the military and outside of it. Nor do the shootings necessarily qualify as acts aimed at undermining the integrity of the state. Extremist groups have spread a wide net to encompass actions by individuals who have sought a convenient last-minute excuse for what used to be called "suicide by police."

At least one leader associated with Al Qaeda, Abu Musab al-Suri, a member of its inner council, has dismissed such publicized acts in Western countries as catering to "the disease of screens, flashes, fans, and applause." The real goal of what Suri calls the "leaderless resistance" is not simply to destroy the current incarnation of the state but to create a new one through a military-style acquisition of territory. "Without confrontation in the field and seizing control of the land," he said in 2006, "we cannot establish a state, which is the strategic goal of the resistance" (Wright 2006). Widely credited as being the inspiration behind ISIS, Suri was released from prison by ISIS's declared enemy, Bashir al Assad.

Characterizing members of these groups as proponents of resistance is not moral equivocation. Representing both an impediment to existing authority and a spur toward a new power structure, they seek to actively rework the process of establishing and maintaining control. That they want change is paradigmatic and it seems almost too facile to describe them as agents of change. But they are indeed that and more. Margaret Mead posited that agents of change operated in a number of ways to alter the perceptions of other individuals and introduce new concepts or technologies. They could attempt to directly influence others, to alter their environments, to create situations within which others will have to act in order to satisfy the needs and emotions or create social support for the individual who adopts the new behaviors (Mead 1955).

The subjugated advocates of resistance, subalterns (Spivak 1988) who seek autonomy as a goal, often attempt to do so through becoming leaders of groups and encouraging collective action. Those who are truly adept at raising consciousness and awareness of powerlessness can stimulate action on the part of others. As opposed to other agents of change, resistant subalterns have limited ability to choose their weapons and their methods. Their primary method is to create a secret discourse that is a critique of power spoken in private. At the same time, the powerful also develop a private dialogue about practices and goals of their rule that cannot be openly avowed. When cultural resistance becomes overt rather than covert, it is often because the "hidden transcripts" of power become public (Scott 1990). Manifest resistance is often the product of knowledge of the dominant culture as well as the realization of one's own inferior position. This involves a process of recognition and replacement—learning the cultural assumptions of the dominator, realizing the fallacy of those assumptions and countering them with apposite ones more indigenous to their own cultures.

In fact, this suggests that many subaltern resistance members know the content of counter messaging and have already rejected it long before their resistance becomes extremist action. As a prerequisite phase to extremism, resistance is a by-product of individual agent decisions (Veldhuis and Staun 2009). It is also a confrontation with the burden of consequences, both positive and negative, that informs the actions of agents who recognize that they are powerless and want to do something about it. In the process of developing cultural resistance, so-called social, economic and political "drivers" are, for the most part, outside of the process. They may contribute to the perceived position of an agent as a subaltern but do not in any sense operate as a spur or a check to violence.

Since some form of unlawful behavior is generally to be imputed to insurgents, extremists and terrorists, it is instructive to offer a definition that addresses the consequences of their resistant behavior in a context outside of political branding. Surprisingly, that venerable mainstay of the legal profession, Black's Law Dictionary, offers fairly even-handed analyses. According to this text, an insurgent is "one who participates in an insurrection; one who opposes the execution of law by force of arms, or who rises in revolt against the constituted authorities." While it is true that most definitions of the term in the literature mirror this one in some fashion, the fact that it is in the very first edition of Black's (1891) tells us that, however current we believe the concept of insurgency to be, it is in fact over 100 years old. This is not the entirety of Black's definition, however, and the second part of it gives us some sense of what we are missing in defining insurgencies today.

"A distinction is often taken between 'insurgent' and 'rebel,' in this: that the former term is not necessarily to be taken in a bad sense," Black's continues, "inasmuch as an insurrection, though extralegal, may be just and timely in itself; as where it is undertaken for the overthrow of tyranny or the reform of gross abuses" (Black's 1891: 633). The term "extremist" does not seem to have achieved an adequate level of criminalization to merit an entry in Black's, but the latest edition does define terrorism in a seemingly neutral way. Black's fairly prosaic statement that terrorism is "the intentional use of terror-induced fear by an individual or group to amplify the effects of a strategic act of violence" is further augmented by the proviso that "[t]errorism has often been associated with actors who are at a distinct military and tactical disadvantage against a larger threat or enemy and who have a limited capacity to strike back" but "it is also possible for dominant actors, including states, to utilize terror based tactics" (Garner 2014: 745). Thus, according to Black's at least, it appears that, contrary to Blum's assumption, a terrorist *can* have an air force.

Insofar as the groups, both ancient and modern, described on the following pages, "extremist" would seem to be the safest shorthand term to apply to proponents of resistance. Although it is not a distinction that is made by security analysts, I would take the position that "terrorist" has a very limited application and, to most people, in spite of Black's assessment, connotes an individual who engages in random acts of deadly mayhem. Extremists, on the other hand, may encompass people who support violent action or who plan such acts. Most certainly, as a historical matter, such individuals are prominent among the founders of modern Western nations. This supports the view espoused by those who study radicalization that the majority of people with radical ideas are not really extremists (Horgan 2014). The best available global polling from organizations such as Pew suggests that there are tens of millions of people worldwide who are sympathetic to "jihadi aspirations," without supporting or engaging in violence (Pew Research 2015). Conversely, some so-called extremists are not ideologues or believers in an "extremist" version of religion. Some have only a cursory knowledge of or commitment to such values and they are drawn to groups and to activities for other reasons (Atran and Gomez 2014; Gelfand et al. 2013).

Anthropologist Scott Atran, who probably has interviewed more presumed terrorists than any person alive, has cautioned that violent extremism "represents not the resurgence of traditional cultures, but their collapse, as young people unmoored from millennial traditions flail about in search of a social identity that gives personal significance and glory. This is the dark side of globalization" (Atran 2010). Cognitive and behavioral psychologists have used the concept of action pathways as scripts for engaging in extremism or violent extremist actions (Atran et al. 2014; Bokhari et al. 2006; Horgan 2008; Taylor and Horgan 2006). Other analysts have implied that this transformation can be especially lethal when the aforementioned processes are combined with moral disengagement that enables individuals, through cognitive distortion, to dehumanize and delegitimize their victims, minimize their suffering and justify violence against them and see complex situations in absolute, black-and-white terms (Liht and Savage 2013).

These cognitive distortions are further augmented by the dynamics of the group's shared belief system as expressed through in-group identification and out-group hatred, and trans-generational suffering, in which "each generation [absorbs] the bitterness of the previous generation" (Post 2007: 39). Under such circumstances, "when hatred is bred in the bone" (Post 2005a: 615), individual identity becomes subsumed by collective identity. Given the diversity of causes and motivation of militant organizations, Post concludes that "group, organizational, and social psychology, with particular emphasis on collective identity, provides the most constructive framework for understanding extremist psychology and behavior" (Post 2005b: 617). Thus, researchers unanimously express discomfort with the notion of an "extremist profile."

Extremist motivation is also the topic of many analyses. Beyond the compelling qualities of the narrative is the discourse that individuals attach to it (Corman 2011). As White has written "[e]ach of the epochs of Western cultural history ... appears to be locked within a specific mode of discourse, which at once provides its access to 'reality' and delimits the horizon of what can possibly appear as real" (1978: 241). White's four tropes, underlying the ways in which the past is constructed by individuals and groups, are instructive in this respect and they are a vital contribution to the organization of that discourse. Tropes, as the historian envisions them, "are especially useful for understanding the operations by which the contents of experience which resist description in unambiguous prose representations can be prefiguratively grasped and prepared for conscious apprehension" (White 1973: 34)

Tropes inform the ways in which source material can be structured and which also contributes to a particular mode of argumentation that is associated with, or expresses, an ideology. It is argued here that historical narratives of extremism in the Middle East are primarily tragically or romantically emplotted. A tragically emplotted narrative generally (although not always) implies, in White's formulation, a mechanistic argument and a radical ideology. Mechanistic refers to an argument that focuses on finding laws or rules that make stories intelligible and meaningful and radical ideology suggests a belief in utopias and revolutions (White 1973). I would also submit that in the cases presented here that it is also invariably associated with a "desired past" (Scham 2009). The story is characterized as one in which heroes are consistently tested and eventually are forced to become resigned to the limitations of the world. This tragic emplotment is associated with a metaphorical trope, which implies a conceptual transition or transfer (White 1973).

The Kurdish narrative is an example of this emplotment, argument and trope. The attempt to find laws that govern human behavior has led them to a belief in the universal recognition of indigenous rights. The utopia they envision is a new and different kind of polity that embodies their long history and ensures their independence (Bruno 2007). Their tragic emplotment is one that has already been recognized by other historians including Henry Kissinger. An entire chapter of his memoirs is devoted to the Kurds whose tragedy, in his view, has been "imposed largely by history and geography" (2012: 113). Given his role in creating a significant part of that tragic history, Kissinger's narrative clearly stems from his "conviction that the world has grown old" (White 1973: 113) or more accurately to a perspective that the limitations of the past that are manifested in the constraints of the present represent the most logical, and defensible, world order. Kissinger's *realpolitik* is most clearly expressed in a satirically emplotted book entitled *Diplomacy* (Kissinger 1994).

A romantic emplotment focuses on somewhat different aspects of the past— the triumph of good over evil, the tribulations of culture heroes and, by its nature, involves struggle. The mode of argument in romantically emplotted stories tends to be formist—that is classificatory and the ideology, anarchist— positing that the government is corrupt and needs to be destroyed. The trope associated with such emplotments is synecdoche where a part of something is used to symbolize the whole. Synecdoche runs rampant in military and government speech—for example, references to "boots on the ground" to represent soldiers uses an article of apparel to represent the whole of an army or military command.

The legends of Early Israelites are demonstrative of a romantically emplotted extremist narrative, embraced by Israel's Hilltop Youth, that makes use of formist argument in which the depiction of "variety, color, and vividness" is the "central aim of the work" (White 1973: 14) and the agents and the events speak for themselves without any additional context or interpretation. These are also stories that employ both metaphor and synecdoche to convey the totality of the actors' personalities and place in the stories—the honeybee, dispensing both sweetness and pain (Deborah) and the ibex, swift and dangerous (Jael), represent the totality of their characters. As extremist narratives, these stories are both naive and insidious and convey the idea that the other "inhabitants of the land" (Joshua 2:9) can quickly be swept away to clear the path for a new regime.

Tragedy and romance have many things in common. Unlike the other emplotments described by White—comedy and satire—they are both authentic and straightforward representations of human hopes and aspirations. There is a high level of seriousness required of those who repeat these kinds of narratives and those who accept them. Both require that the hearers or readers of the narrative have a deep understanding of the culture in order to grasp the tropes of metaphor and synecdoche used. Finally, both the storyteller and the audience must accept the authenticity of the narrative. In order to convince people to embrace a proposition, one must have faith in it—the message can be real or imaginary but it can never be insincere.

At present, archaeological interest in extremists seems to be limited to concern about the security of sites and artifacts. State extremism has been a topic of interest to a number of people in my field, though few of them have defined or distinguished the terms terrorist, extremist and insurgent. In examining the process whereby an extremist/terrorist/insurgent group became a State or Empire, knowing ancient history is a definitive advantage. Adapting symbols of cultural violence that Galtung associates with state and imperial structures seems to be a vital first step. For example, the Bar Kokhba Rebellion, Zenobia's Palmyrene Empire, even Boudica's Iceni Tribal Kingdom, all used coinage to declare their independence from Rome (Gardner 1918). Similarly, ISIS has used it to strike a blow against a different kind of empire, in their words, "the capitalist financial system of enslavement" (Sabah and Alexander 2015). Thus, even though ISIS might have begun as a group that rose up to oppose the postcolonial borders and arbitrarily designated national powers of the region, it now seems to have settled comfortably into the post-insurgent role of rogue state.

Although more traditional archaeologists might say that the number one ethical problem in archaeology today is the illegal antiquities trade, heritage studies are not, as some might believe, preoccupied with preserving sites and artifacts at all costs. Even the prevention of looting has a different focus in this field. While some scholars bemoan the loss of knowledge as its worst consequence, heritage practitioners look at the loss of patrimony, taking the position that effective stewardship over evidence removed from its cultural context places additional burdens on the archaeologist to assure that it is not only preserved but presented for the benefit of those who have the most stake in it (Al Qantar 2017). Further, the evidence of past cultures is not something that exists primarily for us to interpret and promote. Ideally, it should exist to reinforce the connections between the ancient and the modern on a continuum of culture. Even without our collaboration, cultural property furnishes the symbolic hardware for the construction of national and local identities as several archaeologists have suggested (Leone 1992, 1995; Hassan 1998; Dietler 1996). The nature of such identities in the present effectively demands a past with the same characteristics—a past that supports an individual and collective view of how people have come to be where they are.

Today's insurgents and violent extremists would not be unfamiliar figures in the Ancient world. Due to an interesting confluence of new ideas about the empires of the Near East, we are beginning to understand more about the marginalized and resistant peoples living under Akkadian, Babylonian, Assyrian, Hittite, Persian and Roman rule. Lullubi, Gutians and Medes are little known archaeologically even though some of them are historically credited with bringing down empires. Kurdish insurgents have laid claim to some of these ancient insurgents even though few other people have ever heard of them. Interestingly, the sites of resistance associated with these cultures are all within modern Kurdish cultural areas. Is insurgent memory at work here or simply a desire to establish a historical presence based upon geographic coincidence?

In the case of the Settler Movement in Israel, representing the dubious legacy of Meir Kahane, demolitions of their houses—which is tactic usually reserved for Arabs—have been a major stimulus to violent action. Like other such organizations, they recruit online and their message is one of persecution with an invitation to fight the oppression of the state. Their motto is to attack "whenever, wherever and however" in response to any attempt by the Israeli Army or the police to invade their property. The movement began with what is essentially an economic goal—to cost the government as much as possible to remove them and to cost the Palestinians as much as possible to stay in their vicinity. Now they are engaged in a campaign to create a polity that is controlled completely by Jewish law (Pedahzur and Perliger 2011). The superficial resemblances between them and ISIS are made much of in a number of news analyses about them and has earned them a spot on the United States Department of State terrorist list. Yet there is one important distinction that has helped them keep a low profile in the West. Alone among the Abrahamic faiths, Judaism is not a proselytizing religion. There are no dreams of a Caliphate extending from Syria to Spain or of enforcing any adherence to their faith on those who are not already Jewish.

Their targets are the security forces of Israel, Palestinians and, sometimes, sympathizers with either of the above (Pedahzur and Perliger 2011). While both ISIS and radical settler groups speak of theocracy, there is no indication that their actions are intended to lead to that result. The connection of extremism with religion in the Middle East is today, as it was in antiquity, an oversimplification and a diversion. The ancient world seemingly exhibited a strong connection between religion and politics but it was the political that gained the upper hand in every case. True theocracies in antiquity did not exist for very long. Ancient Egypt is often offered as an example but what has become clear from current archaeology in the region is that the authority of the Pharaoh and the priests rested more upon wealth rather than divine sanction.

Nomadic pastoralists are either characterized as the first insurgents in the Middle East or the progenitors of what became Ancient Near Eastern civilizations. When pastoralism began as a way of life, many centuries after farming first appeared, long-distance trading, with its attendant contact between cultures became firmly established. Finding nomads in the archaeological record, however, is still an immense challenge. Even the monumental remains of once-nomadic cultures, such as Petra, have yielded little knowledge of them as individuals. The contrast between the desert and the sown is less apparent today than it once was but the very ancient origins of this dichotomy lend some credence to the view that farmers and herders experience the world in innately different ways. The heritage of nomadism, both past and present, has suffered from romanticization to the point that it is difficult to separate the people from their legends (Marx 1967). Today, the lifestyle of the Biblical patriarchs, whose tombs in Hebron are so contentiously claimed by two religions, is ironically disappearing—a casualty of impermeable national borders (Shryock 1997).

The civilizations of the Ancient Near East—Hittite, Egyptian, Babylonian and Byzantine were seized by peoples who came from elsewhere or arose from the lower ranks of their societies. Insurgents and extremists, as they were characterized by the powers of their time, left their mark upon the archaeological record to the extent that they represented new polities, new gods and new and, sometimes, entirely distinctive language groups. In every sense, however, these cultures also took over most of the important aspects of the cultures that came before.

The Settler and Sinai Insurgents, the Kurdish PKK (Partiya Karkerên Kurdistanê or Kurdistan Workers' Party), the Yemeni Huthis, radical Palestinian organizations and the Islamic State have similarly staked a claim on the ancient world. All are groups representing marginalized peoples and all have come to see themselves as fulfilling historically patterned roles. Their versions of history can be based upon geography, shared historical memory (which may or may not be supported by evidence) or an emotional attachment. The connection that the Kurds have with Early Bronze Age mountain tribes, and especially the association that PKK leaders have with this narrative, encompasses all three. Palestinian beliefs in their descent from the ancient Philistines are less fervently held but geographically and historically compelling. The anti-nationalist Sinai Bedouin and Israeli Settler extremists evidence an enduring cultural connection with the nomads and frontier people of the Iron Age.

Cultures that have a more uneasy relationship with their past, or have a history that has strongly influenced them in ways that they don't necessarily acknowledge, make use of ancient narratives in less direct ways. As ISIS harkens back to the Islamic Caliphate, it is interesting to examine the ideal of Al-Andalus and its appeal to modern Arabs that for much of its history was Berber and not Arab (Fromherz 2010). The relationship of Huthis with their ancestors, the Jewish Himyarites, is geographical and, in part, genetic, historical and cultural. Himyarite history is little known or acknowledged in its country of origin but prominent Middle East historian, Glen Bowersock, has written that the Himyarites had a prominent role in "the tumultuous events in sixth-century Arabia" that, in his words, "were the crucible of Islam" (Bowersock 2013: 18). All of these are what I would consider to be "rooted" narratives—those that have developed naturally from history, legend, belief and landscape.

Given the chronological breadth of this task, it is only possible here to skim the surface of the use of historical narratives by would-be freedom fighters or extremists. In each of the following chapters, only one modern group is represented—it would be difficult in one chapter to explore the myriad militant organizations that have sprung up. This is particularly true in the case of the Bedouin and the Kurds as detailed in Chapters 3 and 4 (this volume). The primary method of focusing on the narrative used by a single group has more to do with the degree of global recognition (or notoriety) that each of them has achieved. Thus, while the PKK is not even fully representative of all groups seeking Kurdish rights in Turkey, it is the most well-known one. The overall objective of each of these chapters is to expose the most ancient narratives of resistance and rebellion that have been documented relating to these cultures.

Arguments based on narrative tend to offer no legitimacy outside of the group of true believers but, nonetheless, can remain powerful for centuries. Studying them through the lens of archaeology rather than history—the supposedly unfiltered story told by material culture and contemporaneous texts— the actions of groups labeled as terrorists, because they defy Western interests, do not achieve rationality so much as recognition that, in fact, there is humanity there beyond the headlines. Similarly, I must conclude that archaeology alone has no power to give voices to ancient peoples any more than the remains of a centuries old temple, in itself, can inspire worship. In simplest terms, it is what people in the present make of their past that gives voice to their ancestors—whether they are adopted or biological. Built into these narratives are, to use a term borrowed from information technology and evolutionary biology, "ancestral structures" composed of resistance to the symbols of cultural violence deployed by states and empires to contain them.

Terrorist, extremist or insurgent—these terms, like most categorizations that define roles and assign activities, are essentially constructed. The term "terrorist," in particular, strikes one as a purely imperial notion—a political, and largely fictitious, construct. In Western society, a "terrorist" is, quite simply, a member of a group that is named by government officials as such. It is thus an ascribed status rather an achieved one. As few people would describe *themselves* as terrorists, the decision of governing bodies to categorize them as such suggests that their actions are divorced from any intent other than to sow chaos and discord. In this sense, there is no such thing as a *narrative* of terrorism except that which is superimposed upon individuals by governments.

In the end, it may not matter which term becomes the consensus one. The cliché that "one person's freedom fighter is another's terrorist," is more about judgments of the past than categorizations of the present. Many American historians have suggested that the Sons of Liberty might be considered extremists today (Kumamoto 2014; Alexander 2011). Two Prime Ministers of the State of Israel were members of groups that have been condemned as terrorists (the Irgun and Lehi) and who were responsible for, among other things, the assassination of a British official and blowing up a hotel. There may well be those who will argue that these figures pale in comparison to ISIS leaders but the latter's brutality is eclipsed, historically, by the ruthlessness of a state that was recognized by the international community—that of Nazi Germany.

Thus, Blum's argument equating state-sponsored callous warfare with terrorism makes sense on many levels but for this to be further understood we will have to wait for the verdict of future generations. Heroism or perfidy—it all depends upon what larger narrative the tale will become a part of and, more importantly, whether the audience for that narrative prevails. In Israel, there are streets and buildings named after the Irgun, Lehi and their members. In the United States, even the most violent of our founding fathers is celebrated in statue and story. Before 1945, there were over 50 streets in Europe named for Adolf Hitler. Now, of course, there are none.

Note

1 ISIS is the name by which most people know the Islamic State (IS), which is also called the Islamic State in Syria (ISIS), the Islamic State in the Levant (ISIL) and Daesh (which is a derogatory name only used by Americans and Europeans).

Bibliography

Al Qantar, S. 2017. Repatriation and the Legacy of Colonialism in the Middle East. *Journal for Eastern Mediterranean Archaeology and Heritage Studies* 5/1: 19–26.

Alexander, J. 2011. *Samuel Adams: The Life of an American Revolutionary*. Lanham, MD: Rowman Littlefield.

Anderson, S. and S. Sloan. 2002. *Terrorism: Assassins to Zealots (The A to Z Guide Series)* (2nd Ed.). Lanham, MD: Rowman & Littlefield.

Archer, J. 2017. *Extremists: Gadflies of American Society*. Santa Barbara, CA: ABO-CLIO.

Atran, S., H. Sheikh and A. Gomez. 2014. *Devoted Actors Sacrifice for Close Comrades and Sacred Cause*. Herndon, VA: Artis Research.

Atran, S. 2010. Pathways to and from Violent Extremism: The Case for Science-Based Field Research. Statement before the Senate Armed Services Subcommittee on Emerging Threats and Capabilities, March 10, 2010.

Ben-Yehuda, N. *Masada Myth: Collective Memory and Mythmaking in Israel*. Madison, WI: University of Wisconsin Press.

Black's Law Dictionary (1st Ed.). 1891. St. Paul, MI: West Publishing.

Blum, W. 2006. *Rogue State: A Guide to the World's Only Superpower*. Monroe, ME: Common Courage Press.

Blum, W. 2010. In Struggle with the American Mind. *The Anti-Empire Report*. Retrieved from: https://williamblum.org/aer/read/86.

Blum, W. 2011. United States Bombings of Other Countries. *The Anti-Empire Report*. Retrieved from: https://williamblum.org/chapters/rogue-state/united-states-bombings-of-other-countries.

Bokhari, L., T. Hegghammer, B. Lia, P. Nesser and T. Tonnessen. 2006. *Paths to Global Jihad: Radicalisation and Recruitment to Terror Networks*. FFI Seminar hosted by the Norwegian Defense Research Establishment (Kjeller, Norway), March 15, 2006.

Bowersock, G. 2013. *The Throne of Adulis*. Oxford: Oxford University Press.

Brighton, M. *The Sicarii in Josephus's Judean War: Rhetorical Analysis and Historical Observations. Early Judaism and Its Literature.* Atlanta, GA: Society for Biblical Literature.

Bruno, G. 2007. Backgrounder: Inside the Kurdistan Workers Party (PKK). Council on Foreign Relations, October 19, 2007. Retrieved from: www.cfr.org/turkey/inside-kurdistan-workers-party-pkk/p14576.

Chaliand, G. and A. Blin. 2007. Introduction in *The History of Terrorism: From Antiquity to al Qœda* (G. Chaliand and A. Blin, eds.), pp vii–viii. Trans. by E. Schneider, K. Pulver and J. Browner. Oakland, CA: University of California Press.

Corman, S. 2011. Understanding the Role of Narrative in Strategic Extremist Communication in *Countering Violent Extremism: Scientific Methods and Strategies* (L. Fenstermacher and T. Leventhal, eds.), pp. 36–43. Topical Strategic Multi-Layer Assessment and Air Force Research Laboratory Multi-Disciplinary White Paper in Support of Counter-Terrorism.

D'Alessio, S. and L. Stolzenberg. 1990. Sicarii and the Rise of Terrorism. *Terrorism* 13/4–5: 329–335.

Dietler, M. 1994. "Our Ancestors the Gauls": Archaeology, Ethnic Nationalism, and the Manipulation of Celtic Identity in Modern Europe. *American Anthropologist* 96/3: 584–605.

Fromherz, A. 2010. *The Almohads: The Rise of An Islamic Empire.* London and New York: I.B. Tauris.

Gardner, P. 1918. *A History of Ancient Coinage: 700–300 B.C.* Chicago, IL: Ares Publishers.

Garner, B. (ed.) 2014. *Black's Law Dictionary* (10th Ed.). St. Paul, MI: West Publishing.

Gelfand, M., G. LaFree, S. Fahey and E. Feinberg. 2013. Cultural Factors in Extremism. *Journal of Social Issues* 69/3: 495–517. Retrieved from http://www.gelfand.umd.edu/Gelfand%20et%20al%20(in%20press).pdf.

Gezari, V. 2013. *The Tender Soldier.* New York: Simon & Schuster.

Goodman, A. 2011. Some Democrats Can't Handle the Truth at Peter King Hearings. *Commentary.* March 10, 2011. Retrieved from: www.commentarymagazine.com/politics-ideas/liberals-democrats/some-democrats-can't-handle-the-truth-at-peter-king-hearings.

Hassan, F. 1998. Memorabilia: Archaeological materiality and national identity in Egypt in *Archaeology Under Fire: Nationalism, Politics and Heritage in the Eastern Mediterranean and Middle East* (Meskell, L., ed.), pp. 200–216. London and New York: Routledge.

Hoenig, S. 1972. Historic Masada and the Halakhah. *A Journal of Orthodox Jewish Thought* 13/2: 100–115.

Horgan, J. 2014. *The Psychology of Terrorism.* New York: Routledge.

Horgan, J. 2008. From Profiles to Pathways and Roots to Routes: Perspectives from Psychology on Radicalization into Terrorism. *The Annals of the American Academy of Political and Social Science* 618: 80–94.

JBS International. 2007. Evaluation of the English Access Microscholarship Program Final Report. December, 2007. Washington, DC: U.S. Department of State.

Josephus, F., W. Whiston and D. Margoliouth. 2004. *The Great Roman-Jewish War.* Mineola, NY: Dover Publications.

Killebrew, A. 2005. *Biblical Peoples and Ethnicity: An Archaeological Study of Egyptians, Canaanites, Philistines, and Early Israel 1300–1100 B.C.E.* Boston, MA: Society of Biblical Literature.

Kissinger, H. 1994. *Diplomacy.* New York: Simon & Schuster.

Kissinger, H. 2012. *Years of Renewal: The Concluding Volume of His Classic Memoirs.* New York: Simon and Schuster.

Kumamoto, R. 2014. *The Historical Origins of Terrorism in America: 1644-1880.* New York: Routledge.

Leone, M. 1992. A Multicultural African-American Historical Archaeology: How to Place Archaeology in the Community in a State Capital. Paper presented at the Annual Meeting of the American Anthropological Association, Washington, DC.

Leone, M. 1995. A Historical Archaeology of Capitalism. *American Anthropologist* 97/2: 251–268.

Lewis, B. 1990. The Roots of Muslim Rage. *The Atlantic* 266/3: 47.

Liht, J. and S. Savage 2013. Preventing Violent Extremism through Value Complexity: Being Muslim Being British. *Journal of Strategic Security* 6/4: 44–66.

Lutz, J. and B. Lutz. 2005. *Terrorism: Origins and Evolution.* New York: Palgrave MacMillan.

McLynn, F. 2011. *Bonnie Prince Charlie: Charles Edward Stuart.* New York: Random House.

Mahan, S. and P. Griset. 2012. *Terrorism in Perspective.* London: Sage Publications.

Marx, E. 1967. *Bedouin of the Negev.* Manchester: Manchester University Press.

Maṭālsī, M. 2000. *The Imperial Cities of Morocco.* Rabat: Terrail.

Mead, M. 1955. *Cultural Patterns and Technical Change.* New York: New American Library.

Milton, J. 1957. *Complete Poems and Major Prose.* New York: Prentice Hall.

Montgomery, D. 2006. The Author Who Got a Big Boost from Bin Laden. *Washington Post*, January 21, 2006. Retrieved from: www.washingtonpost.com/wp-dyn/content/article/2006/01/20/AR2006012001971.html.

National Geographic. 2002. Roper Geographic Literacy Survey. Retrieved from: www.nationalgeographic.com/geosurvey2002/download/RoperSurvey.pdf.

National Geographic. 2006. Geographic Literacy Survey/Roper. Retrieved from: www.nationalgeographic.com/roper2006/pdf/FINALReport2006GeogLitsurvey.pdf.

Pedahzur, A. and A. Perliger. 2011. *Jewish Terrorism in Israel.* New York: Columbia University Press.

Pew Research Center. 2001. The View Before 9/11: America's Place in the World. Retrieved from: www.people-press.org/2001/10/18/the-view-before-911-americas-place-in-the-world/.

Pew Research Center. 2015. State of the Union 2015: How Americans See the Nation, Their Leaders and the Issues. Retrieved from: www.pewresearch.org/fact-tank/2015/01/20/state-of-the-union-2015/.

Pickler, N. "Obama: We will get to bottom of Ford Hood shooting. *San Diego Union Tribune.* April 2, 2014. Retrieved from: http://www.sandiegouniontribune.com/sdut-obama-we-will-get-to-bottom-of-ford-hood-shooting-2014apr02-story.html.

Post, J. 2005a. The Socio-Cultural Underpinnings of Terrorist Psychology in *Root Causes of Terrorism: Myths, Reality and Ways Forward* (T. Bjørgo, ed.), pp. 54–69. London: Routledge.

Post, J. 2005b. When Hatred Is Bred in the Bone: Psycho-Cultural Foundations of Contemporary Terrorism. *Political Psychology* 26/4: 615–636.

Post, J. 2007. *The Mind of the Terrorist: The Psychology of Terrorism from the IRA to al-Qaeda.* New York: Palgrave MacMillan.

Richards, A. 2015. *Conceptualizing Terrorism.* Oxford: Oxford University Press.

Ross, J. 2011. *Religion and Violence: An Encyclopedia of Faith and Conflict from Antiquity to the Present.* London: Routledge

Sabah, Z. and C. Alexander. 2015. Islamic State Flips Gold Coins to Break Fed "Enslavement." *Bloomberg News*, August 29, 2015. Retrieved from: www.bloomberg.com/news/articles/2015-08-29/islamic-state-finds-gold-coins-are-a-steal-as-throwback-currency.

Saul, B. 2008. *Defining Terrorism in International Law.* Oxford: Oxford University Press.

Scham, S. 2009. Diplomacy and Desired Pasts. *Journal of Social Archaeology* 9: 163–199.

Scott, J. 1990. *Domination and the Arts of Resistance: Hidden Transcripts.* New Haven, CT: Yale University Press.

Sharpe, J. 2005. *Remember, Remember: A Cultural History of Guy Fawkes Day*. Cambridge, MA: Harvard University Press.

Shryock, A. 1997. *Nationalism and the Genealogical Imagination: Oral History and Textual Authority in Modern Jordan*. Oakland, CA: University of California Press.

Spivak, G. 1988. Can the subaltern speak? In *Marxism and the Interpretation of Culture* (C. Nelson and L. Grossberg, eds.), pp. 46–111. Champaign, IL: University of Illinois Press.

Taylor, M. and J. Horgan. 2006. A Conceptual Framework for Understanding Psychological Process in the Development of the Terrorist. *Terrorism and Political Violence* 18/5: 585–601.

Townshend, P. 1971. "Won't Get Fooled Again." *The Who's Lyrics*. Retrieved from: www.azlyrics.com/lyrics/who/wontgetfooledagain.html.

Veldhuis, T. and J. Staun. 2009. *Islamist Radicalisation: A Root Cause Model*. The Hague: Netherlands Institute of International Relations Clingendael.

White, H. 1973. *Metahistory: The Historical Imagination in Nineteenth-Century Europe*. Baltimore, MD: Johns Hopkins University Press.

Wright, L. 2006. The Master Plan: For the New Theorists of Jihad, Al Qaeda is Just the Beginning. *The New Yorker*, September 11, 2006. Retrieved from: www.newyorker.com/magazine/2006/09/11/the-master-plan.

Section 2

Tragic emplotments

3 "The fanged serpents of the mountain"

Kurdish separatism in the context of the ancient past

> The Gutians are the fanged serpent of the mountain, who acted with violence against the gods, who carried off the kingship of the land of Sumer to the mountain land, who filled the land of Sumer with wickedness.
>
> (Sumerian Royal Inscription of Uti-Hegal trans. Frayne 1993: 284)

> The Kurdish tragedy was imposed largely by history and geography, but it was also exacerbated by our own national divisions.
>
> (Henry Kissinger 1994)

We looked out upon the iconic site of Carchemish straddling the Turkish-Syrian border from the vantage point of an ancient cemetery high above it. We knew the site well and longed to go there but this was the closest that Turkish border agents would allow, despite the pleas of the government representative who accompanied us. Carchemish—in itself very symbolic of both the Ancient Near East and the archaeologists who "discovered" it, would remain a mystery to us viewed from this distance. However, most of us had seen the reports of T.E. Lawrence (indeed, *that* Lawrence) and Leonard Woolley (Woolley et al. 1914), famed raider of the Royal Tombs of Ur, who dug there. The last bastion of several Ancient Near Eastern Empires, this was the site where all of the great civilizations came together in an epic battle over 2,000 years ago. Babylonians, Persians, Medes and Egyptians struggled for the prize that was the remnant of Assyria, once the greatest power in their known world. It was the place where, according to one Biblical account, the last of Judah's "good" kings, Josiah, was headed, ostensibly to join the battle on behalf of the Babylonians and Medes, when the archers of the Pharaoh Necho II killed him (Seidl 2009).

To the American archaeologists on our team, even this view was exciting. It was not similarly enrapturing for our Turkish colleagues. When our team attempted to persuade army officials stationed on the border to let us visit or take photographs of it from the guard station, the Turkish members of our team were clearly horrified by our request. Having already, they believed, taken their lives into their hands as we made our way through the Kurdish areas of southeastern Turkey in a dilapidated van, they were in no disposition to argue with the military. We had stopped for lunch in a park in Diyarbakir, the "unofficial" capital of Turkish Kurdistan (Guvenc 2011), and even explored what was left of its citadel. Then we did the unthinkable—a Kurdish resident of the city overheard our conversation about archaeology and invited us to see what turned out to be an exquisite restoration of an Ottoman house that he had done himself. We were heedless then of how much this disturbed our companions from Ankara and our driver. Later, when the driver attempted to charge double as reparations for the trauma of going to these places, we got the point.

Nevertheless, this was the first one of many trips we were to take through Turkey's Kurdish region over the five years or so that we conducted this archaeological survey. At least one of our colleagues returned year after year still expressing trepidation about the places we visited but bravely sticking it out. After having flown into Iskenderun a third time to map the ruins of the Hatay Region, I finally began to understand that Turks have a very deeply embedded reverence for two things that we had come dangerously close to treading upon—one of them is the military and the other the integrity of Turkish borders. Our team geologist, also from Ankara, repeatedly referred to a "strong Turkey protected within its borders," a phrase that, at first, made little sense to me.

I later came to understand that southeastern Turkey, on the borders of Iraq and Syria, and with its mixture of Allawites, Kurds, Turks, Muslims, Syrians and Christians, had, in the past, been seen as a model of co-existence but a precariously balanced one. Home to the cities of Tarsus and Antioch, places associated with St. Paul and St. Peter that were regularly visited by pilgrims, it was also the seat of the Bishop of Anatolia whose retreat in the mountains above Iskenderun was our temporary residence. A kind and scholarly man, the Bishop displayed a great interest in all of the early Christian sites we had discovered as a part of our survey. He was restricted by the government in leaving his compound and was always to be accompanied, purportedly for his own safety, by a Turkish national who drove the Bishop's car. He had to provide the authorities with two days' notice before he was permitted to leave, but we managed to covertly arrange a visit to some of our sites using our own driver. The last year of our survey, while the team was on a field trip, Murat Altun, his government assigned driver, attacked and beheaded Bishop Luigi Padovese.

Murat, whom we knew fairly well, was not Kurdish. In fact, his sentence for killing one of the most prominent Christian officials in Turkey angered many Kurds. To anyone who knew the Bishop it sounded preposterous, but Murat claimed that his employer assaulted him and the court determined that, since the Bishop was not available to counter this accusation, they would give the killer the benefit of the doubt. He was given a reduced sentence of 15 years at roughly the same time as the state prosecutor was seeking a 21-year sentence for a French Kurdish woman, Sevim Sevimli, for demonstrating against the government and having alleged links to a leftist organization (Figaro 2013). As one Kurdish website abroad stated, "[t]he only logical conclusion is that Ms. Sevimli poses a far greater danger to Turkish society than a convicted murderer of an innocent man of peace and goodwill" (Australian Kurdish Association 2013).

The cross-border ideology of Kurdish independence has posed a threat to all the nations in which Kurds reside, but most especially to Turkey. The fear felt by Turks in confronting Kurdish autonomy has grown since an independent region of Kurdistan was established in Iraq in 2005 (Salih and Fantappie 2015). One member of our team, a German scholar who was working at a university in Israel, was wont to do his own unique version of ethno-archaeology by bluntly asking people we met in the villages "so, what are you?" Even in Diyarbakir, where there is at least a 70 percent chance that any given person we met would be Kurdish, they invariably answered "Turkish." The aforementioned team geologist was so distressed by this behavior that he complained later to the government that our colleague was an Israeli spy. I do not believe that he was ever able to return to the country.

Turkey has engaged in repeated efforts to tilt the demographic balance in eastern Turkey away from the Kurds, and even indirect questions about language and ethnicity are problematic (van Bruinessen 1996). Kurds in the past have learned, to their great misfortune, that such moves on the part of governments are partly intended to control them. Certainly, revolts by Kurds and subsequent violent suppression by ruling authorities have been a tragically iterative pattern in Iraq, Iran and Turkey for generations. In 1988, only three years before the calamitous Iraqi Kurdish uprisings at the end of the Gulf War, Saddam Hussein had ordered the Iraqi Army to drop mustard and sarin gas on the Kurdish town of Halabja, killing thousands of people, and inflicting cancer, physical deformities and other harm on future generations of the town's population. The Kurdish Peshmerga had liberated Halabja from Iraqi rule at the end of the Iran–Iraq War and the military acted swiftly and ferociously in retaliation (Kelly 2011).

The more recent histories of the different national Kurdish minorities vary, as well as their relationship to the West, but they share an overarching concept of themselves as a people spurned and trampled on by other civilizations. The well-worn expression "Kurds have no friends but the mountains" (Brenneman 2016: 2) summarizes their narrative and in contrast to the equally popular saying in Turkey that "a Turk has no friends but the Turks." For their part, Turks have found that the relentless fighting skills that stem the progress of the ISIS "apocalypse" across the border are being applied by the armed wing of the Kurdistan Workers Party (PKK), the Kurdistan Freedom Hawks (TAK), in multiple violent raids on civilian centers (Gunter 2010).

The United Nations has never declared the PKK and its offshoot organizations to be terrorists, but the United States is very much on board with the Turkish narrative. In January of 2016, Vice President Joe Biden firmly declared that the PKK itself "is a terrorist group plain and simple. And what they continue to do is absolutely outrageous" (BBC News 2016b). This came not long after the deadliest bombing in Turkish history killed almost 100 people, virtually all them Kurdish peace activists. While ISIS was considered to have been the alleged perpetrator, in the resulting confusion over who was responsible, the Turkish government subsequently took swift action to suppress Kurdish militants. In February and March of 2016, as if to confirm Biden's condemnation, the TAK carried out two bombings in Ankara that killed dozens of civilians and seriously injured hundreds more (BBC News 2016a). Needless to say, the body count on both sides since hostilities began has been mounting but, in the eyes of some Western governments, the Kurds, a group that they have a history of misunderstanding, are to blame (Brenneman 2016).

It is a situation that Kurds have come to expect—after centuries of experience. The Taurus and Zagros Mountains, the heights that some archaeologists believe nurtured the world's first farmers (Braidwood and Howe 1960), is their ancestral homeland. Functioning as both a retreat and a fortress, the mountains have fostered Kurdish devotion to ethnic autonomy, egalitarian governance and accommodation to different religious traditions. As the Kurdish saying goes "compared to the unbeliever, the Kurd is a Muslim" (Van Bruinessen 2016) but religion is by no means the primary unifying factor for the Kurds living in different countries. They share a bond of language (albeit with many distinct dialects) and cultural tradition but, more significantly, they are united by a sense of having deep roots in the highlands (Brenneman 2016).

Abdullah Ocalan has echoed this in his observation that all of the historic enemies of the Kurds have labeled them as "the mountain people" (Ocalan 2012: 12). Ocalan is the imprisoned leader of the PKK and he has had nothing but time during his decades of incarceration to reflect upon the ancient causes of the Kurdish struggle. The narrative of the Kurds began, he says "at the outset of class civilization" and, he cautions, while "it would not be scientific to assert that Neolithic society is identical to present-day Kurdishness ... the similarities between the continuing heritage of Neolithic society and the society of 10,000 years ago can be no coincidence" (Ocalan 2012: 15).

Ocalan has also declared this idyllic prehistoric world to be one where the contributions of women were recognized. "Patriarchy has not always existed," he wrote: "[t]here is strong evidence that in the millennia before the rise of statist civilization the position of women in society has been very different. Indeed, the society was matricentric – it was constructed around the women" (Ocalan 2012: 16). These early Kurdish women were warriors as well—just as their modern counterparts are. Many a news source has been obsessed with the sometimes sexualized image of young women fighting the Islamic State in Syria and Iraq on behalf of the PKK in Turkey. Around 40 percent of PKK fighters are female, some of them in the senior command, and their tactics include suicide bombings as well as guerilla warfare (PBS.org 2015).

The first such attack was by a woman in 1996, when Zeynep Kinaci killed ten Turkish soldiers, and herself, by setting off a bomb during a military parade in Dersim to retaliate for the Turkish military attempt to assassinate Ocalan. Kinaci's letter to Ocalan references history five times and speaks of her struggle to defend Kurdish identity and heritage. This was not the last time the name of the famous warrior Queen Zenobia has appeared in connection with militant women, but she is just one of many models revered by young Kurdish women. A writer for the online magazine *Ekurd* asserted a few years back that "Kurdish women are descendants of Queen Vashti of the Medes ... who was one of the first women in the ancient world to stand up for the God given equal status and value of women to men in every society" (Mirwaisi 2013). Vashti, the first wife of the Biblical Persian Emperor Ahaseurus (probably Artaxerxes) who was condemned in the Book of Esther for refusing to come at her husband's bidding, has morphed into a Kurdish feminist hero.

Kurdish identity encompasses a long and varied history beginning with the mountain tribes of the Early Bronze Age, including the Lulubi (mentioned in annals beginning from around 2200 BCE) and the Gutians (who may go back as far as the twenty-fifth century BCE). Unique among the multiple ethnicities of the Islamic Middle East, the mostly Muslim Kurds still enthusiastically embrace their roots in the "days of ignorance" (Jahaliyya) before Mohammed. Although it has been common, as noted previously, for Kurds to trace their ancestry back to the beginning of the Persian Empire (Anderson and Stansfield 2010), the Lulubi and the Gutians are also considered to be a part of Kurdish history (Abd al-Jabbār and Dawod 2006).

The historical authenticity of this narrative matters little as the Kurdish past is not based upon texts but on geography—a geophysical narrative formed in the most mountainous region of the ancient Near East and shaped by centuries of fierce fighting, victories, crushed rebellions and imperial domination. The mountain tribes of antiquity who were able to infiltrate the lowlands and establish small empires of their own have, mysteriously, all disappeared from standard histories. Although the Gutians, the Kassites, the Elamites and the Medians each ruled at one time a large portion of the known world, there was, always, the eventual downfall and ruthless retaliation by lowland powers.

Archaeological projects have not really been able to discern that much about these cultures on the peripheries of ancient empires but, while archaeologists have not uncovered much about the ancient Kurdish past, they have been able to put their skills to work in uncovering the modern one (Pringle 2009). People working in this field have finally come to recognize the importance of human remains to the living and, as if to make up for a past in which they collected them willy-nilly, many are now volunteering for these grisly but, nonetheless, very important assignments. In the Kurdish mountains, the scenes of massacre are numerous and each one is examined if possible and commemorated, in thought if not in deed. The sense of history repeating itself is difficult to ignore especially because the Kurds themselves have adopted even the distant past as their own. In Kurdish folklore, even fairy tales seldom end happily (Jwaideh 2006). Utopias and revolutions are essential to the Kurdish narrative, as the present consistently remains unacceptable. Kurdish identity is built upon a strong belief in direct cause and effect and the Kurdish language is dependent upon metaphors for most aspects of the human experience.

These are not Kurdish narratives, however, but those of the enemies of the Kurds, that is, empires established on insurgencies that were successful.

Kurdish narratives are tragic and radical, mechanistic and anarchist—in many ways, the antithesis of the romantically structured dramas of some of their adversaries, but in others, quite similar. Both emplotments posit heroic struggles and both are revolutionary. Only one, however, succeeds in changing the world. The difference is that, in the one narrative, good triumphs over evil, while in the other, the good just becomes resigned to living in an evil world.

This is perhaps the crux of the issue in finding archaeological evidence of ancient mountain peoples for, just as the winners make the history, they also make the art. The ubiquitous Bronze Age Ancient Near Eastern battle scene, combining the cultural violence of war iconography (Galtung 1990) with the discursive qualities of narrative (White 1980), is the perfect representation of all the qualities of a romantic emplotment. A conquering hero, upending the status quo, is pictured in the final moments of the event. One such battle scene, the Stele of Naram-Sin, shows a devastating defeat of the Lulubi in 2200 BCE at the very site of the massacre of Halabja (Frayne 1990). The iconographic monument commemorating this destruction has become a famous and rare example of Akkadian art showing the doomed denizens of the capital city, Lulubuna, crushed under the giant feet of the Emperor of Akkad.

Erected by the Emperor in the lowland city of Sippar and subsequently taken to Susa by the Elamites, the Stele has intrigued art historians, in particular because of the diagonal orientation of the figure of Naram-Sin shown climbing a mountain that seems to be composed of defeated Lulubi tumbling from its side. There are no depictions or references to divine help in this work—in fact, the king is shown proportionately three times as large as any other figure and is the sole vanquisher. In all, it represents a striking reminder of imperial might and hierarchy. The god-king, who needs no assistance from above or below to conquer his enemy, is the obvious theme (Gates 2013).

In contrast, a few surviving rock reliefs celebrating the battles of Lulubian kings at the site of Sar-e Pol-e Zohab in modern Iran tell a different story. One such example, dedicated to Anubanini, shows a Lulubian leader who might have been one of Naram-Sin's enemies. He is standing on a flat surface with six (probably more originally) vanquished enemies shown in the register beneath him and three in the relief above—one of whom has fallen beneath the king, who is shown facing a goddess who, herself, is leading two captives on a rope. She offers the ring of sovereignty to the leader who is shown in a respectful pose standing before her. There is little doubt that he owes at least part of his victory to her (Potts 1999). According to a number of scholars, the leaders of the Lulubi and their neighbors, the Gutians, were not monarchs in the typical Ancient Near Eastern mode but rather assumed roles that are closer to those of tribal chieftains. This seems to be reflected in these official portrayals of them.

A century later, another tantalizing clue to the Lulubi appears in a Sumerian poem "Lugalbanda and the Anzud Bird," composed during the Ur III Period. The story is of a hero who gains super powers and saves his city by befriending a bird in the "mountains of Lulubi," suggesting that lowlanders were more comfortable with visiting the mountains than they had been in previous periods (Black et al. 2006). Nevertheless, the Lulubi with their herds of goats and sheep were still strange in the eyes of lowland farmers. Shulgi, one of the kings of the Third Dynasty of Ur, claimed to have raided the Lulubi multiple times in revenge for their depredations, which are largely unrecorded. By the time of the late Ur III Period, they appear to have been conscripted into the army of King Amar-Sin, suggesting that they had been conquered once and for all— not by the Semitic-speaking Akkadians, but by a people with whom the Lulubi might formerly have been allied, the Sumerians (Porter 2012).

Many scholars have some difficulty in separating the Lulubi from the Gutians. Some have suggested that both names are just different ways of denoting strange peoples from the hills. Nevertheless, the Gutian historical record is more comprehensive because they successfully established themselves as rulers in lowland Mesopotamia for as long as 100 years after the fall of Akkad. Also, the Akkadians began to write about the fearsome Gutians long before their final defeat by a coalition of mountain tribes. There is some speculation that the Sumerians, who chafed under the rule of the outsiders who spoke a strange language and imposed it upon them, might have joined with the highlanders even though, later, they were to become their mortal enemies (Bar 2003). For a time after the end of the Akkadian Empire, bilingual texts in Sumerian and Akkadian appeared, but the latter began to take precedence after 1700 BCE. Sumerian cuneiform, used to write Akkadian, survived after the demise of Sumerian culture but Sumerian speech, which today remains linguistically unclassified, did not. Akkadian became a *lingua franca* in the Near East during the imperial period and remained so for several centuries thereafter (Ahmed 2012).

Although it is not typical of Akkadian literature to completely denigrate other cultures, a special place is reserved for the Gutians. The author of the *Cursing of Agade* describes the onslaught of "an unbridled people, with human intelligence but canine instincts and monkey's features ... who are not classed among people, not reckoned as part of the land, Gutian people know no inhibitions" (Black et al. 2006: 122). At the time when this piece of literature was written, the Akkadians had not yet completely succumbed to the Gutian offensive but it must have seemed obvious to the author that they would be the instrument of their destruction, just as the prophets of the Kingdom of Judah predicted its destruction by the Neo-Babylonians.

Some historians have suggested that the Gutians began to infiltrate the lowlands slowly, starting with the cities adjacent to their mountain territories and proceeding southwards. Although the city of Erbil, which Kurds claim as their ancient capital as well as their modern one, has never been systematically excavated, the Gutians left a royal monument there. Its inscription details their battle, together with their allies the Lulubi, against Arbela (the city's ancient name) and the capture of its governor Nirishuha, who was probably a Hurrian—another mountain people sometimes allied with the Gutians (Lawler 2014).

Perhaps it is true that, like the emperor Sargon, who putatively began his career as a foreign cup-bearer to the Sumerian King of Kish, the Gutians were a part of the imperial retinue almost from the beginning of Akkadian rule. Some of them are described as "travelers"—more likely messengers—in Akkadian texts, while others were undoubtedly mercenaries in the Akkadian Army. The archives of Adab mention Gutians who received military rations and who were so numerous that the local ruler had to obtain an interpreter for them (Bryce 2009). Exposure to Mesopotamian culture from this experience may have enabled their infiltration and eventual takeover of Akkadian lands. In addition, they also had the impetus from decades of vicious attacks on their fellow Gutians by the rulers of Southern Mesopotamia.

The Akkadians themselves acknowledged the severity of their own rule and the fact that they would quickly suppress any signs of rebellion against it. Their aggressive and expansionist foreign policy left little room for conquered peoples to accommodate to them. Absolute obeisance was required and enforced (De Lillis et al. 2007). Therefore, it is not surprising that the highlands, with its militant people on the periphery who were only of interest as the subjects of scorched earth incursions, became a seething cauldron of resentment. Their parochial enmities became submerged for this period in a growing wave of hatred for the Akkadians and the severe overlords they installed to rule over them.

Nevertheless, Akkadians have largely escaped the harsh judgment of history in part because it is Akkadian texts that are the primary sources for events of this period. Thus, according to those same texts, the Gutians, who left few surviving texts of their own, used terror to control the lands under their sway and conducted periodic and unpredictable raids on the neighbors. While this tactic might have made some sense as long as the Gutians remained a minority attempting to control more numerous Sumerians and Akkadians, it conflicts with the archaeological record which suggests that, after shaking off the yoke of Akkad, the mountain peoples were content to rule the lands that they conquered and avoid unnecessary confrontations.

Akkadian and Sumerian propaganda against the Gutians speak of such bad conditions under their rule that the question naturally arises as to how a small mountain tribal people could have maintained control over their more numerous, and sophisticated, lowland subjects for almost a century. Some of the sources that were contemporary with their period of power compare them unfavorably with the rulers of the city-state of Lagash, which during this same period was a purported model of stability because it was in "native" hands. Yet, despite what the ancient historians characterize as marked differences in their governance, Gudea the King of Lagash seems to have got along well with the Gutians. He allowed the people of Lagash continued access to the Gutian copper mines in the mountains and Gudea's relationship with the Gutian king Erridu-Pizir seems to have been a cordial one.

Some scholars have suggested that, given the short terms of Gutian leaders listed in the Sumerian King List, theirs was an elected rather than dynastic office. The translation of the phrase before the list of kings and the lengths of their reigns reads, "In the army [or land] of Gutium, at first no king was famous; they were their own kings and ruled thus for 3 years" (Electronic Text Corpus of Sumerian Literature 1997: 308–334). In the event, there are no records that the Gutians established a city or administrative center, which might suggest that they maintained a semi-nomadic existence during their reign. They might also have maintained a system that encompassed the appointment of governors from the conquered lands to rule over their own people on behalf of the Gutians (Hallo 2005).

It is ironic that this singular political vision in the Ancient Near East, with its seemingly democratic rule and its forward-looking system of decentralized government, has come down to us in so many histories as a "dark age" (Ahmad 2012). From those rare finds giving us direct evidence of Gutian culture through their own eyes, we have a fragmented picture of what they might have been like as overlords. They suggest to us that, in contrast to other cultures of the region, the Gutians seem to have been reluctant to abandon what might be described as a tribal form of government with a committee of elders and a group composed of other leaders serving as advisors to the supreme leader.

"Who was king? Who was not king?" is the querulous comment on the Sumerian King List about Gutian hegemony (Schneider 2011: 24). As the list seems to have omitted at least half of the Gutian rulers, readers of the list might well ask those questions. One intriguing piece of evidence from a leader who *is* mentioned on the List, one Laerab, is a mace head that is inscribed with a lengthy execration formula. It references the enigmatic "god of Gutium," a deity that is mentioned along with the Sumerian gods Astar (Ishtar) and Sin (the moon god). While a similar curse can be found in earlier Akkadian texts, the one on this artifact, given the concerted effort on the part of subsequent governments to blot out Gutian rule, seems prescient. It warns that for anyone who Laerab calls upon, the aforementioned gods will "tear out his foundations and destroy his progeny" (Van Soldt and Katz 2002: 151).

Most other Gutian inscriptions are from the aforementioned leader Erridu-Pizir who, despite ample evidence of his rule, did not survive the cultural purge to appear on the Sumerian King List. These provide only hints of what Gutian culture was like. One inscribed on the base of a statue refers to the "god Ilaba, the mightiest one of the gods" who is the "clan god" of the ruler (Frayne 1993: 91). Although this particular deity appears to have the same name as an earlier war god of Akkad, this reference does not necessarily mean that the Gutians adopted Akkadian religion. An alternative explanation might be that the name Ilaba in this case was meant to represent the Gutian ruler's own tribal god, whose name, in Gutian, would have been unfamiliar to the audience for this text. The inscription continues with the statement that Erridu-Pizir hunted down and captured the king of Madga (one of those rebellious mountain chiefdoms) and brought him away "by force through the gate of the god of Gutium" (Hamblin 2006: 103).

While it is implied in several inscriptions that the Gutians were eager to emulate the Akkadians with respect to their success in conquest, the Weidner Chronicle confirms that this admiration did not extend to the religious sphere. The Chronicle speaks of the irreverent behavior of the Gutians toward Sumerian gods. "Utuĝal, the fisherman, caught a fish as tribute at the edge of the sea; until that fish was offered to the great lord, Marduk," it reads. "It was not offered to any other god. The Guti took the cooked fish away from him before it was offered" (Grayson 2000: 150). The aforementioned *Curse of Agade* makes the accusation that the Gutians drive "the trusty goats of Enlil from the fold, and make their herdsmen follow; they drive the cows from the pens, and make their cowherds follow" (Frayne 1990). In any event, Gutian religion, according to most accounts, seems to have been an incidental part of their culture. Part of the criticism they received from surrounding cultures with more developed religious traditions is due to this seeming lack of piety.

Gutian control over the Kiš and Adab region appears to have been firm and most probably lasted until the Ur III period. According to the Akkadian and Sumerian authors, they were the most incompetent of rulers—unable to understand the economy of the lowlands, despoiling the cities with their herds and small agricultural plots while the irrigated hinterlands lay fallow, unable to collect taxes or maintain public buildings. One inscription from a Sumerian leader who was later able to defeat the Gutian king laments that they "had blocked (water from) the fields" and "closed off the roads (and) caused tall grass to grow up along the highway(s) of the land" (Frayne 1999).

Nevertheless, as noted above, all of these pejorative epithets and lists of crimes were the products of their enemies. We can only imagine what the Gutian version of their oppression at the hands of the Sumerians and Babylonians had been but, for the lowlanders of Mesopotamia, the horrors of Gutian rule became a hardened narrative passed on with every succeeding empire. Throughout Babylonian history, the name "Gutian" became a standard term for fiends from the mountains. Also, just as Muslims in the Middle East refer to Western armies as "crusaders" in Iraq, the peoples of the Ancient Near East continued to characterize invaders, even up to the fourth century BCE and the Hellenistic Empire, as Gutians (Diakonoff 1951).

The Gutians in the end probably did not manage to control all of Sumer and Akkad. In fact, it does not seem likely that this was their ultimate aim. As the hill peoples who were closest to the Mesopotamian lowlands, they had established themselves as economic as well as military adjuncts to the Akkadian Empire—albeit very ill-regarded ones (Ahmed 2012). They appear to have kept their area of control as close to the mountains as possible. Their royal titles on the Sumerian King List do not include the honorific "King of the four quarters of the world" and "King of the universe." According to the available source material, we know only that the regions of Umma, Kiš and Adab were under (direct) Gutian control and it was in the environs of Adab that the decisive battle that brought the Gutian hegemony to an end took place.

How were they eventually expelled from their lowland fiefdoms? Part of the answer is that they ultimately became as unwelcome to the highlanders as the Akkadians had been, even though the Gutians came to power as part of an alliance with several tribes from the Zagros. It may well be true, as has been proposed, that the Gutians never ruled central Mesopotamia but stayed fairly close to the Zagros—which would account for the fact that the few records we do have of them speak of campaigns against mountain peoples (Liverani 2013). For example, one of the Erridu-Pizir inscriptions tells of the nefarious Ka-Nišba [King of Simurrum—a city of the Zagros] who "caused the mountain lands and cities to revolt, as far as the land of Lulubum" (Frayne 1999), suggesting that the Gutians' old confederates, the Lulubi, were prominent among the rebels.

Nonetheless, it was the Sumerians who brought an end to Gutian rule. The King of Uruk, city of the legendary Gilgamesh, challenged the Gutian King Tirigan and won. The chronicle of this event focuses mostly upon the deficiencies of the Gutians that prompted the otherwise peacefully inclined Sumerian ruler to invade their lands. As a faithful devotee to the god Enlil and the goddess Inanna, Utugal sought divine approval for his mission and seems to have received it. His account takes pains to emphasize, in a paraphrase of those immortal words used by a number of conquerors in the Ancient Near East, as well as in the modern Middle East, that he was greeted as a "liberator."

The Gutians thus passed from dominion, if not completely from memory. Accounts speak of continued efforts on the part of the Kings of the Ur III dynasty (2112 to 2004 BCE) to rout them and the later history of the dynasty might have been different if they had succeeded. The Gutians joined an alliance with another people of the Zagros, the Elamites, who are credited with the destruction of Ur II, the last great Sumerian polity. Those same Elamites are credited with facilitating the rise of another ancestral people claimed by the Kurds. In the great uniting person of Cyrus the Great, archaeologists have found a convergence of Elamite culture with supposed Median civilization.

Sargon II, Assyrian King and putative disperser of the Ten Lost Tribes of Israel in 722 BCE, called the Medes the "Arabs of the East" who "roamed the desert and the mountains like thieves" (Potts 2013). Because they have left few traces behind of their culture, which is clearly discernible from that of others in the region, a number of archaeologists argue that they were a nomadic people whose weaponry, in particular, shows a strong relation to the Scythians. They are also credited as having a seminal role in the development of Zoroastrianism, one of the oldest known monotheist religions. In Iraqi Kurdistan, there has been a resurgence of interest in this religion, which has always been a part of the ethno-religious diversity of Kurdish culture, partly in reaction to the carnage that they are witnessing among their non-Kurdish Muslim neighbors (Fuccaro 1999).

The Magi of Median religion, strongly identified by many scholars as a precursor to Zoroastrianism, bring in a connection with Western religions in particular Christianity. Among Abdullah Ocalan's historical musings is this flattering portrait of his Zoroastrian forebears:

> It was Zoroastrianism which lastingly changed the Kurdish way of thinking in the time between 700 and 550 BC. Zoroastrianism cultivated a way of life that was marked by work in the fields, where men and women were on par with each other. Love of animals had an important position and freedom was a high moral good. Zoroastrian culture equally influenced eastern and western civilization, since both Persians and Hellenes adopted many of these cultural influences. The Persian civilization was founded by the Medes, which are believed to belong to the predecessors of the Kurds.
>
> (Ocalan 2012)

Because of this belief, Turkish President Erdogan's denouncement of the PKK as Zoroastrian and, therefore, an enemy of not just Turkey but Islam itself, could not have come as a complete surprise (Lynch 2016). Indeed, the PKK is, of course, essentially a secular movement, that encompasses many cultural streams both ancient and modern as well as what appears to be a large dose of Marxist thought. Islam is a religion that plays down ethnic barriers among Muslims. Thus, strict adherence to it and veneration for Islamic history would not serve the Kurdish ethnic national project as well as the stories of ancient religions and predecessor cultures.

Kurds who espouse the Median narrative are less interested in either a biological, linguistic or religious link than they are in establishing a regional identity. Archaeologically, the Medes have always represented a conundrum. Distinguishing Median material culture, in particular from Persian, has always been fraught with difficulties. While Mesopotamian sources dating back to the Late Bronze Age speak of the Medes as one of the many tribes occupying the Zagros and Taurus mountains, with which they traded on a regular basis or fought with when necessary, they provide few details as to their location or leaders.

Herodotus, writing in the fifth century BCE, describes Median culture in terms that indicate he was relying more on tradition than fact, explaining that Deioces (the first King of the Medes according to the ancient historian) "collected the Medes into a nation, and ruled over them alone." He continues by stating that the Median tribes were "the Busae, the Paretaceni, the Struchates, the Arizanti, the Budii, and the Magi" (Herodutus trans. by Rawlinson et al. 1875: 27). While little is known about the first five, the Gospel of Matthew succeeded in making the Magi known to the Western world. Herodotus further suggests that the Medes, like the Lulubi and the Gutians, had an elected king. In his retelling of this history, Deioces had distinguished himself as a judge and eventually, like the Biblical tribes of Samuel's day, the Medians agreed to appoint "one of our number to rule us so that we can get on with our work under orderly government, and not lose our homes altogether in the present chaos." Thus, it was the first elected Median monarch who built the Median capital of Ecbatana with its palace and temples (Flory 1987).

The Greek historian seems to have been, in general, an admirer of Median culture, describing their King as "a man of great ability and ambitious for power" (Herodutus trans. by Rawlinson et al. 1875: 225). Three centuries after Herodotus, Strabo took up their cause with even greater enthusiasm declaring that the Medes were the progenitors for all of the cultures, religions, customs and art of everyone who followed them—a claim that, for understandable reasons, is given little credence (Strabo in Dueck 2017).

The archaeological search for the Medes has necessarily centered on the site of Ecbatana (modern Hamadan), which was excavated in the early part of the twentieth century and, once again, in 1977 after the Iranian Revolution. Although the Medes are mentioned in cuneiform sources with some degree of frequency, there is little there to be found about Ecbatana. Further, unlike another conquered city that became part of the Achaemenid Persian Empire, Susa, the Treasury documents from Persepolis are strangely lacking in information. What we do know about the city, similar to what we know about the Medes themselves, comes from the Greeks. Both Susa and Ecbatana are mentioned there, often together, and we must again turn to Herodotus for detailed information about it.

The venerable Greek historian tells us that the walls of the city of Ecbatana were "of great size and strength, rising in circles within each other. The plan of the place is, that each of the walls should out-top the one beyond it by battlements. The nature of the ground, which is a gentle hill, favors this arrangement in some degree, but it was mainly effected by art." "The number of circles is seven," Herodotus continues, "the royal palace and the treasury standing within the last. The circuit of the outer wall is very nearly the same with that of Athens. Of this wall, the battlements are white, of the next black, of the third scarlet, of the fourth blue, of the fifth orange; all these are colored with paint. The two last have their battlements coated respectively with silver and gold" (Herodutus in Rawlinson et al. 1875: 227–229). Even though it does not resemble other cities, the Ecbatana of Herodotus, existing as it did in the heart of the first Persian Empire, cannot really be attributed solely to the Medes.

There seems to be good historical evidence that the city remained associated closely with the Medes. By the time the historian Polybius saw it, over 200 years after Herodotus, Ecbatana was still the royal residence of the Medes. He describes it as having "greatly exceeded all the other cities in wealth and the magnificence of its buildings" (Polybius in Kuhrt 1995: 657), even though precious metals in its walls had been looted by the troops of Alexander and the subsequent Seleucid kings. Anahita, the goddess of healing and wisdom and alleged associate of the god Ahura Mazda (who became the singular focus of Zoroastrian religion) was worshipped with fire rituals there. She was, most surely, a deity of the Medes as the temple to her in Ecbatana is described by several historians of the fifth century BCE (notably Herodotus and his less famous rival Ctesias) as being one of the most luxurious in the known world (Sweeney 2008).

Thus far in this discussion of Median history, I have not alluded to any real evidence of the characteristics of fierce opposition to imperial rule with which the PKK and the Kurdish resistance could identify. The Medes, who were so easily absorbed into the vast Persian Empire with what appears to have been minimal struggle, like the Lulubi and the Gutians have left little trace of their own culture. The appeal of their narrative actually, like many in this book, have been founded upon a fable, mixed with a few known facts, and passed through the filter of modern nation-building. The Medes are credited by Kurds with one important feat in Ancient Near Eastern history—they dog-gedly chipped away at the great Assyrian Empire until they destroyed it.

The victory of the Medes (along with a number of marginalized peoples including the Scythians, Cimmerians and Chaldeans) over the Assyrians is embedded into their nationalist discourse via the Kurds' unique celebration of the Persian New Year (typically called Nowruz) as a holiday of liberation that they call Newroz. According to the PKK narrative about Newroz, the Assyrians were described as follows:

> [T]he most destructive imperialists of the period who prevented our ancestors the Medes from becoming a people and having a homeland. The Medes, by declaring themselves to be "Aryen" [the people of the fire], decided to resist such a ferocious enemy who were a nightmare to every other Middle Eastern people ... To become a people and a homeland the Medes fought against the Assyrians for 300 years and, in the course of this fight, they defeated the Assyrians to establish the foundations of the Kurdish people.
>
> (Gunes 2012: 96; translation of the PKK Manifesto)

Newroz has also been in the past a commemoration of an important Kurdish "charter myth." Zuhak, according to Kurdish legend, was an evil Assyrian king (unattested in Assyrian Archives) who conquered Iran. He is depicted as having serpents growing from his shoulders and is credited with a 1,000-year rule. The King required human sacrifices in the form of the brains of two young men each day. Naturally, the dwindling of their population of youths was a source of major discontent among the Medes, although, as the story is told, the executioner managed to spare one young man each day by substituting the organs of a sheep. There arose from their number two heroes—one a nobleman and the other Kawa the Blacksmith who had lost six sons to Zuhak. They assembled an army of rescued young men who became the ancestors of the Kurds and who were trained by Kawa. They marched to the palace of the evil king where Kawa dispatched him with a hammer, set fire to the hillsides to celebrate and in Spring returned thereafter to the barren land (Galip 2015).

This tale goes back at least to the tenth century CE when it formed a part of the Shahnameh, the national epic of Iran, by the Persian poet Ferdowsi. It is difficult to know where to start in interpreting this story as it is rife with symbols reminiscent of both Greek and Near Eastern mythology. It is an old story but its value as a resistance narrative has only been recognized in recent years. Much as Theseus became an Athenian national hero, Kawa is the progenitor of the Median utopia as the Kurds characterize it. Unlike Theseus, however, Kawa was a man of the people, a humble craftsman who used a tool of his trade to strike a blow for freedom. Like many such myths, it is likely to be based upon a real event—in this case, the Battle of Nineveh in 612 BCE, which was the decisive turning point in the rebellion against the Assyrian Empire.

Nevertheless, the final blow to the Empire took place elsewhere—at the ancient city below the distant promontory from which I took my first and last look at it. Coming full circle to Carchemish (in Kurdish Girgamêş), a dead city adjacent to a dying town of the same name occupied by Kurds, the end of the Median Empire seems pre-figured by the desolation of this spot. When the Medes allied with the Babylonians to finally extinguish Assyrian hegemony in 607 BCE, it enabled them to establish their own empire—although a number of scholars have come to disbelieve the existence of it (Canepa 2015). For our purposes, whether they had an empire or merely a small kingdom is irrelevant. Whatever hegemony they had only lasted about 50 years, after which Cyrus overtook them. Nonetheless, the Medes became, for the Kurds, a symbol of dogged persistence against oppression to add to their ancient lineage of rebellions stretching back to the Early Bronze Age. In the end, the Median connection with Kurdish militants relies not on history but on the narrative that the Medes, like the Lullubi and the Gutians, were an innovative people whose history was subsumed by empires that failed to acknowledge their contributions.

The modern nation of Turkey, which for decades has portrayed itself as under siege by militant Kurds, could surely sympathize with the hapless lowlanders of Mesopotamia who came to regard the denizens of the Zagros and Taurus Mountains with fear and loathing. Turkey's "Kurdish problem" is acknowledged by most of the West and in Europe as a legitimate fear of a terrorist insurgency. The narrative of civilization's dismissal of the "hill peoples" as wild, brutal and sub-human may be as old as the beginnings of civilization, but the new threat is one that challenges more than just imperial rule. The sacred borders of the nation-state are at risk and the Turks, among the countries that harbor significant Kurdish populations, feel this most profoundly.

The Kurds, seeking to establish a place in the largely unknown past, bypass any claims on the well-known Babylonian, Assyrian and Persian Empires. They prefer to distinguish themselves as politically and linguistically distinct from the Semitic-speaking imperial powers of the Middle East and the Turkic speaking peoples of Southeastern Europe and Southwest Asia. Thus, while scholars have argued for years over the question of whether the languages of the Lullubi, the Gutians, the Kassites and the Elamites were Indo-European, Kurdish websites link them all to the very ancient and venerable Indo-Aryan tradition of the Medes from which they consider themselves to be descended. Not only does this provide them with more affinities to the West, but it also speaks to a continuous and very old story of their presence in the land. It matters little to them whether any of these ancient mountain cultures truly represent their ancestry.

What appears not to have changed in roughly 5,000 years of history is the fact that the people of the mountains have been consistently ignored and underestimated by rulers, politicians, historians and archaeologists despite the fact that many of the advances of civilization took place there. The first temple ever erected in human history, Gobekli Tepe, in eastern Turkey, is in traditional Kurdistan (Scham 2010). Some of the oldest agricultural sites in the world and even some of the very first cities are found there. With their mountain streams consistently depleted by lowland irrigation systems, their villages seen as a source for imperial slaves and mercenaries, their herds decimated for sacrifices to alien gods and to feed the cities of the plains and their minerals and timber exhaustively mined by the imperial powers of Mesopotamia, this acknowledged history, although very long, is also bitter.

Another people of the hills, the ancient Israelites, were fortunate enough to enshrine their early insurgencies against the Egyptians and the Canaanites in the world's best-known religious text. The Kurds have little to evidence their own past because it appears that a concerted effort has been made by imperial powers throughout history to eradicate it. Still, there is a sense in Kurdish consciousness of their responsibility for pushing back waves of Semitic migrations since the Early Bronze Age. On occasion, this perspective seems to border on anti-Semitism. A history textbook used by schools in the Kurdistan Regional Government of Iraq states that the definition of Kurd is "the Kurdish nation, of the Aryan race" (Kirmanj 2014: 377).

Their historical narrative gives them a way to assert their role in advancing Middle Eastern history and, also, in taking part in the struggles of the Muslim world to throw off the Crusader yoke. In the aforementioned textbook, their national hero, Saladin, is understandably given a great deal of attention. At the same time because Kurds, like their ancient forebears, have been the victims of policies that have marginalized them in an Arabic and Turkic speaking milieu, non-Kurdish Muslim leaders are barely mentioned. Kurdish rebellions against the Islamic caliphates and the Ottoman Empire are consistently characterized as opposing unjust rulers.

There seems to be little difference between the "always us against them" narrative of Kurdish extremism and the most accepted Kurdish story of their genesis and history. To be a Kurd is to "look death in the eye"—an expression that is the product of a continued battle against the efforts of empires and nations over a period of millennia to change their culture. A history of armed resistance, as well as internal blood feuds, has created a somewhat doleful outlook on life. Further, like other perpetually embattled peoples, the Kurds have a long list of martyrs to their cause—an issue that touches everyone in the community regardless of their politics. Both Turkish and, in the past, Iraqi governments have sought to counter what they view as a cult of martyrdom by disallowing, preventing or completely disposing of the bodies of those who fell in the Kurdish cause against the state.

It is a powerful, and vengeful, political ploy but one that is likely to backfire as this adds yet another highly compelling unresolved grievance to narratives of extremism. Recurring and sometimes violent clashes between Kurds and Turks have emerged on numerous occasions as relatives continue to demand the bodies of dozens of Kurds that have been kept from burial by Turkish authorities. The Turks, for their part, do not seem to understand the significance of this issue and hope that it will go away. For a people whose long and lamentable history has been one of having been erased from history and consistently forgotten, Kurds are unlikely to give up on commemorating their dead any time soon.

A Kurdish documentary, *The Endless Grief*, effectively dramatizes this, as it documents the poignant story of a father's five-year long search for the remains of his son, killed as a PKK fighter in the mountains of eastern Turkey (Candan 2016). It was screened at the Istanbul Film Festival, ostensibly as a gesture of reconciliation, and received a number of awards. A year later, while mothers in Diyarbakir were staging a month-long hunger strike to get back the bodies of their sons, Turkish authorities refused to allow the screening of any films with Kurdish themes. The mountains have been deemed to be a region of violent extremists since the literate world began. This consistent enmity on the part of all lowlanders who tried to expunge the historical record of mountain peoples, from Sumeria to modern Turkey, has contributed to the Kurdish perspective on cultural relations with others in the region.

The lack of recognition of them, even in death, has dramatically altered the prospects for peace between Turks and Kurds. For both Turks and Kurds, there is a strongly felt immediacy to burial of the dead. In Kurdish culture, to leave the dead unburied is a great shame. As one aspect of cultural violence that subsumes all others, this stands out as one of the most significant. The fact that this is almost a universal norm, and one adhered to by the very people who routinely deprive other people of that right, is based upon a particularly malicious belief in Kurdish inferiority (Ergin 2012).

The ancient enemies of the mountain peoples, the civilizations of Mesopotamia, also paid meticulous attention to burial rituals, as the unburied dead were considered to be a primary cause of vengeful spirits. British Assyriologist Reginald Thompson had a special interest in the various spirits and demons that cursed the regions around the Tigris and Euphrates. He wrote that throughout Mesopotamian history "[t]he spirit of an unburied corpse could find no rest and remained prowling about the earth so long as its body was above ground... If for any reason," he continues, "these attentions [proper burial rights] should cease, and the spirit of the dead man be forgotten, then it was forced by hunger and thirst to come forth" (Thompson 1903: 57, republished 2009).

Ghosts, like demons, were the enemies of the living and their visitations were to be avoided. Tellingly, the Sumerians and Babylonians considered the

Zagros and Taurus Mountains to be their special abode. This was undoubtedly used to their advantage by a number of ancient mountain cultures that periodically invaded the lowlands. In the company of demons, ghosts of the unburied dead wandered the earth seeking vengeance for their unenviable state. Especially feared among evil spirits was Lamashtu, the daughter of Anu, who "makes her home in the mountains" (Thompson 1903). A poem in Akkadian describes the sickness and terror that was inflicted upon one man by vengeful mountain spirits:

> Debilitating Disease is let loose upon me:
> An Evil Wind has blown from the horizon,
> Headache has sprung up from the surface of the underworld ....
> The overpowering ghost has left the high lands
> The Lamashtu-demon has come down from the mountain.
> (The Poem of the Righteous Sufferer, after
> the translation of Lambert 1996)

Bibliography

Abd al-Jabbār, F. and H. Dawod. 2006. *The Kurds: Nationalism and Politics*. London: Saqi Books.

Ahmed, K. 2012. *The Beginnings of Ancient Kurdistan (c. 2500–1500 BC): A Historical and Cultural Synthesis*. Dissertation. Leiden: Leiden University. Retrieved from: https://openaccess.leidenuniv.nl/handle/1887/19095.

Anderson, L. and G. Stansfield. 2010. Avoiding Ethnic Conflict in Iraq: Some Lessons from the Åland Islands. *Ethnopolitics* 9/2: 219–238.

Australian Kurdish Association. 2013. Crime & Punishment à la Turka! *Ekurd.net*, January 29, 2013. Retrieved from: http://ekurd.net/mismas/articles/misc2013/1/turkey4480.htm.

Aziz, M. 2014. *The Kurds of Iraq: Nationalism and Identity in Iraqi Kurdistan*. London: I.B. Tauris.

Bär, J. 2003. Sumerians, Gutians and Hurrians at Ashur? A Re-Examination of Ishtar Temples G and F. *Iraq* 65: 143–160.

BBCNews. 2016a. Ankara Blast: Kurdish Group TAK Claims Bombing. 17 March 2016. Retrieved from: http://www.bbc.com/news/world-europe-35829231.

BBCNews. 2016b. Biden: US and Turkey Prepared to Seek IS Military Solution. 23 January 2016. Retrieved from: http://www.bbc.com/news/world-middle-east-35391968.

Black, J., G. Cunningham, E. Robson, G. Zólyomi and E. Loránd. 2006. *The Literature of Ancient Sumer*. Oxford: Oxford University Press.

Braidwood, R. and B. Howe. 1960. *Prehistoric Investigations in Iraqi Kurdistan. The Oriental Institute of the University of Chicago Studies in Ancient Oriental Civilization*. Chicago, IL: The University of Chicago Press.

Brenneman, R. 2016. *As Strong as the Mountains: A Kurdish Cultural Journey*. Longrove, IL: Waveland Press.

Bryce, T. 2009. *The Routledge Handbook of the Peoples and Places of Ancient Western Asia*. London: Routledge.

Candan, C. 2016. *Kurdish Documentary Cinema in Turkey: The Politics and Aesthetics of Identity and Resistance*. Newcastle Upon Tyne: Cambridge Scholars Publishing.

Canepa, M. 2015. Seleukid Sacred Architecture, Royal Cult and the Transformation of Iranian Culture in the Middle Iranian Period. *Iranian Studies* 48/1: 71–97.

De Lillis F., L. Milano and L. Mori 2007. The Akkadian Occupation in the Northwest Area of the Tell Leilan Acropolos. *Kaskal. Rivista di storia, ambienti e culture del Vicino Oriente Antico*. Volume 4. Retrieved from: http://leilan.yale.edu/sites/default/files/publications/article-specific/kaskal_2007.pdf.

Diakonoff, I. 1951. Last Years of the Urartian Empire. *Vestnik Drevnei Istorii (Journal of Ancient History)* 36/2: 143–157.

Dueck, D. (ed.). 2017. *The Routledge Companion to Strabo*. London: Routledge.

Figaro, 2013. L'étudiante franco-turque Sevil Sevimli condamnée mais bientôt en France. Retrieved from: www.20minutes.fr/france/1101725-20130215-etudiante-franco-turque-sevil-sevimli-condamnee-a-5-ans-prison-terrorisme.

Flory, S. 1987. *The Archaic Smile of Herodotus*. Detroit, MI: Wayne State University Press.

Foster, B.1990. The Gutian Letter Again. *Nouvelle Assyrioloques Breves et Utilitaires* 46: 31.

Frayne, D. 1990. *The Old Babylonian Period (2003–1595 BC), Royal Inscriptions of Mesopotamia 4*. Toronto: University of Toronto.

Frayne, D. 1993. *Sargonic and Gutian Periods (2334–2113 BC) (The Royal Inscriptions of Mesopotamia—Early Periods, 2)*. Toronto: University of Toronto Press.

Frayne, D. 1999. *The Zagros Campaigns of Šulgi and Amar-Suena. Studies on the Civilization and Culture of Nuzi and the Hurrians 10*. Ithaca, NY: Cornell University Press.

Fuccaro, N. 1999. *The Other Kurds: Yazidis in Colonial Iraq*. New York: I.B. Tauris.

Gadd, C. 1966. *The Dynasty of Agade and the Gutian Invasion. Cambridge Ancient Histories*. Cambridge: Cambridge University Press.

Galip, O. 2015. *Imagining Kurdistan: Identity, Culture and Society*. London: I.B. Tauris.

Galtung, J. 1990. Cultural Violence. *Journal of Peace Research* 27/3: 291–305.

Gates, C. 2013. *Ancient Cities: The Archaeology of Urban Life in the Ancient Near East*. London: Routledge.

Grayson, A. 2000. *Assyrian and Babylonian Chronicles*. Winona Lake, IN: Eisenbrauns.

Gunes, C. 2012. *The Kurdish National Movement in Turkey: From Protest to Resistance*. London: Routledge.

Gunter, M. 2010. *Historical Dictionary of the Kurds*. Lanham, MD: Scarecrow Press.

Guvenc, M. 2011. Constructing Narratives of Kurdish Nationalism in the Urban Space of Diyarbakır, Turkey. *Traditional Dwellings and Settlements Review* 23/1: 25–40.

Hallo, W. 2005. *New Light on the Gutians: Ethnicity in Ancient Mesopotamia. Papers Read at the 48th Rencontre Assyriologique Internationale*, July 1–4, 2002.

Hamblin, W. 2006. *Warfare in the Ancient Near East to 1600 BC: Holy Warriors at the Dawn of History*. London: Routledge.

Herodotus. 1875 trans. by G. Rawlinson, H. Rawlinson and J. Gardner 1875. *The History of Herodotus: A New English Version*. London: John Murray.

Izady, M. 2015. *The Kurds: A Concise History and Fact Book*. London: Routledge.

Jwaideh, W. 2006. *The Kurdish National Movement: Its Origins and Development*. Syracuse, NY: Syracuse University Press.

Kelly, V. 2011. *The Militant Kurds: A Dual Strategy for Freedom*. Santa Barbara, CA: ABC-CLIO.

Kirmanj, S. 2014. Kurdish History Textbooks: Building a Nation-State Within a Nation-State. *Middle East Journal* 68/3: 367–384.

Kissinger, H. 1994. *Diplomacy*. New York: Simon and Schuster.

Knapp, A. 2015. *Royal Apologetic in the Ancient Near East*. Atlanta, GA: Society for Biblical Literature Press.

Lambert, W. 1996. *Babylonian Wisdom Literature*. Winona Lake, IN: Eisenbrauns.

Lawler, A. 2014. Erbil Revealed. *Archaeology Magazine*. Retrieved from: www.archaeology. org/issues/145-1409/features/2419-kurdistan-erbil-excavations.

Letsch, C. 2013. Syrian Conflict Brings Sectarian Tensions to Turkey's Tolerant Hatay Province. *The Guardian*, September 3, 2013. Retrieved from: www.theguardian.com/ world/2013/sep/03/syria-crisis-threatens-turkish-tolerance.

Liverani, M. 2013. *The Ancient Near East: History, Society and Economy*. London: Routledge.

Lynch, H. 2016. The Changing Face of Islam in Kurdistan. *RUDAW*, February 7, 2016. Retrieved from: www.rudaw.net/english/kurdistan/07022016.

McDowall, D. 2007. *A Modern History of the Kurds*. London: I.B. Tauris.

Miller, J. and J. Hayes. 1986. *A History of Ancient Israel and Judah*. London: Westminster John Knox Press.

Mirwaisi, H. 2103. Cry of Kurdish Women to President Obama Inspired by Queen Vashti of the Ancient Kurds. *Ekurd.net*, June 23, 2013. Retrieved from: http://ekurd.net/ mismas/articles/misc2013/6/state7165.htm.

Ocalan, A. 2012. *Prison Writings III: The Road Map to Negotiations*. Cologne: International Initiative.

PBS.Org. 2015. How Kurdish Women Soldiers are Confronting ISIS on the Front Lines. *PBS Newshour*, May 3, 2015. Retrieved from: www.pbs.org/newshour/bb/ kurdish-women-soldiers-confronting-fears-isis/.

Pelletiere, S. 2016. *Oil and the Kurdish Question: How Democracies Go to War in the Era of Late Capitalism*. Lanham, MD: Lexington Books.

Porter, A. 2012. *Mobile Pastoralism and the Formation of Near Eastern Civilizations: Weaving Together Society*. Cambridge: Cambridge University Press.

Potts, D. 1999. *The Archaeology of Elam: Formation and Transformation of an Ancient Iranian State (Cambridge World Archaeology)*. Cambridge: Cambridge University Press.

Pringle, H. 2009. Witness to Genocide. *Archaeology Magazine*. Retrieved from: http:// archive.archaeology.org/0901/etc/iraq.html.

Salih, C. 2015. *Turkey, the Kurds and the Fight Against the Islamic State*. London: European Council on Foreign Relations.

Salih, C. and M. Fantappie. 2015. Kurds Need More Than Arms. *The New York Times*, October 20, 2015. Retrieved from: https://www.nytimes.com/2015/10/21/opinion/ kurds-need-more-than-arms.html.

Scham, S. 2010. The World's First Temple. *Archaeology Magazine*. Retrieved from: http:// archive.archaeology.org/0811/abstracts/turkey.html.

Schneider, T. 2011. *An Introduction to Ancient Mesopotamian Religion*. Grand Rapids, MI: Eerdmans.

Seidl, T. 2009. Carchemish in Near Eastern Historiography and in the Old Testament. *Old Testament Essays* 22/3: 646–661.

Sweeney, J. 2008. *The Ramessides, Medes, and Persians*. New York: Algora Publishing.

The Electronic Text Corpus of Sumerian Literature. 1997. The Sumerian King List: Translation. Oxford: University of Oxford. Retrieved from: http://etcsl.orinst.ox.ac. uk/section2/tr211.htm.

Thompson, R. 1903. *The Devils and Evil Spirits of Babylonia*. London: Luzac.

van Bruinessen, M. 1996. Diversity and Division Among the Kurds. Warreport, Bulletin of the Institute for War and Peace Reporting #47 (November–December 1996), 29–32.

Reprinted in: van Bruinessen, M. 2000. Kurdish Ethno-Nationalism Versus Nation-Building States. Collected Articles. Piscataway, NJ: Gorgias Press.

van Bruinessen, M. 2016. The Kurds as Objects and Subjects of Historiography: Turkish and Kurdish Nationalists Struggling Over Identity in *Identität Ethnizität und Nationalismus in Kurdistan* (F. Richter, ed.), pp. 13–61. Münster: Lit Verlagpp.

van Soldt, W. and D. Katz. 2002. Ethnicity in Ancient Mesopotamia. Papers Read at the 48th *Rencontre Assyriologique Internationale Leiden*, July 1–4, 2002.

White, H. 1980. The Value of Narrativity in the Representation of Reality. *Critical Inquiry* 7/1: 5–27.

Winter, I. 2010. *Art in the Ancient Near East: From the Third Millennium BCE.* Leiden: Brill.

Woolley, C. 1921. *Carchemish II: Town Defences: Report on the Excavations at Jerablus on Behalf of the British Museum.* London: British Museum Press.

Woolley, C. and R. Barnett. 1952. *Carchemish III: Excavations in the Inner Town: Report on the Excavations at Jerablus on Behalf of the British Museum.* London: British Museum Press.

Woolley, L., T. E. Lawrence and D. Hogarth. 1914. *Carchemish: Report on the Excavations at Djerabis on Behalf of the British Museum.* London: British Museum.

Yanarocak, H. 2014. Turks Have No Friends but the Turks. *Beehive Middle East Social Media.* Tel Aviv: Tel Aviv University Press. Retrieved from: http://dayan.org/content/beehive-"turks-have-no-friends-turks."

4 "A true people like so many others the world has seen"

Bedouin resistance past and present

> But what I can't understand is why those Israelis have to write about how we are so much like they used to be when they lived in their holy book. We never could afford to just wander around with flocks like that anyway, on this land. Our men always had to migrate, but only to work for whatever government ruled us at the moment. Can't they write about us just as we really are?
>
> (Bedouin Chief as quoted by
> Lavie and Rouse 1993)

> The Arab proclivity toward conflict was exported to all the territories that became Arabized or at least Islamicized, and it became a common feature of all Islamic peoples.
>
> (Patai 1981)

I had my first encounter with the ancient conflict between "the desert and the sown" on a Judean Desert hillside in November of 1997. The desultory protest I was participating in had been organized by a Catholic legal society named for Saint Jude—because nothing conveys confidence like the patron saint of lost causes. Certainly, on that day, we were fulfilling the promise of our organization's name. Maale Adumim, a large settlement sprawling over the hills of East Jerusalem, loomed in the distance over the proceedings as a reminder that the Bedouin were being evicted to make way for its expansion. The Jahalin, originally from the Negev Desert further to the south, had been relocated more than three times over the past 20 years. As we watched, they were being herded into prefabricated "homes" by members of the Israel Defense Forces. It was clear that the army recruits were not relishing their task of rounding up men, women and children into what looked like industrial cartons for shipping to another location—too reminiscent of another history they knew all too well. Several of the women soldiers had tears in their eyes.

Sympathy for the Bedouin, however tragically ineffectual it may have seemed in this case, is not really unusual in Israel. Bedouin life has an allure for this people whose claim to the land is based upon a narrative of forced migration. Many Israelis, in fact, have had something of a romance with Bedouin life even as their government seeks to gradually destroy it. This is something that the Bedouin themselves understandably have difficulty in comprehending. For simplistic observers, the Bedouin are a conundrum—fractious, violent, but invariably hospitable and generous, but some Israelis readily admit that they feel an affinity for them as a people who have lived in the deserts of Palestine and Arabia for centuries (Bailey 2002; Marx 2013). They are, to others, somehow reminiscent of the Biblical Patriarchs—but, at the same time, not in any way to be regarded as "indigenous" to Palestine (Frantzman and Kark 2011).

Gertrude Bell's poetic turn of phrase, "the desert and the sown" (Bell 2012) was based upon a dichotomy that was prominent in the work of Medieval Historian Ibn Khaldun (1967). No one really knows how long they have been there but the Bedouin are referred to by various names throughout recorded history in the Negev, Judean and Sinai Deserts and are traditionally associated with three tribes descended from Abraham—the Quedarites, the Midianites and the Amelekites (Levy 2008). "Abraham was a nomad," a sign held by one Jahalin man at the demonstration, was a reminder of this connection and, as it turns out, prescient. Made fully nomadic by the State of Israel, the semi-nomadic Bedouin were moved yet again a few years—this time to the Jordan Valley near Jericho. Once, their tribe was one of the oldest to roam the Negev Desert and Sinai Peninsula. Now they have their own narrative of forced migration, dissolution and dispossession.

Jahalin ancestral lands were originally near the Negev Desert city of Arad. For centuries, they were among the only inhabitants of this area. After 1948, they had the dubious distinction of being the first Bedouin to be removed by the Israeli government. The town of Arad was built in the very center of Bedouin territory and the original occupants of the land were restricted to less than 10 percent of their former area. No one knows how long the Jahalin lived in Arad. In 1879, Claude Reignier Conder, intrepid Palestine Exploration Fund explorer, came upon a Jahalin tribe near Masada. He observed then that they must "derive their name from a remote period as [Jahalin] is the title applied to the Arabs who were 'ignorant' of the religion of Islam" (Conder 1879: 132). Conder was assuming that *Jahalin* and *Jahaliyyah* (the time of ignorance before the Prophet Mohammed) derived from the same root although there is no evidence to support this contention.

Arad itself is the location of an archaeological site that dates back 10,000 years. I visited it not long after the Jahalin demonstration and noted no references to nomadic presence in the numerous informational signs there. The Israeli Government tourist authorities have represented Arad as a stronghold fortified multiple times "[d]uring the reign of the kings of Judah" (Israel Antiquities Authority Arad 2017). Its excavators also documented an impressive Early Bronze Age occupation there but, recognizing the necessity of attaching Biblical significance to it, referred to Arad as an "Israelite" desert stronghold (Aharoni and Amiran 1964) replete with a "horned altar" for its military detachment to offer the requisite animal offerings to Yahweh (Aharoni 1967). The archaeologists did note a Bedouin cemetery there, which they excavated and dismissed with this succinct description: "[T]he top of the mound became a Bedouin cemetery, a fact that evidently contributed to the preservation of its ancient name" (Herzog et al. 1984: 30) the implication being "luckily for us."

Although its Bedouin history seemed to interest a few Israeli investigators, Israel Finkelstein was intrigued by Arad as "an excellent location for the study of the interface of the desert and the sown" (Finkelstein and Prevolotzky 1990: 34). On re-examination of the evidence from the site, Finkelstein concluded that the distinctive house type found at the site, with a pillar and surrounding courtyard, resembled the Bedouin tents found in the region and that, rather than being a desert stronghold, Arad was "a replica in stone" of a Bedouin encampment. He noted further that "in Sinai and the Negev highlands, where it was necessary to defend the inhabitants and the herds" (Finkelstein and Prevolotzky 1990: 43), such encampments have been described by a number of anthropologists (Ben-David 1982: 217; Shmueli and Khamaisi 2015).

The point made by Finkelstein, perhaps unintentionally, is emphasized more clearly by the work of Rosen (2009) and, in particular, Shmueli and Khamaisi (2015) who take the position that "[t]he term Bedouin is connected with seasonal nomadic behavior in arid deserts" (Shmueli and Khamaisi 2015: 5). Despite the fact that it serves the interests of both the Israeli and Egyptian governments to view the Bedouin as an ethnic minority, being Bedouin has little to do with phenotypes or genotypes. To live as a Bedouin, think as a Bedouin, to interact with others as a Bedouin and, importantly, to resolve disputes as a Bedouin is to be Bedouin. In other words, in positing that the Bedouin lifestyle was characteristic of this land since at least the Chalcolithic Period (ca. 3500 BCE) these scholars suggest strongly that they are indigenous by any definition. Perhaps Arad's excavators should have accorded greater respect to that cemetery.

It was not, of course, the only Bedouin cemetery to be desecrated by archaeologists, but it was rare at the time for one to be mentioned in a report. When I was investigating prehistoric nomadic sites surrounding Teleilat Ghassul in Jordan, I found ample evidence of burial sites, characterized only by small piles of stones, and a cemetery near the site that had been excavated by Jesuit scholars in the 1930s. Although it was dated to prehistoric periods for the most part, recent graves were disturbed in that process. I was later to find that at Ghassul itself, there were more than a few disinterments by the Jesuits who dug there.

I was at Ghassul in the winter when sheep and goat herds graze in the temperate lowlands, moving to the cooler highlands in the summer—just as they did during the Chalcolithic Period (Scham 1996). The Bedouin families whose flocks were grazing around the site were hospitable to the point of embarrassment (mine) in their attempts to provide me with food, which they could ill afford to do. Mauss observed about Bedouin culture that, "[t]o refuse to give, or to fail to invite, is—like refusing to accept—the equivalent of a declaration of war; it is a refusal of friendship and intercourse" (Mauss 1970: 11). In my case, refusing to accept was not an option. A group of young women literally herded me from my site into their encampment.

One day, a Bedouin man watching over the herds warned me away from still active land mines (planted 20 years earlier) around the site. He told me that, only one year before, he had lost a goat to one of them. I am not sure if, in Bedouin culture, that constitutes saving a life but I was grateful for the advice. By then, I had some vague notion of the idea of reciprocity and realized that I did not have much to offer in return except for one small act that they would never know about. Working in a small museum in Jerusalem, I was shocked to discover a display of "Arab burials" from Ghassul. The museum was being renovated and the curator and I agreed that the display was offensive. I suggested at the time that I might bring them back to the site in Jordan and rebury them. The legal ramifications of that were somewhat daunting so I believe that we settled on burial in the garden. Not the most noble gesture on my part, but better than having the probable ancestors of the people who had shown me so much kindness moldering in a dilapidated museum case in Israel.

Later, during an archaeological conference in Jerusalem, I talked to an individual who knew more about those landmines than my Bedouin informant. He was an Israeli archaeologist who, like me, was working on Chalcolithic sites. I, of course, mentioned Ghassul and he told me that he had visited the site decades ago. I was surprised because Israelis could not go to Jordan until the two countries made peace with each other. Petra in Jordan was a site particularly beloved by Israelis and members of the Defense Forces reportedly slipped over the border to see it on many occasions. There was even a song written about these events. Petra, however, was a long way from the Dead Sea. When I asked him how he happened to see the site, he said that in the 1970s he was there with other Israeli soldiers planting mines around the site because it was close to the border. "While we were doing that," he said, "I slipped away to take a look at the site." An archaeologist engaged in establishing what are, without argument, the most enduring material remnants of structural and cultural violence in the world, lethal land mines, was a grim harbinger, I thought, for my continuing work in Jordan.

Most of my experiences with Bedouin, including interactions in the desert, collaborations with Bedouin scholars, attending Bedouin social occasions and weekend sojourns with the Bedouin of Petra, were always agreeable ones. While I have witnessed some lively arguments, never once did I see any semblance of a proclivity toward violence. The first time we stayed with a large and lively family living near Petra stands out as an example of what I think of as Bedouin sang-froid when presented with an individual who represents a radically different, perhaps even adversarial, culture. Our host was a traditional Bedouin, clad in a white kamisa and kefiah. He rented rooms to tourists on a number of occasions and charged very little for it.

Later, as we visited the site of Petra, surely a spectacular testament to Jordanian Bedouin history, we encountered an ultra-orthodox man. Dressed fully in black wearing a kippa (skullcap) and sporting payot (sidelocks) he, quite naturally, stood out. Curious about him, my husband struck up a conversation in Hebrew. The man said he was visiting Jordan because he had said almost all of the important Jewish blessings for specific sights except for the one required on seeing a king. Apparently, it is a mitzvah to go and see great rulers, whether they are Jewish or non-Jewish. We were attempting to determine whether he was foolish enough to believe he might get an audience with King Hussein, when he abruptly asked us where we were staying and we told without thinking much about it. Later, we had some misgivings but we reasoned that, if this man turned up at his door, our host would not let him stay. As we trooped into the place later, we found our black clad ultra-orthodox acquaintance seated on one of the floor cushions across from our white clad host and sharing a narjila.

Raphael Patai was wont to believe that tales of Bedouin violence both outside of and within the society reflected real events that were continually occurring. His self-professed understanding of *The Arab Mind* (1981) has enjoyed unwarranted popularity in recent years, mostly among counter-terrorism specialists (few of his fellow anthropologists would ever look to it for enlightenment). It is certainly true that nineteenth-century travelers in the Middle East alluded to brutal "blood feuds" in Bedouin life (Musil 1928)—and some modern social scientists still believe that feuding is a primary masculine pastime (Ginat 1997). Critics of the "wanton destructiveness" of blood feuds in Bedouin culture, like Kressel (1998 and 1999), fail to comprehend that the major reason people of the West have historically exaggerated the brutality of intertribal warfare is that it is damaging to the organizational interests of modern nations.

Disputes over rights to grazing lands have been frequent but each tribe has established legal mechanisms to deal with them that seldom come to the attention of governmental officials. Given the history of horrific combats in the twentieth century among Western nations, however, it is difficult to believe that these small skirmishes are the origin of Bedouin economic and political woes as well as a major obstacle to "the development of individual conscience and thinking" (Hart 1997). In Israel, the dissonant relationship between Bedouins and the government has developed more gradually than its conflict with Palestinians. When the government settled the Negev Bedouins in towns, they simply allocated an insufficient amount of land, utilities and other resources—creating, they hoped, a situation that would indirectly limit Bedouin freedoms. In the vain hope that Western values would take hold and the Bedouin would stop reproducing at a rate that was very likely to overtake that of Jews in the region, this was a subtle form of structural violence that has become something of a ticking time bomb. The Bedouin have responded with building what Israelis consider to be "illegal" settlements that are continually threatened by authorities. The government retaliates by regularly dismantling them (more so, it seems, than they do with Jewish illegal settlements in the West Bank).

Thus, even though they have fulfilled their theoretical bargain by settling down and becoming more or less model second-class citizens, rather than engaging in open rebellion in Israel, they have turned to covert defiance when it comes to the underlying demographic restrictions behind the government's resettlement programs. Polygyny is on the increase in the Negev, even though it is against the law in Israel. The additional children that this marital practice provides are valued for their labor, emotional support and ability to provide security for their parents in old age—to make up in some cases for the patent neglect of their government. The higher the number of children, the more economically productive a family can be. In the Bedouin community, producing more children, especially males, plays an instrumental role in establishing a family's honor and social status. Furthermore, leadership, as well as security, in the "new" Bedouin communities and towns often hinges upon the size of one's family or tribe (Abu-Rabia et al. 2008).

South of the Negev and Judean Deserts, the Tarabin cousins of the Bedouin of Israel are reportedly fiercer in their opposition to structural violence. Members of this large tribe, who are recorded as having inhabited Negev and the Sinai for at least three centuries, are among the poorest people in Israel and Egypt. The Government has accused them frequently of attacking local Egyptian authorities and, according to press reports, the lives of a number of Egyptian soldiers and police officers have been taken by Bedouin tribes people. According to those same reports, Bedouin outrage has been particularly exacerbated by official attempts to stop an age-old Bedouin livelihood—smuggling. In many ways, the economic version of insurgency and a classic example of the reaction of the marginalized to oppressive authority, illegal trade in goods, especially weapons, has been reported for centuries (Pelham 2012; Marx 2013). In the case of the Sinai Bedouin, it has also represented a classic example of their autonomy under both Israeli (from 1967 to 1982) and Egyptian governments.

Of late, the largest concern is that members of Bedouin Tribes who were previously engaged in the smuggling of guns have begun to traffic in people—in this case, Eritrean refugees attempting to get to Israel. Extortion and torture by Bedouin tribesmen, in many cases colluding with Egyptian authorities, has been reported. Arabs have had little regard for the humanity of their southern neighbors and in the far distant past regarded people from the region occupied by Ethiopia and Eritrea as having been corrupted by Christianity and, therefore, historical enemies. Ibn Khaldun, who is somewhat ambivalent about Bedouin, has nothing but harsh words for sub-Saharan Africans, characterizing them as the only people who willingly accept slavery (Lewis 1990).

Although Bedouin have been rarely engaged in any long-term active revolts, they have been historically resistant to attempts to incorporate them into an established political apparatus. At the very least, they have refused to be taxed. At their most unruly, however, they could impose an active embargo on the transport of both goods and people through their desert domains. Some writers have seen the modern condition of the Middle East Bedouin as the natural result of cultural forces within the society (Kressel 1998; Dinero 2002). Bedouin preoccupation with patrilineal kinship, it has been argued, interferes with their "ability to accept cultural pluralism, civil rights, democracy, humanistic principles, individualism, and the full participation of women,"

(Kressel 1998: 34). Other scholars, more honestly, evaluate the changes taking place in Bedouin society as overtly political responses to damaging and alien domination (Dinero 2010). Bedouin identification with the Palestinian struggle and a resurgence of Muslim practice and observance in Israel and Egypt, may be part of this trend (Cole 2003).

There are a lot of reasons to distrust the Egyptian Government's claims that large numbers of Bedouin have been enmeshed within local extremist political organizations. The Wilayet Sinai (Islamic State in the Sinai), formerly known as Ansar Bayt Al Maqdis (defenders of Jerusalem), are certainly active in their recruiting of Bedouin youth but their elders remain steadfast in their opposition. In 2015, for example, some Tarabin in the Sinai launched an armed campaign against Wilayet as retaliation for its attack on a tribal leader whom the extremists had accused of collaboration with Egyptian security agencies. Further, even as these organizations have attempted to obtain recruits from among the tribes, they are encroaching upon Bedouin tribal territory and influential tribespeople are obliged by custom and tradition to push back against Wilayet's territorial expansion. In addition to the fact that these groups profess an allegiance to extra-tribal ideologies, the narrative of Wilayet Sinai does not easily fit in with the Bedouin world view. The attempts of Wilayet to set up a polity in the Sinai, replete with a police force to impose Sharia law, does not sit well. Finally, their new name is too reminiscent of all of the historical entities that attempted, without much success, to control them—from prehistory to the modern nation–state (Aziz 2017).

The first and most important challenge to extremist groups that the Bedouin present is their unorthodox views of religion. Groups that are successful in persuading the religiously unschooled, as well as the disaffected, find in the Bedouin a unique negation of the standard arguments. The concept of the "just ruler," which has come to occupy a central place in the political thought of some fellahin Muslims (particularly Shi'a), is a contradiction in terms for Bedouin. With their acceptance of Islam, the Bedouin did not consider that they accepted all of the practices and restrictions that were developed for sedentary urbanized populations. The polytheist Bedouin accepted the religion primarily as a means of politically and economically integrating into their larger societies. Their pre-Islamic notion of honor, which abjures religious validation of any leader, became incorporated into the version of Islam practiced by Bedouin tribes in the Negev and the Sinai. As the famed pre-Islamic seventh-century Bedouin poet Zuhayr bin Abī Sūlmā wrote, "[h]e who does not cease asking people to carry him, and does not make himself independent of them even for one day of the time, will be regarded with disgust" (Arbery 1957). No state level government could be fully legitimate by that standard.

The much-vaunted tribal awakening of the Sinai Bedouin (Shkolnik 2012) is thus nothing more than a reaction to the recognition that the independence that they have celebrated in poetry since long before the advent of Islam can be infringed upon with increasing effect. Even if the Bedouin have been accorded some autonomy by both Israel and Egypt, alongside of that autonomy has come decades of neglect. Presented with the choice between losing their autonomy and receiving virtually nothing in return has outraged many tribal leaders. Smuggling remains for them a direct assault on the authority of the government, even though it was inevitable that both Israel and Egypt would endeavor to put a stop to it, an action resulting in increasing poverty in places already riddled with it (Marx 2013).

Egypt, in particular, feels compelled under its current anti-Muslim Brotherhood regime to make some effort to provide on-the-ground evidence of its cooperation with Israel under the terms of what has been called a "cold peace" (El-Nawawy 2002). Bedouin commodities and drug smuggling were less of an international issue than the illegal trafficking of arms to Gaza. Smuggling is not an integral part of the Bedouin lifestyle, even though historically they have, like many hard-pressed populations, resorted to brigandage of many kinds when events warrant it.

The fraught relationships between mobile pastoralists, sedentary peoples and state-level societies have interested political, economic and cultural analysts. The idea that conflicts between the "desert and the sown" were ultimately responsible for the disappearance of the nomad in the modern world has congealed into a universal principle. According to this view, the nation-state is also seen as inherently hostile to mobile societies. It has been presumed that borderless cultures, herders and hunters, of necessity have to give way to the needs of countries in the modern world to define and strengthen their borders.

Anthropologists studying pastoralists focus less on outside limitations to the internal systems, but in the 1970s and 1980s, the great "e" concepts, environment and economy, were posited as the factors most likely to bear the responsibility for the "insecurity" of mobile societies. Inspired by the "tragedy of the commons" theory, cultural ecologists speculated that pastoralists pushed their mostly marginal ecosystems beyond the limits of their endurance (Anderson 1996). Others have suggested that mobile systems were inherently unstable because they were fragile economies—ever changing with minor shifts in the environment and ever tuned to the whims of the towns and villages upon which they were assumed to be dependent (Dransart 2003). Vulnerable from within, as posited by the anthropologists, and assaulted from without, as described in the historical and political literature, the demise of mobile cultures when confronted with the superior organization of state-level societies seemed a constant inevitability.

Regardless of the verdict of other scholars, there is no shortage of champions of ancient nomads among archaeologists, which is curious because their sites are notoriously hard to locate and they leave behind few material traces. Nomadic contributions to civilization have been argued since Ibn Khaldun pronounced that "[t]he desert is the basis and reservoir of civilization and cities" (1967: 164). Pastoralists in the Near East often follow the same routes year after year and, over time, develop fixtures such as stone corrals for overnight containment of herds or similar shelters for human occupants at certain sites along those routes. Some archaeologists support the view that the necessity to separate pastoral and farming activities (because animals run roughshod over crops) resulted in an increasing specialization. The latter, they argue, was responsible for improving the flocks to such a great extent that pastoralists could initiate exchanges with farmers because of the superior nature of their animal products compared with those of sedentary villagers (Hole 1978).

Taking this theory a step further, other scholars believe that not only were full-time pastoralists responsible for instituting regional trade relationships, they were also to be credited with the establishment of a regional communications network and the institution of an expanded decision-making organization to coordinate local production and seasonal exchanges (Cribb 2004; Halstead 1996). There has been greater success in locating sites in recent years and, as a result, an increase in speculation about the beginnings of the pastoralist lifestyle going back to periods before the domestication of today's food producing animals. The Natufians, a culture that existed over 14,000 years ago in the Levant, and who have long been considered as the first people to attempt to control the wild wheat population, also appear to have had "proto-domesticated" animals according to some archaeologists—but in their case, the animal in question is the gazelle (Bar-Yosef 1998).

There is ample evidence, however, that the first animal domesticated by the Natufians was not raised for food. Archaeologists working in northern Israel in 1978 made a surprising find in the 12,000-year-old grave of a Natufian woman. She was discovered with her hand embracing a puppy buried above her head. Analysis of the puppy's skeleton showed that, like the woman, it had died of natural causes. Dog bones had been found at Natufian sites as early as 1937 but this was the first indication of a special relationship between dogs and humans. As a result of this find, and later ones from even earlier periods, the dog is now considered to be the first domesticated animal in the Middle East (Tchernov 1997). Apart from the rather touching realization that humans first tamed animals for companionship rather than sustenance, the dog in the Middle East today is one of many touchstones that differentiate herders from farmers. Islamic law has designated the canine species as unclean and, therefore, devout Muslims are abjured from keeping dogs close to their homes. The Bedouin, however, have valued them since pre-Islamic times and were responsible for creating at least two ancient breeds—the Saluqi and the Canaan dog. So disruptive was the difference of opinion between rural and urban Muslims on this subject, early Islamic jurists attempted to distinguish between urban and rural dogs in order to recognize the nomadic tradition (Bailey 1982).

The Natufian canines were not the property of nomads, however. Their keepers were fairly sedentary hunter-gatherers and it was not until sheep and goat species were domesticated later that semi-nomadism came to the Middle East. Sheep and goat bones were discovered in the Middle East at sites dating from the early Neolithic Period (ca. 9500 BCE). The development of the archaeological specialization of analyzing animal bones developed partly as a result of the drive to locate seasonal sites (Cribb 2004). Those who keep sheep and goats in the Middle East are required to move several times during the year to find adequate water and pasturage—a practice that is confirmed by some of the earliest Egyptian texts. Despite the fact that there has been a great deal of progress in locating ancient nomadic sites, most of the information we have on the lifestyle of the Bedouin in the Bronze and Iron Ages (6000 BCE to 1000 BCE) comes from the writings of the inhabitants of the sown.

The Ancient Egyptian view of nomads seemed to depend primarily upon their proximity (not to be desired) and the potential of Bedouin land for exploitation (definitely to be desired). Old Kingdom Egyptian texts refer to "starving" Bedouin, whose culture is utterly foreign to the civilized Nile flood zone dwellers. Other records from the Late Old Kingdom describe expeditions against nomads and record an attack on Egyptians by the Bedouin near the Red Sea (Rosen 2016). The Bedouin who dwelt (and, more importantly, stayed) in Canaan, a place that was devoid of any mineral resources of interest to Egyptians, are distinguishable in the texts from those in the nearby Sinai Peninsula. Although Egyptians clearly saw all Bedouin as inferior, at times, they were considered fairly harmless during most time periods. The famous Middle Kingdom story of the Egyptian official Sinuhe is admiring of the Bedouin of Canaan who were kind to the protagonist and among whom he lived for most of his adult life. Nomads of the Sinai, however, were a completely different matter. Referring specifically to Sinai nomads as "*aamu*" (sand-dwellers), the Ancient Egyptians also branded them as cattle raiders (Weinstein 1975).

In a recent article, Ellen Morris (2017) posited that as early as 2500 BCE, when increasing aridity throughout Africa and the Ancient Near East caused the collapse of the Early Bronze III urban culture in Syria-Palestine, life became more difficult for those who lived in marginal areas such as the Sinai Peninsula. When centralized government in Egypt began to wane at the end of the Old Kingdom, Egyptians began to become more aware of these cultural outsiders as competitors for scarce resources (Hassan 2007: 359–360). During the First Intermediate Period (2181–2055 BCE), *The Prophecies of Neferti* lament "the condition of the east, when the Asiatics raid and terrorize those at the harvest, taking away their teams engaged in plowing" (Lichtheim 1973: 135). At the margins of the Egyptian state, the Sinai had become a political no man's land. The *Instruction of Merikare*, also written during the First Intermediate Period, decries "[t]he vile Asiatic" who, when confronted with the miserable prospect of water shortages and unreliable grazing land:

> [N]ever settled in one place, but plagued by want, he wanders the deserts on foot. He has been fighting ever since the time of Horus. He neither conquers nor can he be conquered. He does not announce the day of fighting, but is like a thief whom society has expelled.
>
> (Faulkner 1973)

These early documents may well be descriptive of the first Sinai Insurgency— at least in the eyes of the Egyptian state.

These fears were not completely unfounded as the later successful attacks of the Hyksos demonstrate. Although it did not originate in the Sinai, the conquest of the Nile Delta ca. 1800 BCE confirmed generations of warnings about the dangers on the borders of "wandering groups of Semites who had long come to Egypt for trade and other peaceful purposes" (Hawkes 1963: 144). While the Hyksos are seldom considered as typical of the nomadic pastoralists of this time, most scholars believe that they had a nomadic past as excavations of the Hyksos capital of Avaris indicate. Most archaeologists accept that they came to Egypt because of famine and instability in Canaan. Analysis of sediments shows that central Canaan was experiencing erosion and arid climatic conditions at this time, while part of the Twelfth Dynasty was marked by extremely high Nile flood levels due to heavy monsoon rains. Drought in Canaan and high Nile flood levels in Egypt could easily have compelled one or more groups of pastoralists from southern Canaan and the Sinai to come in increasingly larger numbers to the Egyptian Delta (Sivertsen 2009).

Hyksos burials have yielded important information as to what they considered to be representative of their values. Significant graves contained the remains of donkey sacrifices or the bones of sheep or goats. In rare instances, the Hyksos also buried their prized horses. They worshipped a combination of Syrian and Egyptian deities but seem to have devoted particular attention to the god Set, who represented the desert and foreigners. In later Egyptian religion, Set became a vilified god, perhaps in part because of his association with these alien rulers. As rulers in the North, the Hyksos were barely tolerated and, even though Egyptians never came to accept them as legitimate rulers, it took centuries to rout them. Hyksos rule did not come to an end until the Seventeenth Dynasty (ca. 1580 BCE); rulers of Upper Egypt mounted a series of military campaigns that resulted in the capture of Avaris (Muscarella 2013).

The humiliating memory of the Hyksos lasted for centuries as attested by the vehemence with which the third century BCE Egyptian historian Manetho describes them. He wrote:

> Unexpectedly, from the regions of the east, invaders of obscure race marched in confidence of victory against our land ... By main force they easily seized it without striking a blow; and having overpowered the rulers of the land, they then burned our cities ruthlessly, razed to the ground the temples of the gods, and treated all the natives with a cruel hostility, massacring some and leading into slavery the wives and children of others.
>
> (Gmirkin 2006: 175)

The Jewish historian Flavius Josephus (first century CE) translated Manetho's name for them as "Shepherd Kings" and that name, with its somewhat scornful implications, was thereafter used by later historians (Josephus 1999, trans. Whiston). It was Josephus who, based upon Manetho's account, first suggested that the Hyksos were the Biblical Israelites—a claim that has been completely rejected by modern historians and archaeologists.

During the New Kingdom, nomads were often associated with the infamous Shasu, itinerant laborers in Ancient Egypt who, according to the Amarna texts, were frequently troublesome. Ancient Egyptians were eager to mine Sinai turquoise, copper and other minerals, but they rarely entered the place except under military protection. The memory of the Hyksos still fresh in their minds, the Egyptians during this period viewed the Sinai as a source of endless needy immigrants. The *Ipuwer Papyrus* (1250 BCE) is considered to be the account of an eyewitness to these events. The eponymous writer of this document bemoans that "the desert pervades the land, the nomes are annihilated, and foreign aliens have come to Egypt... Moreover, all the foreigners claim 'This is our water! These are our crops!'" (Simpson 2003: 192, 193). A number of New Kingdom pharaohs set out to pacify the Shasu once and for all and launched several military campaigns in the Sinai. Eventually, as later texts indicate, the Egyptians ended up hiring Bedouin as guides and scouts. Later texts indicate that the Egyptians relieved them of oppressive taxes and periodically paid them for the protection of trade caravans. Appeasement continued to be the strategy used by subsequent empires. Both the Assyrians and the Persians sought the help of the Bedouin in launching their invasions of Egypt. Accounts from the reigns of Esarhaddon and Cambyses indicate that they consulted with the nomads on how to cross the desert (Morris 2017).

Attacks on the nomadic lifestyle and attacks by nomads on sedentary people became particularly obdurate during the Byzantine Period—the crucible of modern Bedouin relations with external governance. As the first universalist religion to hit the Ancient Near East, Christianity brought with it proliferating monasteries that encroached upon desert areas. Lawlessness among the tribes of the Sinai and a more substantial threat from tribal federations in other parts of the Levant drove those monastic communities to seek protection from the Emperor Justinian, whose response was to build even more monasteries. As a result, some opportunistic banditry by the Bedouin is often recorded and more tensions emerged from the Byzantine project to "occupy" the Holy Land (Parker 1999).

The Nilus account, a narrative of the late fourth or early fifth century, tells of a Bedouin attack at the time when the writer and his son "had come down from the sacred mountain to visit the holy men in the place of the [Burning] Bush" (Hobbs 2001). Another narrative affirms the existence of a tower that was used as a refuge against attacking Bedouins:

> Those (monks) who were found staying near the tower (pyrgos), hearing the uproar and the tumult, ran into the stronghold together with the superior of the place, Doulas by name. He was truly a servant of Christ, for he had more patience and gentleness than anyone else; from this he was popularly called Moses.
>
> (Mayerson 1978: 35).

These accounts appear to indicate that the continuing confrontations in the Byzantine Middle Eastern deserts were more than a matter of simple predation on the part of Bedouin. They suggest that there was real outrage over the growing encroachments of Christians who were the first to "make the desert bloom" (Parker 1999). This was a period in which the semi-arid parts of the Middle East were more productive—resulting in a stable system of local exchange for the most part.

Christian ideology was centered in urban and town areas and on pilgrimage routes that, with the exception of the one to St. Catherine, did not pass through the Bedouin areas very often. Established trade routes were through the cultivated desert highlands. To the extent that they needed to, Byzantine emperors resorted to the solution of previous empires—that of recruiting local Bedouin leaders as "mediators" between the state and the people. With the Islamic shift in ideology, the Bedouin became culturally (if not politically) more integrated into the state. In the Early Islamic Period, the cultural and linguistic similarities between the Bedouin and their putative overlords was such that the "symbolic appropriation" of the desert areas was enough to keep the peace and ensure safety for the Haj and trade routes. Some scholars suggest that with the participation of Bedouin in the Islamic conquest, this population became greatly dispersed and left the countryside to the agriculturalists. There is no evidence that mobile peoples left the Middle East during this time. The hudna (Arab Peace) of the Islamic Periods fell apart with the disruption of the Crusades and the later Ayubbid and Mamluk resumption of Islamic authority was unable to restore good relations between the Bedouin and the Fellahin (town dwellers) (Schick 1998).

The Mamluks tried many strategies, some successful and some not, to reduce Bedouin incursions. Eventually, the Bedouin found the Turks more to their liking but, by this time, they were armed, perhaps even better than the imperial troops, and most of the desert areas had become so marginal that the Ottoman Empire was unable to persuade farmers to live there. As a result, trade relations with local farmers diminished and the resourceful Bedouin came to depend more and more on the "guiding" and "protection" of people who had to travel through desert areas. The empire attempted to fortify the Haj routes, especially against them. The Middle East is not on a major Haj route but the southern Negev and Sinai Peninsula are close to the Sinai route to Mecca taken by pilgrims from North Africa and is decidedly on the minor pilgrimage route to Jerusalem. Through Ottoman land grants, some Bedouin leaders attained large estates, which they paid others to farm, and other Bedouin were forced into itinerant labor (Mikhail 2011).

The Ottoman empire, although Islamic, was not culturally or linguistically affiliated with the Bedouin, however. Further, the decline of settlements in the desert areas during the preceding periods had reduced the trading partnerships and created new tensions between them. Possibly, the contemporaneous introduction of both guns and taxes into the region succeeded in forcing the Bedouin into a more polarized position vis-a-vis the state. The Ottomans by all accounts were more zealous tax collectors than their predecessors (Vorderstrasse 2014). Under the Byzantine and Early Islamic empires, taxes were closely tied to religion and religious law and went largely uncollected, or collected in kind, from mobile pastoralists.

The Ottoman emperors, also, still had a need to maintain the trade and pilgrimage routes, as well as roads through the desert to other Ottoman territories. This resulted in a need to "pacify" the Bedouin but there was felt to be no necessity to completely subjugate them as their leaders served as a conduit between the state and pastoralists elsewhere. Subjugation of the Bedouin in the region finally came about with the establishment of the State of Israel and later its control over the Sinai Peninsula following the Six Day War. Although it can be argued that the Bedouin benefitted from being enfolded within a wealthy Western state, they lost the conduit function that they had served between the desert and the sown for hundreds of years (Abu-Rabia 2001).

There are few records of nomadic groups being, themselves, annexed by any of the empires of the past. Rather, appeasement seems to have been the main method of dealing with them. In terms of maintaining their independence, Bedouin mobility was their greatest asset. A people who neither conquered nor could be conquered, as the *Instruction of Merikare* warned, could be a constant source of anxiety for settled people. In the ancient world, as well as today, the primary symbols of Bedouin refusal to be enclosed or embedded within a state-level apparatus, whether ancient or modern, has been the camel and the tent. Although camels were not always a feature of Bedouin life, the tent appears to be far more ancient. During the Old Babylonian Period, a number of different types of temporary structures are mentioned in connection with the people of the desert. In the famous Middle Kingdom story, mentioned previously, Sinuhe, although an Egyptian, proves his Bedouin credentials by boasting that, after defeating an enemy, he "took what was in his tent; I stripped his camp. Thus I became great, wealthy in goods, rich in herds" (Simpson 2003).

The Mari texts also mention tent dwellings. The famous benediction of the Moabite seer Balaam over the "goodly tents" of Jacob has come down to us in Hebrew transliterated as ohelim, which may be cognate to the Assyrian alu referring to "a place where one dwells." As often happens with emblematic material culture, the tent has also constituted an important focus for imperial cultural violence. The Merneptah Stele, celebrated for containing the first mention of the term Israel, is typical of these expressions of hostility. While the Egyptian Sinuhe just robbed the tent of an enemy, the Pharaoh Merneptah describes his numerous raids on the people of Canaan as including nomads whose tents were burned "to ashes." Setting fire to tents was a particularly popular image to evoke for those rulers who managed to overcome nomadic camps as later Assyrian and Babylonian texts attest (Rosen and Saidel 2010).

The most important components of Bedouin ideology, formed through their contacts with imperial powers, became increasingly difficult for sedentary populations to understand as settled life progressed from villages to large cities. As a result, the possibility of appeasement has disappeared from their relationship with the state only to be replaced by economic privation and repressive policies. The Bedouin relationship between kinship and territory is mistakenly seen by modern nation-states as indicative of communal (and therefore expendable) ownership of land and city dwellers see the appeal of Bedouin life only in very superficial terms (Marx 1977). In effect, to be Bedouin is to be independent in some ways but very dependent in others. The number of bonds and associations that are not apparent to observers, but widely understood within the society, include those between territory and sub-groups in the larger social organization; between the herds as a collective enterprise and both human and divine interactions; and between the pastoral routes and way stations and sacred geography.

The urban societies of both Modern Israel and Modern Egypt have consistently attempted to chip away at Bedouin life, even while remaining reluctant to ever embrace them as their own. Some of the Bedouin of the Sinai, hammered by the Egyptian police and having lost their tourism revenues due to the instability in the region, see the Israel years as having been, if not good, at least prosperous. They have little reason to accord loyalty to either Egyptians or Israelis but at least the latter provided a steady stream of visitors. The ideal of Bedouin history as romantically emplotted and anarchist (Franz 2011) in terms of ideology, to use White's formulation, has probably never been true. Today, their narrative has an essentially tragic emplotment that would suggest that they are now more amenable to a radical ideology. Historically, it has been shown that it is settlement schemes that created this tendency. Both the governments of Israel and Egypt have mistakenly seen settlement as a positive measure in dealing with Bedouin populations when, in fact, it has been sowing the seeds of insurrection.

As a collective society living in a harsh environment, the traditional Bedouin community considers interdependence and group cohesiveness to represent adaptive modes of behavior. This form of ideology provides the primary motivation for intra-familial and intra-tribal contacts—in other words, the aspects of life that are least visible to an outside observer. There is little room in this established and complex interlinking of human relations for simplistic religiously inspired messages that do little to address practical everyday concerns and this is undoubtedly something that accounts for the lack of success for extremists in promoting any large-scale violent Bedouin uprising. Based on the belief that in any location where violence and Bedouin coexist, it is the latter that must be culpable; Egypt has been brutal in its attacks on the Sinai and the Northern Bedouin, predominantly the Tarabin, have borne the brunt. Egypt's new autocracy, pushed by Israel and the United States to stop illegal traffic between the Sinai and Gaza, has also been cracking down on illegal activities in the Sinai.

The Ancient Egyptian hatred of the Bedouin typically surfaced during periods when they were attempting to re-establish hegemony after a time of relative chaos. After the social and political chaos following Akhenaten's reign, the pharaohs that followed him, Horemheb, Ramesses I and Seti I, all set out to "restore" the empire of their forebears. Seti I (1294–1279 BCE) in particular set his sights to the north, mounting a ruthless campaign, to begin with, against the Bedouin of the Sinai to clear the "Way of Horus" to Canaan and Syria. Scenes of war and destruction were a vital part of the cultural violence arsenal of Ancient Near Eastern empires, and Seti's battle reliefs were no exception. Depicting a virtual massacre of unarmed Bedouin who are shown fleeing the scene, the accompanying text explains that the pharaoh had received a report that the Bedouin were plotting rebellion (Morris 2017).

Similarly, in Modern Egypt, while times of restored state control may be welcome to the urban population, they are never good for the Bedouin, considering that maintaining their independence has been part of their world view for millennia. Under the brief governance of the ineffectual Mohamed Morsi, the Sinai Bedouin found their traditional, and highly cherished, Urf legal system was "discouraged" by the government because it did not always comport with Sharia. That, however, was a period of relative freedom. Deposing the democratically elected Morsi, Abdel Fattah el-Sisi established a regime more repressive, according to some analysts, than Egypt had yet seen in modern times. When he came to power, Sisi immediately announced an all-out campaign against "terror in the Sinai" that uprooted thousands of Bedouin who had little or nothing to do with the groups they were accused of aiding and abetting. The Sisi government is so determined to bring Islamic State actors in the Sinai Desert to heel that they have "accidentally" killed groups of tourists (Bassiouni 2016).

Acts of resistance in the Sinai have been labeled by some reporters as Bedouin exacting vengeance "old style" and executing a return to their age-old roles as enemies of authority at all cost. In truth, the so-called Sinai Bedouin Insurgency, on closer inspection, is neither Bedouin nor, strictly speaking, a true insurgency. To the extent that it does include Bedouin leaders, among non-Bedouins coming from the Nile Delta, Palestine and North Africa, they are primarily people who have rejected the lifestyle lived for generations in cities. Tribal leaders and other individuals leading lives that are more traditional have been remarkably impervious to extremist messaging in the Sinai. About two years ago, the Sinai Tribal Union even took the unprecedented step of recommending tribes deny protection to extremist members—with the exception of those who reject militancy and return to the fold. Rather than indicating a breakdown of solidarity, this was actually an assertion of traditional "shunning" methods adopted in the past against those who threaten the collective by drawing the unwanted attention of authorities (Gold 2015).

In contrast to most histories, the vision of the past that the Bedouin accept is not expressed through prose narratives of grand events. They have come into contact with, and for the most part cast off, all of the great Ancient Near

Eastern civilizations. Neither is their history known primarily through the accounts of conquerors. Theirs is not an "alternative subaltern" narrative that they are struggling to bring to light. The creation of their culture and the episodes they have witnessed are expressed in poetry, as has been well documented by anthropologists (Bailey 2002; Abu-Lughod 1986). Poetry continues to be a mode of expressing their views on many different subjects, including world affairs, criticism of government policies, the problems of poverty and marginalization and the corruption of officials. This practice began long before the advent of Christianity or Islam.

The poetry of the Jahilaya (pre-Islamic past) enshrines the ethics of life in the desert and extolls the community's traditions, beliefs and, very importantly, its past. Bedouin monuments to their battles in verse often contain the same elements as Ancient Near Eastern battle monuments in stone. They present an ideal version of events and describe the heroic exploits of leaders and their loyal men. Unlike other Near Eastern texts, their poetry, extending back to before the Byzantine Period, also speaks of chivalry and generosity and the sacrifices that had been made (Bailey 2002). Battle imagery is ubiquitous in these poems and has been misunderstood by some readers as expressing a predilection for conflict. Even before the concept of Jihad (in terms of inner struggle) entered their lives, however, the Bedouin had a sense of how metaphors for conflict convey multi-layered meanings.

Living on the cusp of the transition of the Arabian Peninsula from polytheism to Islam, the seventh-century Bedouin poet, Duraid ibn al-Simma, well understood the nature of violence in Bedouin culture. Two of his brothers died during inter-tribal conflagrations. The frequency with which these events are recorded should not be understood as any sense on the part of Bedouin that people are expendable. Each death is felt—and expressed. Duraid showed a marked fatalist outlook on the continual struggles within, and between, tribes cautioning his audience to "[t]ake for thy brother whom thou wilt in the days of peace, but know that when fighting comes thy kinsman alone is near." Duraid is sometimes seen as an "anti-Islamic" poet but, in truth, his religion was not that different from the fairly relaxed version of Islam now practiced by the Bedouin. He practiced what has been called the "religion of the desert" (Izutsu 2002). Tribal collective spirit came before everything. "When they [his kinsman] disobeyed me I made myself one of them holding that their error was right and I was not right," he wrote following a disastrous skirmish (Pedersen 2013).

At his most philosophical, the poet might admit the toll that his tribal solidarity could take. On witnessing the death of a friend in battle, he describes himself as being "like a camel that has lost its foal and is terrified" but he never questioned the importance of *asabiyyah*, as Ibn Khaldun (1967) labeled the cohesive quality of nomadic tribalism. Late in life, the battle-hardened veteran followed his kin, against his better judgment, into a battle that cost him his life. Many years earlier he had composed verses that could provide a fitting epitaph:

Then we, no doubt, are meat for the sword and, doubtless, sometimes we feed it meat,

By a foe bent on vengeance, we are attacked. Our fall, his cure or we vengeance bent, attack the foe.

Thus have we divided time in two between us and our foe 'til not a day goes by when we're in one half or the other.

(Duraid ibn al-Simma quoted in Brown 2003: 31–32)

Bibliography

Abu-Lughod, L. 1986. *Veiled Sentiments: Honor and Poetry in a Bedouin Society*. Berkeley, CA: University of California Press.

Abu-Rabia, A. 2001. *A Bedouin Century: Education and Development Among the Negev Tribes*. New York: Berghahn.

Abu-Rabia, A., S. Elbedour and S. Scham 2008. Polygyny and Post-nomadism among the Bedouin in Israel. *Anthropology of the Middle East* 3/2: 20–37.

Aharoni, M. 1985. Short Notes. On the Israelite Fortress at Arad. *Bulletin of the American Schools Oriental Research* 258: 73.

Aharoni, Y. 1967. Excavations at Tel Arad. *Israel Exploration Journal* 17: 233–249.

Aharoni, Y. and R. Amiran. 1964 Excavations at Tel Arad. Preliminary Report. *Bulletin of the American Schools of Oriental Research* 90: 263.

Alexandrani, I. 2014. Jihad and Jihadism in the Armed Conflicts in Contemporary Sinai in *Proceedings of the Multidisciplinary Conference on the Sinai Desert* (R. de Jong, T. van Gool, C. Moors, Z. El Houbba, eds.), pp. 119–141. Cairo: The Netherlands–Flemish Institute in Cairo.

Anderson, E. 1996. *Ecologies of the Heart: Emotion, Belief, and the Environment*. Oxford: Oxford University Press.

Arberry, A. 1957. *The Seven Odes: The First Chapter in Arabic Literature*. London: George Allen and Unwin Ltd.

Azis, S. 2017. *De-Securitizing Counterterrorism in the Sinai Peninsula*. Doha: Brookings Doha Center.

Bailey, C. 1974. Bedouin Star-Lore in Sinai and the Negev. *Bulletin of the School of Oriental and African Studies, University of London* 37/3: 580–596.

Bailey, C. 1982. Bedouin Religious Practices in Sinai and the Negev. *Anthropos* 77/1-2: 65–88.

Bailey, C. 1985. Dating the Arrival of the Bedouin Tribes in Sinai and the Negev. *Journal of the Economic and Social History of the Orient* 28/1: 20–49.

Bailey, C. 2002. *Bedouin Poetry: From Sinai and the Negev*. London: Saqi Books.

Bailey, C. 2009. Justice without Government in *Bedouin Law from Sinai and the Negev*, pp. 9–22. New Haven, CT: Yale University Press.

Bar-Yosef, O. 1998. The Natufian Culture in the Levant, Threshold to the Origins of Agriculture. *Evolutionary Anthropology* 6/5: 159–177.

Bassiouni, C. 2016. *Chronicles of the Egyptian Revolution and its Aftermath: 2011–2016*. Cambridge: Cambridge University Press.

Beit-Arieh, I. 1986. Two Cultures in Southern Sinai in the Third Millennium B.C. *Bulletin of the American Schools of Oriental Research* 263: 27–54.

Bell, G. 2012. *The Desert and the Sown*. New York: Cooper Square Press.

Ben David, Y. 1982. *Stages in the Development of the Bedouin Spontaneous Settlement in the Negev – in the Transformation from Semi-Nomadism to Permanent Settlement.* Jerusalem (Hebrew): PhD in the department of Geography, The Hebrew University.

Bernard, H. 2009. The Archaeology of Pastoral Nomads between the Nile and the Red Sea in *Nomads, Tribes, and the State in the Ancient Near East* (J. Szuchman, ed.), pp. 15–42. Chicago, IL: University of Chicago.

Brown, J. 2003. The Social Context of Pre-Islamic Poetry: Poetic Imagery and Social Reality in the Mju'allaqat. *Arab Studies Quarterly* 25/3: 29–48.

Cole, D. 2003. Where Have the Bedouin Gone? *Anthropological Quarterly* 76/2: 235–267.

Cole, D. and S. Altorki. 2014. *Bedouin, Settlers, and Holiday-Makers.* Cairo: American University in Cairo Press.

Conder, C. 1879. *Palestine Exploration Fund Quarterly Statement.* London: Palestine Exploration Fund.

Cribb, R. 2004. *Nomads in Archaeology.* Cambridge: Cambridge University Press.

Dinero, S. 2002. Image is Everything: The Development of the Negev Bedouin as a Tourist Attraction. *Nomadic Peoples* 6/1:69–94.

Dinero, S. 2010. *Settling for Less: The Planned Resettlement of Israel's Negev Bedouin.* New York: Berghahn.

Dransart, P. 2003. *Earth, Water, Fleece and Fabric: An Ethnography and Archaeology of Andean Camelid Herding.* London and New York: Routledge.

El-Nawawy, M. 2002. *The Israeli-Egyptian Peace Process in the Reporting of Western Journalists.* London: Weblex.

Faulkner, R. (Trans.) 1973. The Instruction of Merikare in *The Literature of Ancient Egypt* (W. Simpson, ed.), pp. 180–192. New Haven, CT: Yale University Press.

Finkelstein, I. and A. Perevolotsky. 1990. Processes of Sedentarization and Nomadization in the History of Sinai and the Negev. *Bulletin of the American Schools of Oriental Research* 279: 67–88.

Frantzman, S. and R. Kark. 2011. Bedouin Settlement in Late Ottoman and British Mandatory Palestine: Influence on the Cultural and Environmental Landscape, 1870–1948. *New Middle Eastern Studies* 1/2011. Retrieved from: www.brismes.ac.uk/nmes/archives/268.

Franz, K. 2011. The Bedouin in History or Bedouin History. *Nomadic Peoples* 15/I: 11–53.

Ginat, J. 1997. *Blood Revenge Family Honor, Mediation and Outcasting.* Portland, OR: Sussex Academic Press.

Gmirkin, R. 2006. *Berossus and Genesis, Manetho and Exodus: Hellenistic Histories and the Date of the Pentateuch.* New York: T and T Clark International.

Gold, Z. 2015. *Sinai Tribes: Between the Egyptian State and the Islamic State.* Institute for National Security Studies. Tel Aviv: Tel Aviv University.

Halstead, P. 1996. Pastoralism or Household Herding? Problems of Scale and Specialization in Early Greek Animal Husbandry. *World Archaeology* 28/1: 20–42.

Hart, D. 1997. *Traditional Society and Feud in the Moroccan Rif.* Rabat: Editions La Poste.

Hassan, F. 2007. Droughts, Famine and the Collapse of the Old Kingdom: Re-reading Ipuwer in *The Archaeology and Art of Ancient Egypt: Essays in Honor of David B. O'Connor* (Zahi Hawass and Janet Richards, eds.), pp. 357–377. Cairo: ANNALES DU SERVICE DES ANTIQUITES DE L'EGYPTE . CAHIER No. 36.

Hawkes, J. 1963. *The World of the Past.* New York: Random House.

Herzog, Z., M. Aharoni, A. Rainey and S. Moshkovitz. 1984. The Israelite Fortress at Arad. *Bulletin of the American Schools of Oriental Research* 254: 1–34.

Hobbs, J. 2001. Exploration and Discovery with the Bedouin of Egypt. *Geographical Review* 91/1–2: 285–294.

Hole, E. 1978. Pastoral Nomadism in Western Iran in *Explorations in Ethnoarchaeology* (R. Gould, ed.), pp. 127–167. Albuquerque, NM: University of New Mexico Press.

Hunaiti, H. 2008. *The Jahalin from the Nakba to the Wall*. Ramallah: Palestinian Grassroots Anti-Apartheid Campaign.

Ibn Khaldun, A. 1967. *The Muqaddimah: An Introduction to History*. Trans. by F. Rosenthal. Princeton, NJ: Princeton University Press. Retrieved from: https://asadullahali.files. wordpress.com/2012/10/ibn_khaldun-al_muqaddimah.pdf.

Israel Antiquities Authority Arad. 2017. Retrieved from: www.antiquities.org.il/Article_ eng.aspx?sec_id=17&subj_id=475&id=862.

Izutsu, T. 2002. *Ethico-Religious Concepts in the Qur'an*. Montreal: McGill–Queen's University Press.

Jacobs, J. 2014. Traditional Tourists and Modern Bedouin: Tourism and Development in the South Sinai in *Proceedings of the Multidisciplinary Conference on the Sinai Desert* (R. de Jong, T. van Gool, C. Moors, Z. El Houbba, eds.), pp. 34–49. Cairo: The Netherlands-Flemish Institute in Cairo.

Josephus, F. 1999. *The New Complete Works of Josephus*. Trans. W. Whiston. Grand Rapids, MI: Kregel Publications.

Konczacki, Z. 2014. *The Economics of Pastoralism: A Case Study of Sub-Saharan Africa*. London: Routledge.

Kressel, G. 1998. The Arab World's Travails: The Desert's Burden. *Middle East Quarterly* March 5/1: 49–57.

Kressel, G. 2003. *Let Shepherding Endure: Applied Anthropology and the Preservation of a Cultural Tradition in Israel and The Middle East*. Albany, NY: State University of New York Press.

Kreutzmann, H. (ed.). 2012. *Pastoral Practices in High Asia*. Berlin: Springer.

Lavie, S. and F. Rouse. 1993. Notes on the Fantastic Journey of the Hajj, His Anthropologist, and Her American Passport. *American Ethnologist* 20/2: 363–384.

Levy, T. 2008. Ethnic Identity in Bibical Edom, Israel and Midian: Some Insights from Mortuary Contexts in the Lowlands of Edom in *Exploring the Longue Durée: Essays in Honor of Lawrence E Stager* (D. Schloen, ed.), pp. 251–261. Winona Lake, WI: Eisenbrauns.

Lewis, B. 1990. *Race and Slavery in the Middle East: An Historical Enquiry*. Oxford: Oxford University Press.

Lichtheim, M. 1973. *Ancient Egyptian Literature: A Book of Readings*. Volume 1. Berkeley, CA: University of California.

Magness, J. 2003. *The Archaeology of the Early Islamic Settlement in Palestine*. Volume 1. Winona Lake, WI: Eisenbrauns.

Marx, E. 1977. The Tribe as a Unit of Subsistence: Nomadic Pastoralism in the Middle East. *American Anthropologist* 79/2: 343–363.

Marx, E. 2013. *Bedouin of Mount Sinai: An Anthropological Study of their Political Economy*. New York: Berghahn Books.

Mauss, M. 1970. *The Gift: Forms and Functions of Exchange in Archaic Society*. London: Routledge.

Mayerson, P. 1978. Procopius or Eutychius on the Construction of the Monastery at Mount Sinai: Which Is the More Reliable Source? *Bulletin of the American Schools of Oriental Research* 230: 33–38.

Mikhail, A. 2011. *Nature and Empire in Ottoman Egypt: An Environmental History*. Cambridge: Cambridge University Press.

Morris, E. 2017. Prevention through Deterrence along Egypt's Northeastern Border: Or the Politics of a Weaponized Desert. *Journal of Eastern Mediterranean Archaeology and Heritage Studies* 5/2: 133–147.

Mumford, G. 2006. Tell Ras Budran (Site 345): Defining Egypt's Eastern Frontier and Mining Operations in South Sinai during the Late Old Kingdom (Early EB IV/MB I). *Bulletin of the American Schools of Oriental Research* 342: 13–67.

Muscarella, O. 2013. *Archaeology, Artifacts and Antiquities of the Ancient Near East.* Leiden: Brill.

Musil, A. 1928. *The Manners and Customs of the Rwala Bedouins (American Geographical Society Oriental Explorations and Studies No.6).* New York: American Geographical Society.

Parker, T. 1999. An Empire's New Holy Land: The Byzantine Period. *Near Eastern Archaeology* 62/3: 134–180.

Patai, R. 1981. *The Arab Mind.* New York: Charles Scribner and Sons.

Pederson, J. 2013. *Ibn Duraid. Encyclopedia of Islam* (M. Th. Houtsma, T.W. Arnold, R. Basset and R. Hartmann, eds.). Brill Online, Retrieved from: http://referenceworks.brillonline.com/entries/encyclopaedia-of-islam-1/ibn-duraid-SIM_2981?s.num=0&s.f.s2_parent=s.f.book.encyclopaedia-of-islam-1&s.q=Ibn+Duraid.

Pelham, N. 2012. In Sinai: The Uprising of the Bedouin. *New York Review of Books,* December 8, 2012.

Racy, A. 1996. Heroes, Lovers, and Poet-Singers: The Bedouin Ethos in the Music of the Arab Near-East. *The Journal of American Folklore* 109/434: 404–424.

Rapport, N. 1992. Discourse and Individuality: Bedouin Talk in the Western Desert and the South Sinai. *Anthropology Today* 8/1: 18–21.

Ritner, R. 2009. Egypt and the Vanishing Libyan: Institutional Responses to a Nomadic People in *Nomads, Tribes, and the State in the Ancient Near East* (J. Szuchman, ed.), pp. 43–56. Chicago, IL: University of Chicago.

Rosen, S. 1988. Notes on the Origins of Pastoral Nomadism: A Case Study from the Negev and Sinai. *Current Anthropology* 29/3: 498–506.

Rosen, S. 1992. Nomads in Archaeology: A Response to Finkelstein and Perevolotsky. *Bulletin of the American Schools of Oriental Research* 287: 75–85.

Rosen, S. 2009. History Does Not Repeat Itself: Cyclicity and Particularism in Nomad-Sedentary Relations in the Negev in the Long Term in *Nomads, Tribes, and the State in the Ancient Near East* (J. Szuchman, ed.), pp. 57–86. Chicago, IL: University of Chicago.

Rosen, S. 2016. *Revolutions in the Desert: The Rise of Mobile Pastoralism in the Southern Levant.* London: Routledge.

Rosen, S. and B. Saidel 2010. The Camel and the Tent: An Exploration of Technological Change among Early Pastoralists. *Journal of Near Eastern Studies* 69/1: 63–77.

Saidel, B. and A. Barakat. 2007. The Pillars of Hercules as Metaphors for Fertility and Health among Bedouin and Fellahin in the Southern Levant. *Anthropos* 102/H.1: 220–224.

Scham 1996. Teleilat Ghassul Site Survey in P. Bikai and V. Egan. Archaeology in Jordan. *American Journal of Archaeology* 101/3: 507–508.

Schick, R. 1998. Palestine in the Early Islamic Period: Luxuriant Legace. *Near Eastern Archaeology* 61: 74–108.

Scholz, M. 2013. *Egypt's Sinai since the Uprising 2011: Explaining the Differences in the Amount of Violence between North and South.* Unpublished Thesis. Leiden: Leiden University and the Clingendael Institute.

Shkolnik, M. 2012. *Tribal Culture and the Islamic Awakening.* Ottawa: United Nations Association in Canada.

Shmueli, D. and R. Khamaisi. 2015. *Israel's Invisible Negev Bedouin*. Cham: Springer International Publishing AG.

Simpson, W. 2003. The Story of Sinuhe in *The Literature of Ancient Egypt*, pp. 55–66. New Haven, CT: Yale University Press.

Sivertsen, B. 2009. The Coming of the Hyksos in *The Parting of the Sea: How Volcanoes, Earthquakes and Plagues Shaped the Story of Exodus*, pp. 10–22. Princeton, NJ: Princeton University Press.

Stewart, F. 1991. The Woman, Her Guardian, and Her Husband in the Law of the Sinai Bedouin. *Arabica* 38/1: 102–129.

Szuchman, J. 2009. Integrating Approaches to Nomads, Tribes, and the State in the Ancient Near East in *Nomads, Tribes, and the State in the Ancient Near East* (J. Szuchman, ed.), pp. 1–13. Chicago, IL: University of Chicago.

Tchernov, E. 1997. Two New Dogs, and Other Natufian Dogs, from the Southern Levant. *Journal of Archaeological Science* 24/1: 65–95.

Tobias, M. 1980. Sinai. *The Kenyon Review, New Series* 2/4: 65–74.

Vorderstrasse, T. 2014. The Archaeology of the Ottoman Empire and Its Aftermath in the Middle East. *Near Eastern Archaeology* 77/4: 292–298.

Webb, P. 2016. *Imagining the Arabs: Arab Identity and the Rise of Islam*. Edinburgh: Edinburgh University Press.

Weinstein, J. 1975. Egyptian Relations with Palestine in the Middle Kingdom. *Bulletin of the American Schools of Oriental Research* 217/Feb: 1–16.

Zachova, A. 2016. *Bedouins and Sinai Insurgency: Political Causes of Violence*. Brno: Masaryk University Faculty of Social Studies, Department of International Relations and European Studies International Relations.

5 "Their hearts were confident, full of their plans"
Philistines and Palestinians

> This temple was built by 'Akish, son of Padi, son of Yasid, son of Ada, son of Ya'ir, ruler of Ekron, for Ptgyh, his (divine) lady. May she bless him, and guard him, and prolong his days, and bless his land.
>
> (Philistine Inscription from Ekron Gitin 1996)

> They spent their time going about the land, fighting to fill their bodies daily; they came to the land of Egypt seeking the necessities of their mouths.
>
> (Merneptah Inscription Breasted 1905)

Most Americans do not really understand the trauma of displacement. In a society built on mobility of many kinds, our attachment to places seldom lasts for more than two generations. Perhaps this is what explains my consistent irritation with an otherwise close Palestinian friend who persists in describing me as being "from Alabama" when I was born in Washington, DC. Nevertheless, to him, I am from Alabama every bit as much as he is from Nazareth, even though he has lived almost his entire adult life elsewhere. My parents were born there and I have visited the state. Other Palestinian friends who have virtually never set foot in Yafa or Akka still have no compunction about saying that they are from those cities and in the truest sense—that of heritage, tradition and ties to the land—they are.

These places are where their families lived for generations and, just as importantly, where their family names were formed—names that identify them so accurately that they can pinpoint an individual, based on his or her name, within ten kilometers of the village, town or city where their forebears lived. The plight of the refugee is ever a hard one but theirs is made even more painful by the fact that their families were involuntarily ejected in generations past from homes that they will never return to. They cannot go home again nor, indeed, even try. The places they once inhabited, as evidenced by the ruins of abandoned villages in the countryside and elegant and enduring houses in cities, are now enfolded within Israel—and their land is now collectively owned by the Jewish People, on behalf of whom the government holds it in trust (Cook 2013).

Our daughter, Anat, spent a good part of her childhood in the State of Israel. She was accustomed to being surrounded by houses that are described as "Arab built" in real estate advertisements—one of the rare good implications attached to the word "Arab" in Israel. She was named after a fierce warrior goddess who successfully challenged death and its minions for the life of her brother, and the gruesome myths about Anat were a favorite, particularly the descriptions of the goddess wading "knee-deep in warriors' blood" (Matthews and Moyer 2012: 167). Children enjoy these kinds of horrors—if they do not have to experience real-life versions of them. Jerusalem in those years was relatively calm and one day as I was walking with her through a "historic" part of the city, we passed several old houses with foundation stones inscribed with Arabic numerals and letters. Even though she was only about six years old at the time, she had lived in Jordan where she was used to seeing the Arabic script. She also had friends and babysitters who spoke and read Arabic with her so she knew what the written language looked like.

On the other hand, what she did not know was the recent history of the city she lived in. In Jerusalem, there is ancient history to be found on every street corner but history after the eighteenth century? Not so much. Unexpectedly, she asked *why* Arabic was appearing out of the context she had become accustomed to. I explained that those houses were built by Arabs and were once lived in by Arab families. She then asked the inevitable question of "why did they leave?" Hard questions from young children are to be expected but the answer to this one was complicated by the fact that we lived in one of those "abandoned" houses. I knew if I explained to her that the people who had once lived in those houses were forced to leave and that their houses were taken away, she might notice that our house, which was also old, did not look very different from them. At least, I told myself, we were only renters, but that would hardly assuage the conscience of a morally scrupulous six-year-old. Theft is theft—even if you are only in possession of stolen goods for a short time.

This was but one of many moments that reminded me that living in Israel could easily become an exercise in constantly repressing one's conscience. Indeed, I am always surprised that the presence of any Westerner in Palestine is not greeted with hostility even though my colleagues and I often thought we were, to use the cliché about the scariest words in the English language, "there to help." The kind of help I had in mind was optimistically called "shared heritage" at the time—an oxymoron in the Middle East if there ever was one. I first became involved in this rather pointless endeavor by working on several workshops, featuring Israeli and Palestinian archaeologists, and titled rather ungrammatically "Who was here first? and Does It Matter?" (Scham 2001:183). We got news coverage for these events, some of it sympathetic—and some, vitriolic. One writer featured our little meeting on the cover of her magazine under the tabloid title "Demolishing David" (Gross 2000).

In the article, she dismissed as "ridiculous" the Palestinian assertions that they are descendants of the Canaanites and Philistines who came to the land before the Israelites. She also alleged that Israelis and Palestinians during our workshop almost came to blows over the topic. She described one Palestinian antiquities official as banging his shoe on the table to make his point. For people of my generation, this fictitious incident seems to have been copied from the Cold War Playbook as Khrushchev famously did this during a speech at the UN (Taubman 2003: 657). The reporter's fable brought some small element of celebrity to our proceedings and later engendered the outrage of prominent Biblical Archaeologist, William Dever. In Dever's view, the "detailed and explicit report… of a clash between Israeli and Palestinian archaeologists at a symposium in Gaza" was yet another example of "meddling revisionists" who "have succeeded in undoing the efforts of two generations of Palestinian archaeologists," which is apparently what he considers himself to be, despite his Anglo-Saxon protestant Kentucky origins (Dever 2001: 294).

Few observers of this supposed battleground noted that, in fact, the floodgates of claiming descent from ancient peoples in Palestine had been opened some five decades before our workshops took place (Silberman 1995). Although they may be accused of lack of originality in one sense, Palestinians have every reason to believe that they have origins in the land that are equal to, if not greater than, those of Jews. Palestinian Authority (PA) Chairman Mahmoud Abbas, declared as much in a recent interview with an Israeli news reporter stating that "Our narrative says that we were in this land since before Abraham. I am not saying it. The Bible says it. The Bible says, in these words, that the Palestinians existed before Abraham. So why don't you recognize my right?" (Abbas 2016). In Israel, a national religious television channel reported this statement as patently false, only one among many other right-wing media sources that were outraged by the remark. They were obliged to note that the Biblical reference Abbas was talking about was that Abraham dwelt "many days in the land of the Philistines" (Genesis 21: 34), but their report continued, "the Philistines have no connection to today's Palestinian Arabs… The Palestinians who are Arabs could not have had ancestors in the land from biblical times predating Israelite and Judean statehood because Arabs only arrived in the land in 637 CE with the Muslim invasion" (Palestinian Media Watch 2016). Belief in the ridiculous proposition of mass migration into an empty land aside, this statement is utterly striking in its lack of historic validity.

Palestinian Christians, represented most prominently by Hanan Ashrawi, the first woman to be elected to the Palestinian National Council, are similarly excoriated for claiming their own ties to the land. In her 1995 memoir, Ashrawi spoke of the ancient heritage of Christians in Palestine and how her mother had lectured missionaries that they did not have to preach to Palestinians because "we are the ones who know Christianity directly, culturally and historically. Jesus was born next door" (1995: 24). She also lamented that Zionists had declared the Palestinian "ancient narrative" (Ashrawi 1995: 303) as completely ahistorical. The Zionist Organization of America attacked Ashrawi for her "Lies About Palestinian Arab History" (Zionist Organization of America 2002) but most Western Christians would not take issue with her remarks.

Today, there are fewer Christians in the Palestinian government and they are finding themselves increasingly marginalized as they have been in other Middle Eastern countries. In response, they are leaving the region in ever-growing numbers (Kershner 2007). These individuals care little for the Dome of the Rock or the Al-Aqsa Mosque and cannot be persuaded to deny the existence or significance of the Hebrew Bible—their Old Testament, even though they might be somewhat uncomfortable with the sections of that text quoted most often by Israeli nationalists (Scham 2004).

Since the Islamicization of the Palestinian cause, beginning with the Al-Aqsa Intifada, these kinds of measured scholarly arguments for Palestinian claims to the land have been eclipsed by more extreme measures intended to make the point. Violent political suicides have become a tragic commonplace (the term "suicide bombing" does not really describe the majority of these attacks, which are accomplished by other means). In a real sense, these attacks have cost more Palestinian than Israeli lives when one considers swift and deadly government retaliation (Ali and Post 2008). At one time, there were a number of organizations implicated in these attacks but, in recent years, two events have hampered the ability of groups to sponsor planned individual strikes against Israeli targets. One is the construction of the Wall ("security barrier" to Israelis) between Israel and the West Bank and the other is the Israeli absolute embargo on goods and people entering (or leaving) the Gaza strip—both fairly literal examples of "structural" violence. Hamas dominates politics in Gaza as a result of an internationally acknowledged free and fair democratic election and although its members were chief among the ranks of Palestinian suicide attackers for many years, most of the recent activities attributed to the organization appear to have been organized by individuals on social media.

Like Hezbollah, Hamas is now effectively engaged in a more conventional war with Israel with occasional and mostly ineffectual rocket fire from the Gaza Strip or Lebanon. Attacks by individuals are responsible for the majority of political suicide attacks that have occurred in recent years. A 2016 bus bombing in Jerusalem by an individual identified as a Hamas member gave no appearance of having been planned by the group, which patently denied involvement. In early 2017, five Palestinians from an alleged Hamas cell in the West Bank were arrested on suspicion of planning a number of attacks. So great is the Israeli fear of Hamas taking over the West Bank that at least one hapless soul was deprived of his freedom because his uncles belonged to the organization (Brenner 2017).

The Hamas narrative, while it avoids emphasizing Palestinian descent from idolatrous ancient cultures, also references the Biblical past. The organization's Charter is notorious for its call for the destruction of Israel but in May 2017, the group published a new policy document for the first time since its founding that declared a willingness to accept an interim Palestinian state within pre-1967 boundaries. Although it did not mention recognition of Israel, it did not repeat the anti-Jewish language of its original 1988 charter (Al-Mughrabi and Finn 2017). The text was seen as an effort by Hamas to soften its image, although the group made clear it did not replace the Charter. The latter document, among other things, outlines their principles for the historical education of the young. Article Sixteen requires that every child receive "an Islamic education based on the implementation of religious precepts, on the conscientious study of the Book of Allah, on the Study of the Prophetic Tradition, on the study of Islamic history and heritage from its reliable sources, under the guidance of experts and scientists," stating further that "It is also necessary to study conscientiously the enemy and its material ... to detect its weak and strong spots, and to recognize the powers that support it and stand by it" (Hamas 1988).

In its views of the distant past, Hamas effectively seeks to combine the ideas of both religious and secular Palestinian Muslims. According to the organization's American wing (which was disbanded as a result of American government pressures) the history of the region can be summed up as follows:

> Palestine is the heart of the cradle of prophethood and revelations, where many prophets were born, lived, visited, and/or died. Father of Prophets, Ebraheem [Abraham], who was welcomed by the Canaanites (old Palestinians) when he migrated from Ur, Iraq to their historical land, was promised by God to make the Holy Land inherited, not by a chosen people, but by good believers regardless of their race or ethnicity. Palestine was conquered and occupied by several ancient and new forces, but the only people that had never ceased to be the majority and to continually live on its land, is its Arab population starting with the Canaanites and ending with today's Palestinians.
>
> (Islamic Association for Palestine 1992)

Although traditional Islam may recognize the existence of Ancient Israelite history, Hamas' brand of Islamic nationalism does not (Scham 2009). Furthermore, regardless of normative religious views, Hamas has come to realize that the past that has the greatest impact on the street is that which stakes a claim on history either by asserting the supremacy of one group's past over another's or by suppressing alternative views. In this regard, it should be also pointed out that, despite the hue and cry over Palestinian textbooks' denigration of Israeli history, few texts and curricula for schools and universities, and even fewer media discussions or political speeches, in Israel reference the Palestinian past at all (Rogan and Shlaim 2001; Segev 1999; Sternhell 1999; Wasserstein 2001).

The unshakeable belief in their ancient Israelite origins on the part of Israelis and the view of Palestinians that they are the resolute guardians of the land, fending off invader after invader, are the approaches accepted by the majority on both sides—and, as should be clear, they ultimately succeed in canceling out any hope of future coexistence. For Israelis, the Bible and a host of loaded symbols that intrude upon daily life reinforce these entrenched beliefs (Masalha 2014). Israeli coinage, the basic unit of which is the Biblically name "shekel," features numerous ancient motifs including the Menorah, the Lyre, the pomegranate and the lily (all of which symbolize the Temple) and the "Israelite" helmet and war galley. Some of these coins reproduce ancient ones minted during the second most important Jewish monarchy—that of the Hasmonaeans (140 to 37 BCE). The Magen David has only been used as a Jewish symbol since the Middle Ages but few Israelis would deny that it is also an "ancient" symbol of nationhood (Mayer 2005).

Palestinians have fewer collectivizing symbols. The kefiah and the olive tree, both demonstrating rural culture and ties to the land, the Eagle of Salahadin, vanquisher of the Crusader enemy, and the Palestinian flag, modeled on the flag of the Arab Revolt against the Ottoman Empire, represent various aspects of the Palestinian desired past (Swedenburg 2003). With the Bible having been appropriated by Israelis, Palestinians have little in the way of ancient historical documents to work with. As a result, they have turned to oral history in formulating and reinforcing their national narrative even of the very distant past (Ziadeh 1995; Ziadeh-Seely 1999). The rationale for using oral data as historical evidence is the fact that Palestinians have not been able to do otherwise. Also, in terms of both language and position, Palestinians are far better placed than Israelis to record the observations of other Palestinians which, as a few Israeli scholars (Benvenisti 2000; Pappe 1994) have also noted, are the vital elements lacking in Israel's national chronicles.

Among both Israelis and Palestinians, the folklore of nationhood has assumed a deep familiarity that can counter any scholarly contentions to the contrary. Concrete symbols, repetition and reenactment are the characteristics of ritual behavior (Kertzer 1988; Durkheim 1974; D'Andrade 1986) and so, indeed, do these three things convert national narratives into sacred pseudo-memories—origin myths that have become all the more vital because the most significant modern historical memories for each side are stories of crushing defeat. For Israelis, this is the Holocaust—an event that retains the immediacy of post-trauma and one that also exposed, as far as Israelis are concerned, the "slim reed" of diaspora existence. For Palestinians, it is the Naqba, the end of a way of life that was embedded in the land and, once severed from it, almost ceased to exist. Outside of scholarly circles, speeches, books and articles much more clearly reflect the past that the public desires. On the one hand, it is a past without Palestinians (like the "land without a people") and, on the other hand, a past that demonstrates, once and for all, the falsehood of the premise upon which the Israeli state was established.

The relationship between Palestinians and Philistines has been the subject of tweets and blogposts aplenty but the majority of them completely miss the point that those who link the two cultures intend to make. The Israeli Jewish obsession with establishing a genealogical attachment to the land is one that causes the citizens of many other countries to scratch their heads in consternation. Americans, in a cultural and historical sense, feel that the Anglo-Saxon founding fathers (and mothers) of the country are their ancestors but few of them would claim direct descent from that population. In no sense do Palestinians believe that they are directly descended from Philistines, among the many different cultural and historical populations in the land that contributed to their culture. In this instance, Abbas focused on the Philistines for both historical and linguistic reasons. Yasser Arafat helped to explain this in an interview 35 years ago. Referencing "good relations between Jews and Arabs in Palestine" in times past as evidence that there could be peaceful coexistence between Israelis and Palestinians, he turned, like Abbas, to the Jewish Bible for inspiration. David, he pointed out, was given refuge from Saul by the Palestinians because, he reasoned, the Arabic name for Palestine is Filistin, a name that was directly derived from the Greco-Roman term for the "land of the Philistines" (Kelman 1983).

That linguistic association may strike many as fantasy but the insistence of some Israelis and American Jews that Arabs arrived in Palestine en masse at the end of the seventh century is pure myth. The extent to which people cling to this idea, even today, is remarkable. During one of the meetings that our Shared History group held for a Jewish audience was in an orthodox synagogue in Jerusalem. My colleague, Adel Yahya, stated that he had come to believe that Palestinians are descendants of a mix of local and regional peoples, including the Canaanites, Philistines, Hebrews, Samaritans, Greeks, Romans and pre-Islamic and Muslim Arabs (Yahya 2005). This has become the dominant view among other Palestinian academics (Farsoun and Aruri 2006) and, considering that Arabs (i.e., those who speak various forms of the Arabic language) were known to have been in Syria as early as the ninth century BCE it makes some sense. The audience, many of whom would support their own affinity of Iron Age Israelites, found this idea unbelievable.

This battle of the ancestors is older than one might suppose. Although some Israelis have dismissed Palestinian nationhood as an "invented" twentieth-century idea (as if all nationhoods were not invented) (Gelvin 2014), most scholars agree that the history of the Palestinian people goes back to long before the Islamic conquest (Masalha 2007). In effect, Palestinians were the Arabic speaking sedentary farming (fellahin) culture that existed alongside the Arabic speaking nomadic Bedouin culture in the Levant. There is an ancient tension between Palestinians and Bedouin that persists to this day and many Bedouin suspect that Palestinians look down upon them as "country cousins," who are less educated and less sophisticated. Both of these cultures existed side by side with Jews and later Christians in the region, mostly peacefully at the sites of Dura-Europos in Syria and Um er-Rasas in Jordan indicate. All of these cultures were subjected to the same waves of conquest that affected Jewish historical narratives but Jews were the only ones that maintained a consistent historical memory of these events passed down from generation to generation—a memory, and a nationhood, that was primarily formed by displacement. While the Arabs remained in the land, the Jews, at least those that were capable of recording events, for the most part did not. If one conceives nation as an "imagined community," Jews in the diaspora may constitute the oldest example.

Arnold Toynbee in 1961 took a different perspective on the formation of the Israeli state in an article published in the *Jewish Quarterly Review*, a rather provocative venue considering the nature of his arguments. He pronounced that Israelis are simply the last of the groups that conquered Palestine throughout its history. Israelis, Toynbee argued, were following on the heels of Middle Kingdom Egypt, the Amorites, New Kingdom of

Egypt, "the Hebrew peoples and the Philistines" (presumably at the same time) and "the Assyrians, Babylonians, Persians, Macedonians, Romans, Arabs, Saljuq Turks and Crusader Franks, Saladin and his Mamluk successors, the Ottoman Turks and their British successors." Modern Israel was, according to him, only the "latest but not necessarily the last" conquerors (Toynbee 1961: 9). His conclusion that "[N]one of the successive occupying peoples has any title unless we accept the barbarous claim that a valid legal claim can be derived from an act of military conquest" (Toynbee 1961: 9) was the *coup de grâce* to any hopes that the editors might have had that he would support Jewish claims to Palestine. Presumably, they thought that getting Toynbee to contribute to their very insignificant journal was a coup of their own. The publishers of the journal, assailed by the readership, were forced to apologize and explain that Toynbee was invited to present his views but not asked to write anything specifically about the validity of the Israeli state. Professor Solomon Zeitlin charged that the essay did not conform "to scholarly standards either in form or in substance," had "no documentation and none of the allegations was based on primary sources" (*Jewish Telegraphic Agency Daily News Bulletin*, December 1, 1961). As co-editor of *the Jewish Quarterly Review*, Zeitlin did not offer an explanation as to why he published the article anyway.

Scholars who identify themselves as Biblical archaeologists, like William Dever, reject outright any Palestinian ancient claims to indigenousness. An article written by archaeologists Hallote and Joffe is representative of this genre:

> More recently (mid 1990s to present) the tendency has been to discount, excise, or wholly revise the questions of ancient Israel and any Jewish presence. Elite promotion of the ideas that Palestinians were descended from Canaanites, Philistines, or third millennium B.C.E. Arabian migrants, has been considerable, despite the lack of evidence or logic to support these claims, and their inherent contradiction with Islamic mythology.
>
> (Hallote and Joffe 2002: 87)

The term "mythology," used here to describe one of the world's major religions, suggests that the authors are not entirely neutral in their approach to this question.

Hallote and Joffe further note that Palestinian narratives of the past traditionally exclude the story of Ancient Israel or treated it as a mere historical episode of no greater importance than any other. They make little mention of the fact that Ancient Israel is, in itself, a construction of an Iron Age occupation in Palestine that is, at least in part, subject to question. There is little in the way of evidence to support the existence of a United Monarchy of David and Solomon as Finkelstein and Silberman (2007) and others have noted. Rather, if these kingdoms existed at all, they were tribal chiefdoms, which is precisely how the Bible describes them. Leadership in Ancient Israel was an achieved rather than an ascribed status. There were no firm lines of succession, at least in the Kingdom of David, and the so-called "king" was subject to religious authority and limited in his ability to make laws or even decide cases.

Albert Glock, a notable exception among Western Biblical archaeologists, was one of the first to question the "Ancient Israelite" narrative. A minister as well as an archaeologist, Glock is unfortunately known primarily because of his violent death. Two Palestinian men gunned him down in in the West Bank, possibly because of an honor-related offense. Working among Arabs primarily, Glock came to see himself as a champion of their heritage (Glock 1999a). His main concern was not in fashioning an ancient Palestinian narrative in the land so much as it was to point out the destruction of the evidence of their history. As Glock was the first Western scholar to point out, the Palestinian past has been diverted from its original scholarly roots. During the British Mandatory Period (1917–1948), Palestinians literally invented ethnographic archaeological studies, at a time when American and European archaeologists were uninterested in looking at comparisons between modern and ancient cultures.

Studies of ancient farming methods and settlement patterns by scholars such as Tawfiq Canaan (1927), Dimitri Baramki (1961) and Stephan Hanna Stephan were also remarkable for the period. Forced into exile after 1948, these archaeologists were responsible for establishing major field schools and programs in universities all over the Middle East (Glock 1999b). The work of these scholars, like that of so many others working in the "Holy Land," was informed by the Biblical text but they tended to use it more as an ethnographic analogy than as a historical guide. Today, there is a more pronounced effort on the part of Palestinians to write themselves into Biblical history, a situation decried by Maher Al-Sherif, a professor at King Fahd University in Saudi Arabia. Al-Sherif has written that, "Zionism not only forced the Palestinians and their Arab brothers to make history a weapon of war. It imposed the subject matter for their writing of history and the agenda for their research" and concludes that "Arab historiography must free itself from the terms of reference imposed by the Zionist reading of history" (Al-Sherif 1998).

The motives have clearly not changed and, although there are not many published accounts from would-be perpetrators of failed suicide attacks, those that have been brought to light clearly delineate them. For example, Momammed Rezaq, the only surviving hijacker of EgyptAir Flight 648 and a member of Nidal, spoke at his trial about how he became affiliated with increasingly violent groups. In 1948, his mother, then a child, was living in Jaffa, the Arab suburb of Tel Aviv, when she and her family fled to her grandparents' farm in the West Bank. When Rezaq was exactly the same age, in 1967, his family was forced to flee again, eventually ending up in a Jordanian refugee camp. As they were leaving, his mother, understandably bitter at the prospect of two displacements in her life told him, "This is the second time they have stolen my family lands" (Post 2005: 60). Later, while he was attending school, his teacher, a member of the Palestinian Liberation Organization, taught him that the only way for a Palestinian youth to become a man was to become a "soldier for the revolution" to take back the lands stolen from previous generations. It was a matter of lost honor, confiscated property and negated rights. In a sense, in the words of the song, with "nothing left to lose," he was "free" to do anything within his power to restore what was lost. From generation to generation, his family had suffered and he was the only one who could address it. His father was opposed to him becoming a political activist and, to Rezaq's mind, had acquiesced in his own subjugation (Post 2005). More recent interviews with others who have attempted and failed to accomplish suicide attacks show that the motivations have changed very little over the years.

One individual, who spent several years in prison for his attempted crime, explained that "I didn't have anything to do with the factions, it wasn't religious. I just didn't feel alright with the life I was living and I needed to do something about it." This is consistent with studies of both men and women would-be suicide bombers. Although some of them express regret over having landed in prison as a result of their actions, they still believe that they were "driven" to it by a complete lack of autonomy. As Pape concluded in his book *Dying to Win* (Pape 2004):The data show that there is little connection between suicide terrorism and Islamic fundamentalism, or any one of the world's religions ... Rather, what nearly all suicide terrorist attacks have in common is a specific secular and strategic goal: to compel modern democracies to withdraw military forces from territory that the terrorists consider to be their homeland. (Pape 2004: 2).This suggests that what I have called "rooted extremism" in Palestine is a response to alien occupation and its deleterious effects on human agency.

Looking at ancient prototypes for Palestinian political suicide, one returns once again to the subject of the Philistines as the first recorded "suicide terrorist": was the famous Philistine frenemy, Samson. Samson, by far the strongest of putative Israelite heroes (Judg. 13–17), was a genetic "sport" as well. Before entering the womb, he was dedicated to God as a Nazirite and, thus, had to abstain from wine, haircuts and touching "any unclean thing" (13.4, 7, 14). With a name derived from that of the Canaanite sun god and a predilection for, as it turns out, many "unclean things," including Philistine women, honey made in the rotting carcass of a lion and water from the jawbone of an ass, he seemed to be a greedy and thoughtless man—closer in fact to animal than human (Scham 2002). He was an anomaly as an Israelite leader, acting alone against the Philistines with whom he seems to have been extraordinarily cozy. Samson redeems himself through martyrdom and, not content to end only his own miserable life, he takes out an entire city with him by pulling down the pillars of the Philistine temple on the heads of the hapless worshippers. The Rabbis have, helpfully, added commentary to this story to the effect that, even though Samson committed suicide, it was not a sin because he threw his body clear of the destruction and could thus receive a decent Jewish burial.

The parallels between Samson and modern extremists have, of course, not been lost on other scholars. His celebration in Israel as a hero has caused some to debate the morality of applauding the ancient religious fanatic while condemning the modern ones. Seymour Hersh dubbed Israel's nuclear deterrence strategy as the "Samson Option" in 1991 (Hersh 1991) and, since then, the Israel Defense Forces have used the name of this mythical hero for several "super weapons." With the arrival of Lockheed's Super Hercules airlifter at an Israeli airbase, the Israel Defense Forces enthusiastically changed its name to Shimshon (Hebrew for Samson). The theme was enthusiastically taken up by Marilyn Hewson, Lockheed's CEO:

> This aircraft is worthy of its given name, Shimshon, a leader whose power was thought to be as mighty as the sun. Shimshon used his power to combat the enemies of Israel and perform heroic feats. In the same way, this aircraft will support the defense of Israel and the men and women who are the heroes of the Israeli Defense Force.
>
> (Cohen 2014)

It is not clear whether Hewson was aware of Samson's lamentable end but this is certainly not the first time that the Israel Defense Forces adopted a nationalist myth exalting suicide. Moshe Dayan began the practice of swearing-in Israeli soldiers who had completed their basic training on top of Masada, site of the alleged suicide of Jewish zealots, in order to avoid being taken captive by the Romans, in 73 CE (Bitan 1960).

The example of Samson also came up some years back in the context of a film called *Paradise Now* by a Palestinian cinematographer. A recipient of several awards, and an Oscar nomination, the filmmaker tells the story of two fictional Palestinian youths who choose to become suicide bombers. In an interview in which he discussed his work with a Palestinian reporter he said, "I feel that we have reached a very painful point in which there are few choices, especially for youths. They now find themselves sacrificing themselves and taking their victims with them. This is a painful reality. In Jewish mythology," he continued, "the mighty Samson was the first to take suicide action against his enemies. In this sense, the Palestinian suicide bombers represent Samson. They live the legend every day. This is the tragedy of suicide bombers regardless of how Israel or the United States see them" (Saad 2004).

In the Biblical account, Samson is presented as merely an "instrument" of God in annihilating the Philistines, ostensibly for the crimes of hating the Israelites but permitting them to fraternize with their women. Bringing down the wrath of God against the subjugators of believers by unbelievers is not a secondary matter in the eschatology of political suicides (Drury 2003). In Islamic thought, as well as in Judaism and Christianity, there are often questions about the status of Samson (Shamsun in Arabic). As with many Biblical stories, Muslim sources provide different details than those contained in the Book of Judges. The early eighth-century writer, Al-Iraqi, and the ninth-century historian al-Tabari in his *History of Prophets and Kings*, discuss the story of Shamsun as a man who struggled in the way of God for over a century. Islamic sources compare the incident of Samson using the jawbone of an ass as a weapon to a companion of the prophet who used the jawbone of a camel to mow down the enemies of Islam.

Rippin (2008) points out that the interpretations of Samson by medieval Muslim scholars paint him as a mythic hero striving to enact God's will throughout his life. Different views of the Samson narrative in Islam, Rippin concludes, depend upon the cultural circumstances at the time in which these views are expressed. For Medieval scholars, he writes, Samson's story "[takes] on a Muslim character in its emphasis on the role of a prophet to struggle against the unbelievers" (Rippin 2008: 244). Modern scholars from Muslim cultural contexts, depending upon their orientation toward what has been dubbed "Islamic fundamentalism," take different positions on the subject of Samson. Some have used the fact that Samson is not explicitly mentioned in the Quran as proof that political suicide is not part of the Muslim ethos (Murad 2008), while others have suggested that Samson is a symbol of jihad (Dunning 2016).

The tale of Samson suggests that, even though he is specifically mentioned in the Bible as being from the Tribe of Dan, his story has close ties to the Philistines and the land of the Philistines. According to the text, he married one Philistine woman and, after her death, turned to another—the infamous Delilah. Although as a suicide attacker prototype, Samson is a powerful symbol, his story and others in the Bible do not necessarily shed any light on the culture of the Philistines. Also, whether the Biblical text supports the proposition that the Philistines preceded the Israelites in the land (to the extent that anyone is interested in the answer to that question any more) is subject to interpretation. For example, although people tend to associate the period of Abraham, Isaac and Jacob (the Patriarchal Period) with the Israelites, they are more correctly identified as the ancestors of the Israelites. Jacob received the name "Israel" after struggling with the angel (Genesis 32:28) but only his 12 sons, progenitors of the 12 tribes, could officially be considered as Israelites, even by Biblical terms. On the other hand, the "Israelite Period," a term in use only by very conservative Biblical scholars and nationalist Israeli archaeologists (Davies 2015), is identified as the Iron Age (1200 to 550 BCE), which is some centuries after the time generally ascribed to the Patriarchal narratives.

The earliest extra-Biblical text mentioning "Israel" is the Stele of the Egyptian Pharaoh Merneptah that dates to around 1200 BCE. The earliest extra-Biblical text referencing the "Sea Peoples" is from roughly the same period as not all of the references to them in Egyptian texts have been dated with certainty. Because the Bible notes the presence of Philistines in the land during the Patriarchal Period, it could be argued that the Biblical sources suggest that the Philistines *did* precede the Israelites in the land but archaeology posits a simultaneous ethnogenesis. In Genesis 10:13–14, the Philistine origins are said to have been in Egypt, although later sources (see Amos 9:7 and Jeremiah 47:4) state that they originated in Caphtor (some sources place Caphtor in the region of the Nile Delta, however, modern sources tend to associate it with Cilicia, Cyprus or Crete). Biblical scholars believe that the Patriarchal narratives referencing the Philistines were probably added later—again, very close in time to the appearance of the Israelites in the Bible (Killebrew 2005).

The archaeology of Samson, and of the Philistines themselves, can perhaps provide some insight into the formation of this legend and the culture that provided the backdrop for it. Beyond the mysterious allusions that scholars began to identify in Egyptian texts on the Sea Peoples in the late nineteenth century, it was not until the 1980s that archaeologists began the quest to determine the origins of the Philistines in earnest. They are generally supposed to have been the *Peleset*, one of the groups of perhaps mixed origin "Sea Peoples" (Maeir et al. 2017). Prior to most of the significant excavations of Philistine sites, in an article that has largely been disregarded by both Biblical scholars and archaeologists, Yigael Yadin, excavator of Masada, suggested in 1968, a hypothesis for the origin of the real Samson. Looking at the story and the description of the Danites in the Old Testament, he argued that the tribe of Dan was really the Denyen who, along with the Philistines (Peleset in Egyptian), formed part of the Sea Peoples, one of Ancient Egypt's Late Bronze Age adversaries. The name Dan he asserted was related not only to the Denyen but also to the Danaoi, Greek seafarers of the Mycenaean Age. It seemed an outlandish idea at the time but Yadin was writing before archeologists had firmly established the identity of the Sea Peoples as Indo-European, in all probability of Aegean origin (Betancourt 2000)—although scholars disagree as to whether or not they were Greek. Yadin saw in the Samson story a reiteration of the tale of the Greek hero Heracles and further contended that Samson's easy proximity to the Philistines, as described in the Book of Judges, clearly indicated that he was one of them (Yadin 1968).

Archaeologists in Palestine have, of course, long ceased looking for such persons in the archaeological record so, even though it was somewhat prescient, Yadin's argument, based as it is on the Biblical text, has become unfashionable. But it is not to be discounted that Samson may yet emerge from an archaeological site. Indeed, other finds have appeared that confirm the existence of some of the Bible's more implausible characters. In the 1980s, a text was found at Deir Alla, the ancient Moabite site of Heshbon, that contains a story of "Balaam the Seer"—a character in the Exodus narrative who was persuaded by the unlikely team of an angel and a talking donkey to bless the Israelites (Hackett 1984). In 2005, an incised potsherd was found at the site of Tell es-Safi, identified as the Biblical Gath, containing the name of the Biblical giant Goliath (Maeir et al. 2017). The latter, added to other Philistine texts that have been recovered, appears to confirm the Aegean origins of the Sea Peoples. The first identifiably Philistine burials were discovered several years ago at Ashkelon. The finds are still being analyzed but it is expected that they may resolve the question of Philistine origins and identity once and for all, and more than one blogger has posed the question of whether DNA from these remains can be compared with the modern Palestinian population. If a Samson/Shimsun/Shimshon is found somewhere in Jordan, Israel or the West Bank to take his place as a Greek hero, it would not be surprising. For now, though, Yadin's view that Samson was a Philistine, by the standard of Biblical exegesis, does not seem as unlikely as it once did (Finkelstein 1996).

Yadin was only one of a large number of archaeologists who have been interested in the Philistines and Philistine sites. Partly this is due to their identification as the perpetual adversaries of Israel. The Biblical narrative, in fact, suggests that the first Israelite state rose in juxtaposition to the Philistine presence in Palestine. They are mentioned over 250 times in the Bible and, among these references, are verses referencing their foreign origins, their urban centers of Gath, Ashdod, Ashkelon, Ekron and Gaza, the cities of the Philistine Pentapolis. Four of these cities have been excavated. The fifth, Gaza, is the site connected to the Biblical Samson (Killebrew 2005). Perhaps the most crowded and beleaguered place on the globe, Gaza has not been really explored since Tel Harube, identified as the site of Ancient Philistine Gaza, is today underneath the modern city. In 1922, Pythian-Adams excavated a small part of the site but never fully published his findings (Maeir 2013).

The Philistines who came to the shores of the Levant might well have spoken a number of different languages or could even have been familiarized via trade relations with the Canaanite language (Knapp 2008). The foreign origin of the Philistines, however, is reflected in all aspects of their Aegean-inspired material culture, including pottery style and manufacture, cuisine, architecture, religious practices and the layout of their urban spaces. The distinction between Philistine material culture and that of the preceding Late Bronze Age occupations at or near their sites is significant and seems to suggest that the Canaanites at those sites were fairly quickly displaced (Drews 1998). Within several generations, Philistine material culture traditions began to demonstrate that they were beginning to assimilate to their new milieu. There are a number of differing interpretations of the character of these newcomers. These "urban colonists of the Early Iron Age" (Killebrew 2005: 197) could have arrived as a well-organized prosperous group, perhaps representing more of a mercantile than military incursion. There are disagreements as to whether they originated in the West Aegean or Crete or the Eastern Aegean, Northern Levant, Cyprus or Cilicia. The fact that they were able to rapidly settle and construct urban centers may demonstrate that they were colonizers rather than conquerors or migrants (Killebrew 2005).

According to some scholars (Hitchcock and Maeir 2014), the Sea Peoples may have been multiethnic Mediterranean pirates. Others have characterized them as migrants or even impoverished refugees (Karageorghis 1992 and 1994). The consensus of all is that they were not native to the region—but they were, by far, not the only groups on the move in the Mediterranean during this period. According to Killebrew:

> The final centuries of the Late Bronze Age, spanning ca. 1400–1200 B.C.E., have often been characterized as an "age of internationalism." But as the 13th century drew to a close, this interconnected world of the

eastern Mediterranean witnesses irreversible changes and crises that led to the collapse or gradual decline of imperial aspirations and the "old order" that had prevailed throughout much of the second millennium B.C.E.

(Killebrew 2005:21)

The resulting migrations stemming from upheavals, and ethnic (and religious) conflict, have made it tempting for archaeologists to see this period as an ancient mirror of our own new global order (Cline 2014).

The question of why the Philistines came to the Levant and how they settled into their new homes (whether by peaceful or military means) is not really answered in the scant texts we have outside of the Bible. The Philistines appear in four important New Kingdom Egyptian texts. Two, during the reign of Ramesses III at Medinet Habu and Deir el-Medineh, one papyrus composed shortly after the death of Ramesses III (Papyrus Harris I) and two dating to the end of the twelfth or early eleventh century BCE. The reliefs and accompanying hieroglyphs on the temple at Medinet Habu are the most significant of any ancient references to the Philistines and provide the following commentary on the Philistine incursions:

Not one stood before their hands, from Kheta, Kode, Carchemish, Arvad, Alashia, they were wasted ... They desolated his people and his land like that which is not. They came with fire prepared before them, forward to Egypt ... they laid their hands upon the land as far as the Circle of the Earth. Their hearts were confident, full of their plans ... Those who reached my boundary, their seed is not; their heart and their soul are finished forever and ever.

(Henry 2003: 231)

The feathered headdress considered characteristic of Philistine warriors is shown on this and other reliefs that refer specifically to the Denyen—the tribe that, in Yadin's view, corresponds to the Israelite tribe of Dan and the Tjekker as well as the Peleset (Philistines). It seems that this particular item of attire was associated with the Sea Peoples in general. A relief showing the chief of the Philistines wearing such a chapeau can be seen with accompanying hieroglyphic text in the first court of the Medinet Habu Temple. The Harris Papyrus, composed shortly after the death of Ramesses III, supplements the Medinet Habu evidence on the Philistines (Killebrew 2005). Referring to Ramesses III's battle against the Sea Peoples, the Harris Papyrus I declares that the Peleset were "reduced to ashes" (Breasted 1905: 201; Erichsen 1933). It also adds the details that Ramesses apparently drove them back "to their strongholds" but it is not clear whether this refers to an actual Philistine fortress in Canaan or just to the places where they had been before their skirmish with the Egyptians.

Like most Ancient Near Eastern rulers, Rameses III makes it clear that the Egyptians prevailed in battles against the Peleset on land and sea but parts of the Medinet Habu texts describe them as a formidable military force. On the other hand, these battles do not appear to have been significant events but, rather, a series of small skirmishes, suggesting the Sea Peoples represented more of a nuisance than a threat (Cifola 1988)—much like the Shasu and Habiru of the Amarna Period. These texts seem to indicate that the majority of the Sea Peoples was composed of the Peleset and the Tjekker. Egyptian depiction of the land battles shows that both sides had chariots, although those used by the Sea Peoples had three soldiers per chariot to the Egyptian one, or less frequently, two. The Philistines are shown as armed with long spears and straight swords (Killebrew 2005).

It is difficult to tell how organized the Philistine warriors were as it was the Egyptian convention to show the enemy as a chaotic jumble—much as depictions of Alexander the Great's battles show the Persians in complete disarray (O'Conner 2000: 95). Further, the Philistine camp is shown in a very unusual manner. Ox-carts carrying women and children appear in the midst of the frenetic battle. There are two possible interpretations for this. Either it is intended to show that the Egyptians, who are seen in this relief slaughtering warriors right and left, would not deign to attack women and children (doubtful) or to hammer home the idea that they were just another incarnation of the hated nomads that plagued Egypt since the Old Kingdom (Chapter 4, this volume). Another well-known relief from Medinet Habu shows a battle at sea as even more disordered but provides another interesting detail about Philistine ships and weaponry. Both sides used vessels with sails but the Philistine ships are not shown with oars (Dothan 1982: 7). The prows of the Philistine ships were effigies of bird heads—similar to some of the motifs appearing on Philistine Aegean style pottery.

Excavations at Philistine sites add some important details to our knowledge of their culture once known mostly from the Egyptian texts. The Philistines were an urban culture and their sites reveal definite urban plans of a type not seen before in the Levant, and they were replete with fortifications and impressive public buildings. Philistine hearths and megaron hearth rooms are considered to be a hallmark of the culture and are modeled on similar features found in the Aegean world. Stone and terracotta basins resembling bathtubs are also features that are unique to the Philistine sites and are found near throne rooms and sanctuaries. While water is an element of both Canaanite and Israelite ritual practices, these kinds of fixtures are unknown at those sites. Hundreds of loom weights show that the Philistines had a burgeoning textiles industry and others have suggested that the bathtubs were also used for dyeing (Mazow 2006).

Much has been made of the fact that pig bones abound at these sites as opposed to "Israelite" hill country settlements where they are rare. Some archaeologists have asserted that the pigs were of a European variety brought to the Levant by the Philistines. Also, it appears that the Philistines were not above indulging in the occasional dog—although it was not a staple of their diet. Both animals are, of course, forbidden to Israelites according to the Bible. Based on the number of cow bones discovered at Philistine sites, they ate them as well as using them for traction, although pigs make up the largest single species among animal bones found at Philistine sites. Incised decorations on numerous cow shoulder bones found at Philistine sites have been a source of interest for archaeologists who have interpreted them as either tools for divination or pieces of musical instruments (Webb 1985).

Material evidence for Philistine religion consists primarily of large buildings designated as temples, altars and a plethora of clay fertility figurines, cups shaped like lion heads and the aforementioned incised cow bones. The figurines all represent females although they are not in female form. The best-known type, called "Ashdoda," shows a chair with a stylized head and breasts decorated in geometric Mycenaean style designs. Another lesser known figurine type shows a form with upraised arms resembling the Greek letter Psi and quite similar to Mycenaean figurines of the same name. The Ashdoda, on the other hand, are completely unique to Philistine culture, and although it is seen as evidence that the Philistines worshiped a Great Mother Goddess, this is by no means an accepted interpretation. The small number of Philistine temples that have been identified show that two central columns, a feature that Samson made use of in his suicide demolition, were actually features of Philistine religious structures. Central hearths, much larger than those found in other structures, also figured in Philistine worship (Killebrew 2005).

Philistine religion thus remains enigmatic. The Bible states that they were worshippers of the ubiquitous Baal, probably the goddess Astarte and, more unusually, Dagon—a deity that is thought to have originated in Ugarit. Dagon, who was later characterized as a "fish god," appeared in Mesopotamia as early as the third millennium BCE, but was virtually unknown in the Levant during the Iron Age. The Philistines may have encountered Dagon along their route to the Southern Levant (which assumes that they did not come directly to its shores by sea) and integrated him into their pantheon (Machinist 2000). There is no material or written evidence for Dagon worship in Canaan, however, so this is purely speculation. An Early Iron Age kingdom named Palistin, near Tell Ta'yinat in southeastern Turkey, might be associated with the Philistines and, if so, this could support the theory that the Philistines picked up Dagon worship there and also the speculation that they arrived in the Levant by way of Cilicia. The first evidence for Palastin was excavated in 1936, however, and no real firm connections have been established since then. As for Israelites, it is equally true that the Bible remains the main source of information distinguishing them as a culture of the Iron Age (Killebrew 2005). Despite years of work and a fortune in funds expended on Israelite sites, most archaeologists have come to the conclusion that Israelites were simply a rural manifestation of the Canaanites and their differences in culture were not any greater than the differences between a small country village and New York.

This may be why Palestinians often choose to discuss their ancient presence in the land as Philistine in origin even though the Semitic-speaking Canaanites are the more obvious choice. Beyond the linguistic similarities between the names of the two peoples or the Biblical example of the pious suicide bomber Samson, the Philistines were the primary adversaries of the Israelites. Further, the Canaanites disappeared from history only to arise later as a part of Phoenician civilization. In essence, it is believed that they were either permanently driven from Palestine or gradually moved north to join their relatives—a situation repeated in 1948 with Palestinian refugees flooding to Lebanon. Like the Palestinians, the Philistines were also migrants (if not necessarily refugees) but they easily put down roots in the most geographically desirable part of Palestine—the coast, where the modern cities of Ashdod, Ashkelon, Gaza and Tel Aviv/Jaffa are—and the fertile Shephelah, known as Modern Israel's most agriculturally productive region. Whether they accomplished this by conquest, colonization or simply hunkering down and refusing to move, the Philistines stayed put for centuries—outlasting the Israelites by at least 100 years and the United Monarchy by 600 years.

On the other hand, in the absence of more definitive archaeological evidence, we are left with the conclusion that most of what we know about the Philistines consists of polemic and propaganda composed by their enemies. In other words, while they may have been "winners" among the contenders for local power during the fractious years of the Late Bronze Age (Killebrew 2005), they are historical losers—a people whose memory has been obliterated except for the survival of some material evidence and geographical place names. Their affinities with the Palestinians, whose similarly tragically emplotted history as a people has been denied by Israeli leaders and others as fictitious, have more to do with that than they do with the linguistic similarities between their names or pointless arguments over who came first. There is nothing to indicate in the details of either Philistine or Palestinian history that they sought to become "historically significant" by conquering their neighbors or that they wanted to do anything other than settle down, hold onto their land and become prosperous—which was, in fact, what both of these cultures did for generations. The one gave their name to the geographical region in which they lived and the other derived their name from it. In the end, that may be the fullest measure of their relationship.

There is another strong link between the ancient and modern cultures—one that speaks to their tragically emplotted history and, in effect, confirms the statement by Arafat with respect to the bond between David and the Philistines (Bauck 2008). Like the Palestinians whose continued resistance enabled the Land of Israel to extend its borders far beyond the territory originally allotted to them during the mandatory period, the Philistines played a part in defining one of the most important national narratives of their worst enemies. In addition to providing a modus vivendi for Samson's suicide attack, they became, in fact, the "power behind the throne" of the once and future King David. It was in order to defend themselves against the Philistines that the Israelites begged the prophet Samuel to give them a king but it was to the Philistines that David turned in order to escape the wrath and jealousy of that same king. David fled to Philistine territory and was gladly received by King Akish, who welcomed him as a rebel against the monarchy of his enemy, Saul. In order to avoid yet another skirmish with the Philistines, Saul refrained from following David and permitted the Israelite exile to enjoy the considerable luxury of the Philistine court for years (Halbertal and Holmes 2017).

They even effectively awarded David his own Philistine city. Having once killed so many of their number, David was an object of suspicion among the Philistine courtiers and disingenuously asked the king to give him "a place in some town in the country" where he might be of greater service to him. As soon as David was settled at the Philistine town of Ziklag in the Negev, he began raids on various groups of Canaanites who, at this point in their history, were easy pickings. Accordingly, he was able to use the spoils of his successful predations to build his own army of mercenaries. To retain the confidence of the Philistine King, David gave him the impression that his expeditions were directed against his own countrymen and their allies, even though he was still afraid to set foot in Israelite territory. It was in the city of Ziklag that David first began to rule and the lessons of deceit and faithlessness that he learned there served him well later in life. He became King of the Twelve Tribes of Israel, celebrated in his own time, and revered far into the future, for having done virtually nothing for his people except unite them for a brief time.

"So that's what happened. The Israelites turned Philistine and the Philistines became the Jews of their day. If it weren't so tragic it would be funny." These are parting words of Maurice Yacowar's Delilah in his fascinating turnabout narrative of the story of Samson, *The Bold Testament* (Yacowar 1999: 249). Indeed, it *is* true that the two Israelite champions who were divinely intended to stand in moral opposition to the Philistines, Samson and David, were, on closer inspection, Philistine pawns. Isaiah was later to chide the people of Israel for these close associations to the enemy and prophesied their doom "because they be replenished from the East and are soothsayers like the Philistines, and they please themselves in the children of strangers" (Isaiah 2:6 KJV). The monarchy of Ancient Israel, begun with Samson's recklessness and David's fecklessness, did not stray far from their path.

Saul and Jonathan and virtually all of their family, with the exception of David's wife Michal, whom he treated abominably, and Saul's lame son, were collateral damage. After colluding with the Philistines for years and just narrowly escaping having to serve in their army when they went against the Israelites at Mount Gilboa, David was distressed to learn that the Philistines killed Jonathan and wounded Saul, who subsequently committed suicide. Father and son were beheaded and their corpses were displayed on the walls of the city of Beth Shean. After murdering the hapless young man who informed him of the deaths of his monarch and his closest friend, David wrote a touching tribute purportedly in an excess of grief. The next verse appearing in the Biblical text describes David making his way quickly to Hebron to collect his kingship. The best-known phrase from this lament has worked its way into common parlance as an ironic comment on a prominent person having been demeaned by his own acts or by outside circumstances (Attridge 2006). It is an eloquent elegy but one that still, somehow, rings emotionally hollow:

The beauty of Israel is slain upon thy high places: how are the mighty fallen!

Tell it not in Gath, publish it not in the streets of Askelon; lest the daughters of the Philistines rejoice, lest the daughters of the uncircumcised triumph.

Ye mountains of Gilboa, let there be no dew, neither let there be rain, upon you, nor fields of offerings: for there the shield of the mighty is vilely cast away, the shield of Saul, as though he had not been anointed with oil.

From the blood of the slain, from the fat of the mighty, the bow of Jonathan turned not back, and the sword of Saul returned not empty.

Saul and Jonathan were lovely and pleasant in their lives, and in their death they were not divided: they were swifter than eagles, they were stronger than lions.

Ye daughters of Israel, weep over Saul, who clothed you in scarlet, with other delights, who put on ornaments of gold upon your apparel.

How are the mighty fallen in the midst of the battle!

O Jonathan, thou wast slain in thine high places. I am distressed for thee, my brother Jonathan: very pleasant hast thou been unto me: thy love to me was wonderful, passing the love of women.

How are the mighty fallen, and the weapons of war perished!

(2 Samuel 1: 19–27 KJV)

Bibliography

Abbas, M. 2016. PA TV. March 21, 2016.

Al-Mughrabi, N. and T. Finn. 2017. Hamas Softens Stance on Israel, Drops Muslim Brotherhood Link. *US News*, May 1, 2017. Retrieved from: www.usnews.com/news/world/articles/2017-05-01/hamas-to-soften-stance-on-israel-muslim-brotherhood-in-policy-document-sources.

Al-Sherif, M. 1998. Palestinian history, Israeli terms. *Al-Ahram Weekly*. Retrieved from: http://weekly.ahram.org.eg/Archive/1998/1948/383_mahe.htm.

Ali, F. and J. Post. 2008. The History and Evolution of Martyrdom in the Service of Defensive Jihad: An Analysis of Suicide Bombers in Current Conflicts. *Social Research: An International Quarterly* 75/2: 615–654.

Ashrawi, H. 1995. *This Side of Peace: A Personal Account*. New York: Touchstone Books.

Attridge, H.2006. *The HarperCollins Study Bible--Old Testament*. Atlanta, GA: Society of Biblical Literature.

Baramki, D. 1961. *Phoenicia and the Phoenicians*. Beirut: Khayats.

Bauck, P. 2008. 1 Samuel 19: David and the Teraphim. and the Emplotted Narrative. *Scandinavian Journal of the Old Testament* 22/2: 212–236.

Benvenisti, M. 2000. *Sacred Landscape: The Buried History of the Holy Land Since 1948*. Trans. by M. Kaufman-Lacusta and M. Benvenisti. Berkeley, CA: University of California Press.

Betancourt, P. 2000. The Aegean and the Origin of the Sea Peoples in *The Sea Peoples and Their World: A Reassessment* (E.D. Oren, ed.), University Museum Monograph 108. University Museum Symposium Series 11, pp. 297–303. Philadelphia, PA: University Museum: University of Pennsylvania

Bitan, D. 1960. *Masada the Symbol and the Legend, the Dead Sea and the Judean Desert.* Jerusalem: Yad Ben Zvi.

Breasted, J. 1905. *A History of Egypt from the Earliest Times to the Persian Conquest.* New York: Charles Scribner and Sons.

Brenner, B. 2017. *Gaza Under Hamas: From Islamic Democracy to Islamist Governance.* New York: I.B. Tauris.

Canaan, T. 1927. Mohammedan Saints and Sanctuaries in Palestine. Jerusalem: The Syrian Orphanage Press.

Cifola, B. 1988. Ramses III and the Sea Peoples: A Structural Analysis of the Medinet Habu Inscriptions. *Or* 57: 275–306.

Cline, E. 2014. *1177 B.C.: The Year Civilization Collapsed.* Princeton, NJ: Princeton University Press.

Cohen, M. 2014. The Details Behind Israel's Purchase of Lockheed's "Samson" Airlifter. *LobeLog.* Retrieved from: https://lobelog.com/the-details-behind-israels-purchase-of-lockheeds-samson-airlifter/.

Cook, J. 2013. *Disappearing Palestine: Israel's Experiments in Human Despair.* New York: Zed Books.

D'Andrade, R. 1986. Cultural Meaning Systems in *Culture Theory: Essays on Mind, Self, and Emotion* (R. Schweder and R. LeVine, eds.), pp. 88–119. Cambridge: Cambridge University Press.

Davies, P. 2015. *In Search of "Ancient Israel": A Study in Biblical Origins.* London: Bloomsbury T and T Clark.

Dever, W. 2001. *What did the Biblical Writers Know and When Did They Know It?* Grand Rapids, MI: Eerdmans.

Dever, W. 1998. Archaeology, Ideology and the Quest for an Ancient or Biblical Israel. *Near Eastern Archaeology* 61/1: 39–52.

Dothan, Trude. 1982. *The Philistines and their Material Culture.* Jerusalem: Israel Exploration Society.

Drews, Robert. 1998. Canaanites and Philistines. *Journal for the Study of the Old Testament* 81: 39–61.

Drury, S. 2003. Terrorism from Samson to Atta, *Arab Studies Quarterly* 25/1&2: 1–12.

Dunning, T. 2016. *Hamas, Jihad and Popular Legitimacy: Reinterpreting Resistance in Palestine.* London: Routledge.

Durkheim, E. 1974. The Elementary Forms of the Religious Life. Trans. by J. Swain. Glencoe, IL: Free Press.

Erichsen, W. 1933. *Papyrus Harris I: Hieroglyphische Transkription.* Bibliotheca Aegyptiaca V. Brussels: Fondation Égyptologique Reine Élisabeth.

Farsoun, S. and N. Aruri. 2006. Palestine and the Palestinians: A Social and Political History. Boulder, CO: Westview Press.

Finkelstein, I. 1996. The Philistine Countryside. *Israel Exploration Journal* 46: 225–242 .

Finkelstein, I. and N. Silberman 2007. *David and Solomon: In Search of the Bible's Sacred Kings and the Roots of the Western Tradition.* New York: Touchstone.

Gelvin, J. 2014. *The Israel-Palestine Conflict: One Hundred Years of War.* Cambridge: Cambridge University Press.

Gitin, S. 1996. Royal Philistine Temple Inscription Found at Ekron. *Biblical Archaeologist* 59: 101–102.

Glock, A. 1999a. Cultural Bias in Archaeology. Republished in *Archaeology, History and Culture in Palestine and the Near East: Essays in Memory of Albert E. Glock* (T. Kapitan, ed.), pp. 324–342. Atlanta. GA: Scholars Press.

Glock, A. 1999b. Archaeology as cultural survival: The future of the Palestinian past. Republished in *Archaeology, History and Culture in Palestine and the Near East: Essays in Memory of Albert E. Glock* (T. Kapitan, ed.), pp. 343–365. Atlanta, GA: Scholars Press.

Gross, N. 2000. Demolishing David. *Jerusalem Report*, September 11, 2000: 41–42.

Hackett, J. 1984. *Balaam Text from Deir 'Alla*. Harvard Semitic Mongraphs. Cambridge: Scholars Press.

Halbertal, M. and S. Holmes 2017. *The Beginning of Politics: Power in the Biblical Book of Samuel*. Princeton, NJ: Princeton University Press.

Hallote, R. and A. Joffe. 2002. Between "Nationalism" and "Science" in the Age of the Second Republic. *Israel Studies* 7/3: 84–116.

Hamas. 1988. Yale Law School. The Avalon Project. Retrieved from: http://avalon.law. yale.edu/20th_century/hamas.asp.

Henry, R. 2003. *Synchronized Chronology: Rethinking Middle East Antiquity*. New York: Algora Publishing.

Hersh, S. 2001. *The Samson Option: Israel's Nuclear Arsenal and American Foreign Policy*. New York: Random House.

Hitchcock, L. A. and A. M. Maeir. 2014. Yo Ho, Yo Ho, A *Seren*'s Life for Me! *World Archaeology* 46: 624–640.

Islamic Association for Palestine. 1992. Internal Memorandum, October 1, 1992. Retrieved from: www.investigativeproject.org/document/23-internal-memo-of-the-iap.

Jewish Telegraphic Agency Daily News Bulletin. 1961. Toynbee Equates Zionism with Anti-Semitism: Attacked by Jewish Leaders, December 1, 1961.

Karageorghis, V. 1990. Miscellanea from Late Bronze Age Cyprus. *Levant* 22: 157–159.

Karageorghis, V. 1992. The Greeks on Cyprus in *50 Years of Polish Excavations in Egypt and the Near East: Acts of the Symposium at the Warsaw University 1986* (Stefan Jakobielski and Janus Karkowski, eds.), pp. 137–154. Warsaw: PAN.

Karageorghis, V. 1994. The Prehistory of Ethnogenesis in *Cyprus in the 11th Century B.C.: Proceedings of the International Symposium Organized by the Archaeological Research Unit of the University of Cyprus and the Anastasios G. Leventis Nicosia, October 30–31, 1993* (V. Karageorghis, ed.), pp. 1–10. Nicosia: A. G. Leventis Foundation.

Kelman, H. 1983. Conversations with Arafat: A Social-Psychological Assessment of the Prospects for Israeli-Palestinian Peace. *American Psychologist* 38/2: 205–216.

Kershner, I. 2007. Palestinian Christians Look Back on a Year of Troubles. *New York Times*, March 11, 2007. Retrieved from: www.nytimes.com/2007/03/11/world/ middleeast/11christians.html.

Kertzer, D. 1988. *Ritual, Politics and Power*. New Haven, CT: Yale University Press.

Killebrew, A. 2005. *Biblical Peoples and Ethnicity*. Atlanta, GA: Society for Biblical Literature.

Knapp, A. 2008. *Prehistoric and Protohistoric Cyprus: Identity, Insularity, and Connectivity*. Oxford: Oxford University Press.

Machinist, P. 2000. Biblical Traditions: The Philistines and Israelite History in *The Sea Peoples and Their World: A Reassessment* (E.D. Oren, ed.), University Museum Monograph 108. University Museum Symposium Series 11, pp. 53–83. Philadelphia, PA: University Museum: University of Pennsylvania.

Maeir, A. 2013. Gaza in *The Oxford Encyclopedia of the Bible and Archaeology* (D. Master, ed.), pp. 451–453. New York: Oxford University Press.

Maeir, A., B. Davis and L. Hitchcock. 2017. Philistine Names and Terms Once Again: A Recent Perspective. *The Journal of Eastern Mediterranean Archaeology and Heritage Studies* 4/4: 321–340.

Masalha, N. 2007. *The Bible and Zionism: Invented Traditions, Archaeology and Post-Colonialism in Palestine-Israel.* London: Routledge.

Masalha, N. 2014. Reading the Bible with the eyes of the Philistines, the Canaanites and the Amelekites in *Theologies of Liberation in Palestine-Israel: Indigenous, Contextual, and Postcolonial Perspectives* (N. Masalha and L. Isherwood, eds.), pp. 57–114. Eugene, OR: Pickwick Publications.

Matthews, V. and J. Moyer. 2012. *The Old Testament: Text and Context.* Grand Rapids, MI: Eerdmans.

Mayer, T. 2005. National Symbols in Jewish Israel: Representation and Collective Memory in *National Symbols, Fractured Identities: Contesting the National Narrative* (M. Geisler, ed.), pp. 3–34. Lebanon, NH: Middlebury College Press.

Mazow, L. 2006. The Industrious Sea Peoples: The Evidence of Aegean-Style Textile Production. *Cyprus and the Southern Levant. Scripta Mediterranea* 27/8: 291–321.

Murad, A. 2001. Recapturing Islam from the Terrorists. Retrieved from: http://masud.co.uk/ISLAM/ahm/recapturing.htm.

Murad, A. H. 2008. *Bombing Without Moonlight: The Origins of Suicidal Terrorism.* Cairo: Amal Press.

O'Connor, D. 2000. The Sea Peoples and the Egyptian Sources in *The Sea Peoples and Their World: A Reassessment* (E.D. Oren, ed.), University Museum Monograph 108. University Museum Symposium Series 11, pp. 85–102. Philadelphia, PA: University Museum: University of Pennsylvania.

Palestinian Media Watch. 2016. Mahmoud Abbas Fabricates History. Retrieved from: www.palwatch.org/main.aspx?fi=709&fld_id=709&doc_id=18124.

Pape, R. 2004. *Dying to Win: The Strategic Logic of Suicide Terrorism.* New York: Random House.

Pappe, I. 1994. *The Making of the Arab-Israeli Conflict, 1947–1951.* London: I B Tauris & Co Ltd.

Post, J. 2005. When Hatred Is Bred in the Bone: Psycho-Cultural Foundations of Contemporary Terrorism. *Political Psychology* 26/4: 615–636.

Rippin, A. 2008. The Muslim Samson: Medieval, Modern and Scholarly Interpretations. *Bulletin of the School of Oriental and African Studies* 71/2: 239–253.

Rogan, E. and A. Shlaim. 2001. *The War for Palestine: Rewriting the History of 1948.* Cambridge: Cambridge University Press.

Saad, A. 2004. Paradise Now. *Palestine Report,* June 2, 2014. Retrieved from: www.palestinereport.ps/article.php?article=386.

Scham, S. 2001. The Archaeology of the Disenfranchised. *Journal of Archaeological Method and Theory* 8/2: 183–213.

Scham, S. 2002. The Days of the Judges When Men and Women Were Animals and Trees Were Kings. *Journal for the Study of the Old Testament* 97: 37–64.

Scham, S. 2003. From the River unto the Land of the Philistines: The "Memory" of Iron Age Landscapes in Modern Visions of Palestine in *Deterritorializations—Revisioning Landscapes and Politics* (M. Dorrian, ed.), pp. 73–79. Edinburgh: Black Dog Press.

Scham, S. 2004. High Place: Symbolism and Monumentality on Mount Moriah, Jerusalem. *Antiquity* 78/301: 647–660.

Scham, S. 2009. Diplomacy and Desired Pasts. *Journal of Social Archaeology* 3/3: 399–416.

Segev, T. 1999. *One Palestine Complete.* New York: Henry Holt.

Silberman, N. 1995. Promised Lands and Chosen Peoples in *Nationalism, Politics and the Practice of Archaeology* (P. Kohl, ed.), pp. 249–262. Cambridge: Cambridge University Press.

Sternhell, Z. 1999. *The Founding Myths of Israel*. Princeton, NJ: Princeton University Press.

Swedenburg, T. 2003. *Memories of Revolt: The 1936–1939 Rebellion and the Palestinian National Past*. Fayetteville, AR: University of Arkansas Press.

Taubman, W. 2003. *Khrushchev: The Man and His Era*. New York: W.W. Norton & Co.

Toynbee, A. 1961. Jewish Rights in Palestine. *Jewish Quarterly Review* LII: 1: 1–11.

Wasserstein, B. 2001. *Israelis and Palestinians: Why Do They Fight?* Can They Stop? New Haven, CT: Yale University Press, 2001.

Webb, J.M. 1985. The Incised Scapulae in *Excavations at Kition V: The Pre-Phoenician Levels, Part II* (V. Karageorghis, ed.), pp. 317–328. Nicosia: Department of Antiquities, Cyprus.

Yacowar, M. 1999. *The Bold Testament*. Calgary: Bayeux Arts Incorporated.

Yadin, Y. 1968. And Dan, Why Did He Remain in Ships? *American Journal of Biblical Archaeology* 1: 9–23.

Yahya, A. 2005. Archaeology and Nationalism in the Holy Land in *Archaeologies of the Middle East: Critical Perspectives* (R. Bernbeck & S. Pollock eds.), pp. 66–77. Oxford: Wiley-Blackwell.

Ziadeh-Seely, G. 1999. Abandonment and Site Formation Processes: An Ethnographic and Archaeological Study in *Archaeology, History and Culture in Palestine and the Near East: Essays in Memory of Albert E. Glock* (T. Kapitan, ed.), pp. 127–150. Atlanta, GA: Scholars Press .

Ziadeh, G. 1995. Ethno-history and "Reverse Chronology" at Ti'innik, a Palestinian Village. *Antiquity* 69/266: 999–1014.

Zionist Organization of America. 2002. Hanan Ashrawi, Apologist for Terror, Should be Disinvited from Colorado Symposium on 9/11 Anniversary. Retrieved from: http://zoa.org/2002/08/102248-hanan-ashrawi-apologist-for-terror-should-be-disinvited-from-colorado-symposium-on-911-anniversary/#ixzz4hpqi4P5i.

Section 3

Romantic emplotments

6 "There was no king in Israel"

Early Israel in settler movement narratives

In those days there was no king in Israel: every man did that which was right in his own eyes.

(Judges 21:25)

The only way to bring viable and long-term peace on this land is to deepen our roots into this land, into the source of the Jewish nation. The source of the Bible is here. If, God forbid, we uproot ourselves, there'll never be peace. They'll say, "man these Jews don't feel any connection. So how about wiping them out of this country altogether." If we're not in Jerusalem, if we're not in Hebron, if we're not in Bethel, we won't be in Tel Aviv.

(Mitchell and Stahl 2011; Statement from Naftali Bennett,
as Leader of the Settler Yesha Council)

It is difficult to believe now that I once travelled to the West Bank by car with American students from Jerusalem several times a week without even being stopped at the border. In the spring of the year 2000, three months before the cataclysm, I taught a class entitled "The Archaeology of the West Bank," which I envisioned as an on-site course—and an excuse to visit ancient sites that I had not had much of an opportunity to explore. My students were attending a fundamentalist Christian college located on Mount Zion in Jerusalem. It was housed in a British Mandate building next to the Jerusalem Mount Zion Protestant Cemetery where the body of Flinders Petrie is interred *sans tête* (his head went to the Royal College of Surgeons in London at his request). Although I was not ideologically in tune with the "mission" of the college, its location in a century-old compound with a garden overlooking the Old City was an inducement. Its amiable Dean had a standard lecture for those of us who were not quite on board with their Christian values—"it is your responsibility to give your students the consensus of opinion about Biblical archaeology but we are *not* here to test their faith."

At the time, letting the sites speak for themselves seemed to me to be an inspired notion for accomplishing this balancing act. The first site we decided to visit was Bethel. Located adjacent to a small village near Ramallah, Bethel is purportedly sacred to Jews as the place where Jacob became Israel (Genesis

32:28)—the first mention of that name in the Hebrew Bible. I had been to the site several times but in those pre-GPS years, I had to depend upon maps and my own very flawed sense of direction to find it again. Naturally, we got lost and we found ourselves near the settlement of Beit El. I had not visited that many settlements but I wasn't surprised to see that this one was heavily guarded.

At the entrance to the settlement, I asked the guards, who were wearing kippas (yarmulkes) and obviously residents, where the archaeological site could be found. After questioning several people there, I found that none of them seemed to know. Later, one of our group spied a Palestinian man harvesting olives in a nearby orchard. We asked him in Arabic if he knew the location of the site—the Biblical place name of this site, like so many in Palestine (Benvenisti 2002), was preserved in the Arabic name Beitin. As it is also a largeish town, we asked for the location of the site using the English and then the Hebrew pronunciation. "You mean the place where Yacoub (Jacob) fell asleep and fought the angel?" he asked us. He continued with further stories about the significance of the site but our Arabic was not up to the task of comprehending it. Finally, he gave us very exact directions on how to get there.

Perhaps it is not to be wondered at that a Palestinian Muslim would know the location of an important Israelite archaeological site better than the relative newcomer settlers, but the settlement had been there for almost 30 years. Ostensibly, the reason for religious settlers to occupy this land rested on the story of Biblical events that occurred there but it didn't much matter to them where that was. Perhaps they were interested in Beit El lemala (Bethel above or in the heavens) rather than its earthly remains but I suspect that their presence there had more to do with an aggressive land acquisition program that was anchored by this site rather than its proximity to the Biblical location of their people's origins.

Three years before our visit, Beit El settlers had temporarily occupied the nearby privately owned Palestinian site of Jabal Artis of no known Biblical significance, the hill on which we encountered our Palestinian informant. They camped out at the site and renamed it in honor of their fellow settlers Ita and Ephraim Tzur, a mother and her 12-year-old son who were killed by Palestinians. Maoz Tzur, as they called it, is also the name of a well-known Hebrew song associated with what may be the most xenophobic of Jewish Holidays, Hanukkah. The squatters eventually evacuated voluntarily but, later, it was revealed that this was due to a government promise to expand their permanent settlement. Jabal Artis, renamed Pisgat Ya'akov (Mount of Jacob), was reoccupied a year after our visit and, with the blessing of the Ministry of Housing and Construction, it became a part of Beit El without ever having gone through even a sham legal process to establish a change in ownership. The land had belonged to the Farahat family and was registered with forged documents signed by the family patriarch who had been dead for over 30 years when the documents were drawn up (Al-Hadi 1997).

Not long after our visit, the site of Bethel/Beitin became an important part of my life for almost five years. Between 2001 and 2005, we worked on a project, funded by the United States Department of State, that among other things, brought the Arab community together to maintain and appreciate the site they had lived with their entire lives. The late Adel Yahya was the primary force behind this project and he spent years collecting stories and memories about the site and employing Beitin residents to work on restoring and protecting it. In 2004, I visited Bethel/Beitin for the last time with Adel. I brought my daughter with me over the border into the West Bank and went through no less than three checkpoints, receiving a lecture at each one on the dangers of taking a child with me to Ramallah. Adel picked us up in a United Nations vehicle, brought my daughter to his house to play with his own daughter of the same age and we proceeded to the site of Bethel. It was a ten-minute drive in 2000. In 2004, it took us two hours. Israeli roadblocks put up to protect settlements and cut off routes for Palestinians barred our way at every turn.

Even while we were working to make the site of Beitin/Bethel into a tourist destination, a new movement that probably had its beginnings at Jabal Artis was growing that would crush any Palestinian hopes for visitors from abroad and hamper efforts to make peace between Israelis and Palestinians (Jones 2013). A year after the Beit El settlers had evacuated Maoz Tzur, then-Israeli Defense Minister Ariel Sharon urged settler youth to "grab the hilltops." He was channeling their frustration of the Wye River Accords calling for miniscule relinquishments of West Bank land to the Palestinian Authority. Coincidentally, this was the same Israeli-Palestinian agreement under which our project was financed. Adding to his Horace Greeley moment, Sharon urged the rest of the settlers so that they "should move, should run ... expand the territory. Everything that's grabbed will be in our hands. Everything we don't grab will be in their hands" (Kershner 2014: 184).

Retaliatory occupation was once part of the story of how Palestinian land became Jewish in the West Bank. As acts of violence against settlers on the part of Palestinians desperate to keep their land continued, however, Israelis living within the recognized borders of Israel started to resent the funds expended for settler protection. A housing shortage, coupled with a large influx of immigrants in the 1990s, added to the numbers of people living in the settlements where housing was cheap—and as a result, the numbers of children raised in fortress-like conditions surrounded by hostile neighbors grew (Rivlin 2010). For the most part, these "economic" settlers were not part of the ideological settlement movement but their children are susceptible to the appeal of radicalism (Sprinzak 1991). Growing up in this fraught environment, feeling themselves to be under siege with no way out, members of the younger generation have turned to more extreme actions (Byman 2011; Byman and Sachs 2012).

They call themselves the Hilltop Youth, although it is clear that they are not unified, nor necessarily even organized (Taub 2010 and Jones 2013). They are radical religious xenophobes who revere the example of Rabbi Meir Kahane (Jones 2013), possibly the most extreme Jewish leader in modern history.

Kahane's Jewish Defense League (JDL), an American organization that has been linked to violent attacks since the late 1960s, became the Kach Movement in Israel and subsequently Kahane Chai. In the United States, JDL members were implicated in the murder of Alex Odeh, the head of the American-Arab Anti-Discrimination Committee, in 1985.

In Israel, Kach member Baruch Goldstein massacred 29 Muslims worshipping at the Cave of the Patriarchs in 1994. In 2001, JDL members were arrested after allegedly plotting to blow up a Culver City mosque and the office of Darrell Issa. The JDL in the West is moribund but the Kach Movement and Kahane Chai are the only Jewish organizations to be designated as terrorists by the United States, the State of Israel and the European Union. Kahane's assassination in 1990 by an Egyptian gunman has only added to the reverence for his message by extremist Jews (Friedman 1990).

In terms of socioeconomic status, the Hilltop Youth are mostly from impoverished families and a number of them are school drop outs. They are from groups who consider themselves outside of Israel's Ashkenazi founding elites and include Yemenites, Moroccans, Russians and new Israelis of many nationalities, including Americans, who find it difficult to break into a society that is by now firmly established. They live in isolated temporary camps, like nomads and "work the land, to harvest olives and to ride freely on horses" (Shafran 2002). They represent a stark contrast to the Westernized large settlements where they were raised. They grew up in settlement schools singing "David, Melech Yisrael, Chai, Chai, Israel" (David, King of Israel, lives and endures) and studying the stories of Biblical heroes living in the land and slaughtering its previous occupants on a regular basis (Hirschhorn 2017).

Israel's authorized settlements sit on the tops of hills surrounded by walls, built of white stone, concrete and stucco—a glaring intrusion into the natural landscape. These are urbanized strongholds, built with large donations from abroad and Israeli Government funds. To call them "settlements" seems to belie their physical aspect, particularly in comparison to neighboring Arab villages with brown weathered "Jerusalem stone" houses built decades, even centuries, ago. They spill down the hillside surrounded by native stone buttressed terraces, many of which have been farmed continuously since the Bronze Age (Gibson 2001), and olive groves. Sheep and goats graze in pens or freely on the outskirts of the villages. It is difficult not to conclude that the second-generation settlers who joined the Hilltop Youth, raised in huge anonymous housing blocks or identical "villas" walled off from the landscape, must have felt some sense of imprisonment there.

Perhaps they looked upon their elders, with the exception of some of the venerated and rapidly aging founders of the Hilltop Youth Movement, as their jailers. Most of all, they were taught that it is the neighboring Palestinians who have hindered their freedom of movement (Halevi 1995, 2014). They may have seen the Arab villages from their manufactured white prisons with a sense of envy. Among the settlers, there was once a diversity of opinion about Arabs—with some believing in the possibility of coexistence—but increasingly, the younger generations, at least those that have been attracted to the

Hilltop Youth, are quite unanimous in their ingrained enmity. While they have probably reached the point of hating the Israelis who want to stop them, they do feel a distinct sense of outrage against them (Caton 2011).

Their illegal outposts are ramshackle temporary shelters, mostly caravans. They seem to have been put there in the expectation that they will be forced to remove them one day. More importantly, few of them have the least idea of how to construct permanent shelter because, in Israel, building is Avodah Aravit (Arab Work). They practice some form of desultory agriculture, growing a few scraggly crops, stealing sheep and goats from their Palestinian neighbors, perhaps raising a few chickens. They have come to the hills not just to take back the land but go back to it. They are incapable of doing this at present, partly because they have never been taught these skills. While some of their older mentors have engaged in successful farming activities, the young people of the movement are increasingly left to their own devices (Glanz 2016).

The Hilltop Youth are wont to speak to reporters in platitudes and proclamations, if at all (Remnick 2013). A reporter for the *New Yorker* visiting the West Bank about ten years ago attempted to get a young man from Yitzhar to explain why he was destroying the olive trees of Arab villagers and was told by him emphatically that "I'm not hearing you, I'm not hearing what you're saying. You don't understand me. I'm not hearing and I will continue not to hear." A religious authority in the settlement later told the reporter that the owner of the olive trees "is an Arab. He shouldn't be here at all. All this land is Jewish land. It is meant for the Jews by God Himself" (Goldberg 2004). The story was written in 2004, right after Yitzar had become a battleground for a skirmish between settlers and the Israel Defense Force. No one was killed but a number of settlers were arrested. Israeli soldiers are cautioned not to use dangerous weapons against fellow Jews and settlers, in any case, they are not so easily deterred. After the dismantling of their colony, they returned practically the next day to rebuild (Goldberg 2004). To this day, Yitzar and its satellites still stand in the hills overlooking the Palestinian city of Nablus.

Several years ago, it looked like the movement was waning in the wake of several violent incidents that called attention to them and stimulated the government to bring them to heel. Now they have been given new life by the rise of right-wing politics in Israel and in the United States as well (Pedahzur 2012; Pedahzur and Perliger 2009). Jordanians often refer to Israel as "America's fifty-first state" and settlements, with an influx of American wealth from individuals such as the ultra-conservative Sheldon Adelson and a complicit administration in Israel, are moving forward at a faster pace than ever (Reinl 2016). While the Hilltop Youth scorn establishment settlements they, like their elders, see some encouragement in these developments. "Make Israel Great Again" hats and t-shirts are appearing in these outposts (Zeveloff 2017).

Of late, although many of them are still somewhat suspicious of the media, some representatives of the Hilltop Youth have stepped forward to explain their cause. Arutz Sheva (Channel Seven), the right-wing religious Israeli station, was, not surprisingly, more successful than others in getting them to open up. This media outlet also had an interesting connection to what is becoming a consistent theme in this chapter—the settlement of Beit El. At the height of the *Al-Aqsa Intifada*, ten of their employees were convicted of operating an illegal radio station from there. In addition to prosecuting the employees, the Israeli court convicted the director of the station for perjury after having lied about the location of the broadcasts (Izenberg 2006).

An interviewer for the voice of religious nationalism in Israel questioned a representative of what he referred to as "the much-maligned Jewish youths strengthening Israel's presence in Judea and Samaria" one Friday afternoon about two years ago (Tucker 2015). His subject was a woman leader of an outpost of Yitzar in the West Bank. Ayelet Hashahar-Hakohen, whose first name is derived from that of the Biblical woman warrior Jael (Yael), was a founder of one of those outposts, Givat Shalhevetya (the Hill of God's flame), possibly named in honor of a ten-month-old Jewish girl named Shalhevet Pass, who was shot by a Palestinian in 2001. Hakohen spoke to the sympathetic news outlet in order to "stop the persecution of the Hilltop Youth." Bemoaning that "[w]e suffered a lot from the system in the past—arrests, administrative distancing orders, we experienced it ourselves," she called out the Israeli Government for this mistreatment.

Although many of the founding members of the movement, she pointed out, are now too old to be called "youth," she looks to their children as keepers of the flame. "[W]hen at their age most children are busy with computer and iPhone screens, that doesn't interest them, they are interested in the land, the land of Israel, agriculture, building and a connection to our roots ... It moves you to tears," she said, "to see the self-sacrifice of the children who day and night study Torah, guard their towns, remove rocks, weeds and thorns and want to settle the land of Israel." Later in the interview she lamented that their lives could be easier:

> [I]f only the security system and the state would do what is needed against the Arab terror threat, but unfortunately it isn't happening ...[we] cannot stand it that every day blood is spilled, it's very painful, and because the system doesn't do its job, these children are confused ... It's true that they make mistakes, but...these are children who are ready to sacrifice themselves just for the land of Israel.
>
> (Tucker 2015)

Hakohen represents the Hilltop Youth as the "only sheriff in town" willing to deal with the lethal threat represented by largely unarmed Arab villagers, while preserving the integrity of the Land of Israel for future generations. Palestinians have killed a number of West Bank settlers, including young children, so her concern is understandable, but the fact that they are occupying land that no national or international authority recognizes as theirs and are daily harassing and threatening the people who do own the land might have a great deal to do with these tragic instances. The Hilltop Youth also does not constitute a harmless group of pacific "back to the landers" who simply want to farm in peace. The Biblical prophecy that the Lord would drive out "the inhabitants of the mountain" (Judges 1:19 KJV), they believe, is simply a signal for them to do as Joshua had done and take "all that land, the hills, and all the south country" (Joshua 11:16 KJV). Hakohen and her disparaged compatriots have little sympathy for the victims of the Duma village arson attack that, in July of 2015, resulted in three deaths including that of an 18-month-old child.

In general, both settler politicians and their favorite news organ gloss over most violent episodes associated with the Hilltop Youth and have even gone so far as to allege "rumors" of "internal clan feuds in the village" that raise doubts about the guilt of Jewish youths who were, supposedly, tortured into confessing. Similarly, they suggest that many instances of reported attacks by Jews on Palestinians are fabricated (Arutz Sheva 2016). But if some supporters of the Hilltop Youth doubt the official stories of these incidents, the Israeli filmmaker of *The Settlers* (2016), Shimon Dotan, has proof that should convince everyone else. After having spent months in the hills of the West Bank, he branded the Hilltop Youth, although very small in number, as the new face of West Bank settlement. His film provides a close-up view of the motivations and backgrounds of the group and concludes that, although mainstream settler leaders try to distance themselves from them, they are, in fact, a natural outgrowth of the Settler Movement. "Those who push it forward today are the hilltop youth," Dotan said, "And it seems to me a very dangerous direction" (Glanz 2016).

The Hilltop Youth Movement has made and disseminated their own films, which not only confirm Dotan's conclusion but also suggest that it does not go far enough. A video seized by police in 2015 shows them dancing around and stabbing a photo of Ali Dawabsheh, the toddler who was killed in the Duma attack. The film was made at a Jewish wedding (now often referred to as "the blood wedding" or "wedding of hate"). The songs in the video include such perennial favorites as "Burn down the mosque" and "We will avenge one of the two eyes of Palestine, curse them" (an allusion to the story of Samson). But the most popular music at affairs of this kind is provided by Dov Shurin, a favorite of the radical Israeli settlement movement, who has written most of his songs about what he believes is the existential "struggle for Israel."

Shurin based his song, *Zochreini Na* (I remember it well), upon the myths of Early Israel recounted in the Book of Judges (Ettinger 2003). It was this song that the Hilltop Youth danced to in the "Blood Wedding" video, with their automatic weapons waving in the air, a custom actually originated by their "fellow" nomads of Israeli wilderness, the Bedouin (Thompson 1999). As the perfect accompaniment to this celebration of a vicious attack upon a Palestinian family, in which a child died, it has also become something of an anthem for the group. The Biblical verses that the song is based on speak of killing Philistines—a reference that Shurin often changes in his performances to Palestinians, suggesting that at least one Israeli traditionalist believes that the two are connected (see Chapter 5, this volume).

Many Israelis were shocked to see this obvious display of hatred but, as has been pointed out, are not shocked when the perpetrators of this violence are not brought to justice. Known Jewish assailants in several deadly attacks on Palestinians have gone free and youth gangs have set upon Israeli Jewish peace movement protestors with impunity (Ascherman 2017). Farmers and olive gatherers have frequently experienced predations from Jews toting stun grenades, clubs and explosives—and *ex officio* appropriation of Palestinian land by settlers, with the approval of Israeli courts, goes on and on. All of these incidents have resulted, according to veteran reporter, Amira Hass, in a culture in Israel of "unknown offenders, insufficient evidence and do-nothing soldiers." Their messianism, she alleges "was born of the incessant secular Israeli disregard for international law" (Hass 2015).

There are a number of theories about how the Hilltop Youth originated. Mostly these explanations follow a similar pattern to those that analysts provide about the formation of other groups labeled as terrorists. Supposedly, relative deprivation, marginalization and a belief in the efficacy of violence, born of fear and deeply instilled hatred, have all been cited as contributing to their radicalization (Gurr 1970). Limited access to employment and a lot of time on their hands is also a factor. Their creed is described in the simplest terms—they hate Arabs and want to drive them out but these are actions not values (Caton 2011). Their ideology is essentially anarchistic but it is also steeped in a religious tradition, Jewish Religious Zionism, that instills suspicion and animosity toward those who are outside of the community. This includes other Jews but, most importantly, it is aimed at Arabs.

It was the evacuation of settlements in Gaza in 2005 that was really the catalyst for the movement. For many Jews, the sight of the Israel Defense Forces roughing up their own fellow citizens was disturbing but, for settlers in the West Bank, it was at once both outrageous and ominous. The idea that they could be treated in the same manner probably crossed many of their minds. The weakness of the Yesha Council in protesting the Gaza disengagement convinced these disaffected young people that they could trust neither the government nor their own representatives. They consider the Council members, along with their parents, to be collaborators with a corrupt state (Taub 2010: 127). They began creating a number of outposts on isolated hilltops throughout the West Bank for which they neither sought nor acknowledged the approval of the government. Isolated in their nomadic camps they plotted raids on settled Arab townspeople—a practice that they have called "Price Tagging" (Kraft 2007: 33).

B'Tselem, the Israeli Information Centre for Human Rights in the Occupied Territories, defines a "price tag" attack as an "act of violence aimed at the Palestinian population and/or Israeli security forces" that occur often in response to actions by Israeli authorities that are perceived as harming the settlement enterprise (B'Tselem 2010). Price-tag attacks are of two types—one is in retaliation for attempts by the Israeli military to demolish illegal encampments and the other is against specific targets, such as Palestinians, representatives of the Israeli Peace Movement or the Yesha Council. The second type is simply violence, pure and simple, against Palestinians, in particular, the destruction of their olive trees, arson and, in the past few years, assault and murder (Tranas 2012: 48).

Quite naturally, as religiously inspired extremists, the Hilltop Youth have their supporters among the rabbinical ranks. One affiliate of the Chabad Movement in Israel, which generally attempts to maintain a low political profile and has disclaimed his teachings, is considered to be the putative "father" of "price tagging." During a speech in protest over the removal of the Gush Katif settlement from Gaza, he famously referred to a metaphor of the "shell and the fruit," encouraging his followers to remove the hard shell (i.e., state institutions) from the fruit, which is the heart of the Jewish people. It was a clever inference derived from Kabbalistic teachings but, also, a play on an old Zionist saying that Israelis are like the Sabra fruit (prickly pear cactus), spiky and tough on the outside but "sweet" on the inside. According to Rabbi Ginsburgh, the time had come to break the shells, overthrow the secular ideology of Zionism and oppose the government until a new religious Jewish regime is restored to the Land of Israel (Harel 2017).

They have the advantage of being much better armed and organized than their Palestinian neighbors and more or less constitute a "civilian militia," a number of whom have been trained while serving the Israel Defense Forces, which they believe they are now forced to oppose (on occasion). Settlers who engage in violence in the West Bank are taking advantage of the lax law enforcement in the occupied territories and the general view on the part of Israeli authorities that they can take care of themselves (Feige 2009: 232). It is a frontier mentality and, as such, it is easy for the occupants of "civilized" regions to forget what their co-religionists are doing in the colonies (Scham 2006).

Each time one of these attacks occurs, the solid citizens of "Green line Israel" ask why the state does not cut off support or otherwise crack down on this behavior. During my most recent fieldwork in Israel, in 2014, the country was reeling from the virulent outbreak of violence by Israeli settlers in retaliation for the killing of three Jewish teenagers in the West Bank. Several children were killed, including one Palestinian teenager who was kidnapped and burned alive (Beaumont 2014). Arabs who are victims of lawlessness in the West Bank believe that they are in the same position that Native Americans were in the American Old West. As one Palestinian official said "[w]hen the attack targets Jews, you can see how efficient the Israeli security forces are. They solve the crime and capture the people responsible within days or weeks at most. Then suddenly, when the attack goes the other way, and it is Jews who murder Arabs, nothing happens" (Caspit 2015).

The Hilltop Youth identify most with the Israelite pioneers, Joshua and the Judges (Gilbert 2009), the first warrior leaders of Israel. The Bible is essentially the only source attesting to the existence of Early Ancient Israel and many scholars doubt that they were in any way distinguishable from the surrounding Canaanites except with respect to differences that can be attributed to urban versus rural surroundings (Thompson 1999; Whitelam 1996). It was Joshua who initiated the concept of "holy war," which might be surprising to many people who believe this idea to have originated with Islam (Mayes 1974). The term "herem" is used in the Hebrew Bible to denote absolute destruction of the enemy. The Early Israelites were told to kill "every living thing" (animals and humans) but to spare the crops and the trees that they would need in the future when they settled down in their conquered territories (Borowski 1998, 2002). Although the events of the conquest of Canaan are rendered differently in the Books of Joshua and Judges, the two offer insights into the making of the myth of Early Israel (Aharoni 1976).

The emergence of Early Israel in the Bible began with Moses, a stern but mostly peaceful man who was prohibited from entering the Holy Land because he struck a rock, and ended with David, who was prohibited from building the temple because he had killed "thousands." It is hard to find any continuity in these accounts and in the stories of the Books of Joshua and Judges (Guest 1998), but the theme that primarily surfaces is that of obedience. Moses was instructed to talk to the rock and it would bring forth water and he struck it instead. David could not erect the house of God because he had "shed blood abundantly and made great wars" (I Chronicles 22:8), suggesting that his violence was excessive even by Old Testament standards (Brettler 1989). These are the bookended narratives of the primary heroes of the Zionist imagination but the Hilltop Youth with their "back to nature" ideology most recall the Days of the Judges (Hareuveni 1980).

The Bible records 40 years as the time that the Israelites spent living as nomads and making their way through Transjordan to Mount Nebo. After that, Joshua and Judges present two differing accounts as to the settlement of the tribes of Israel (Dever 1990 and 1998). The first chapters of Joshua describe Israelite battles with the Canaanites, while Judges depicts the Israelite presence as growing gradually with small tribal groups arising here and there to take over (Killebrew 2005). Joshua himself represents a transitional figure between Moses and the Judges—as the person most responsible for drawing the borders of their tribal territories. Joshua, like most Biblical heroes, is the conduit of miracles, parting the Jordan River as Moses had parted the Red Sea, demolishing the walls of Jericho with the sound of shofars and causing the sun and moon to stand still at Gibeon. He had defeats but these were always attributable to the disobedience of his warriors. Most importantly, Joshua was the first of the Israelite leaders to exhort the Israelites to shun the Canaanites and "other" inhabitants of the land.

As noted in Chapter 5, the earliest (and only) textual evidence that exists for an entity called Israel in the Early Iron Age is the Merneptah Stele. From the late thirteenth century BCE, this inscription describes Merneptah's victories over a number of towns and peoples in Canaan. The text as translated reads, "Israel is laid waste, his seed is not." There are many disagreements among scholars as to whether the term Israel refers to a person, a people or a city. Based more on a lack of textual evidence from Canaan during this period than on other material culture, scholars have presumed that the term refers to a tribe. Not all researchers agree that the text refers to Israel, as others have proposed that the better-known Canaanite geographical term Jezreel is more likely (Margalith 1990). Others have simply suggested that the Egyptian transliterated term bears no relationship to the name Israel (Nibbi 1989).

Most Egyptologists seem to agree, however, that the term should be translated as Israel. Whether this refers to the Biblical Israel is another question, one that cannot be resolved based upon currently existing evidence. Biblical researchers were the most eager to make a connection between Merneptah's Israel and Biblical Israel and believe that the Merneptah Stele provides a chronological datum for the emergence of Israel in the Iron Age. One scholar believes that the reference to "seed" in the text refers to the destruction of flocks and their progeny, indicating that the "Israel" of the inscription was a nomadic pastoral society (Rainey 2001).

The Merneptah Stele and the Biblical text are really the only explicit evidence for the culture of Early Israel—the first being very limited but contemporaneous with the Iron Age and the second more explanatory but not contemporaneous. Thus, the symbolism that could help to identify the ideology of Early Israel must be sought in the material culture of the time in comparison to the Bible, which must be acknowledged as the dominant narrative for both the ancient inhabitants of the hill country of Palestine and its modern usurpers. Beginning with the text, we see that the Judges narratives follow several themes that would make them likely archetypes for the ideology of rural Jewish radicalism.

Like the Judges, the Hilltop Youth characterize themselves as "sons of the soil," as opposed to the residents of Israel's towns and cities who have no idea of how to live off the land and are wont to think of raising olive trees and sheep herding as Palestinian occupations (Faust 2000). The "halutzim" (pioneers) of Israel's early years, the subsistence farmers who began to immigrate there beginning in the late nineteenth century, are remembered only in old Zionist anthems and agricultural kibbutzim are now engaged in industry. These secular Zionists do not inspire the radical Jews of the West Bank. Instead, they look to the Bible. As one of them replied to a reporter who asked who gave the land to them, "[f]or starters, God did. It says so explicitly in the Bible. It says, 'All the land which thou seest'" [from Genesis 13:15 KJV) (Glanz 2016). That these words were actually said to the man who is the ancestor of both Jews and Muslims, Abram (before he was Abraham/Ibrahim), would not have struck the settler as ironic—there is no sharing of patriarchs in the Holy Land.

It is true that some of them have adopted Biblical farming and herding methods—possibly because the Bible represents their only source of knowledge on how to raise crops and animals. But if they had studied more history and less Torah, the Hilltop Youth might have been inspired by the notion that the central hill country of Palestine has one of the oldest agricultural traditions in the world (Bunimovitz 1994). The land they have chosen has experienced 9,000 to 10,000 years of plant domestication, 7,000 to 8,000 years of animal domestication and 3,000 to 4,000 years of using the "secondary products" of domestic animals (milk, wool, traction and so on) (McCorriston and Hole

1991; Sherratt 1981) and domesticating fruit trees (olives, grapes, dates, figs) (Zohary et al. 1975).

The Biblical hero of the Hilltop Youth, Joshua, is never recorded as having settled down to raise crops or indeed to do anything other than lead the Israelites into battle. Joshua died and was buried in the land of Ephraim. Thereafter, the Biblical writers record a period of chaos during which the Israelites won and lost a number of Canaanite cities and, thereafter, a period of sporadic apostasy during which God "raised up" heroes referred to in the English Bible as "Judges" but, more likely, tribal chiefs who managed at various times to form confederations. This was the true frontier of Early Israel, according to Judges, where the Israelites established their settlements and began to live as farmers and herders in the hill country of Palestine (Hopkins1985; Scham 2002).

In addition to plant and animal domestication, the Iron Age denizens of the central hill country had the benefit of two important innovations from the Late Bronze Age that enabled them to survive and flourish—slaked lime plastered cisterns and domesticated camels (Baumgarten 1992). Although there is a controversy as to how much these two events impacted the expansion of settlements in the Iron Age, it seems clear that the cisterns made it possible for people to live further away from perennial springs and wells, such as in the hill country of Palestine where water sources are numerous but not entirely reliable (Finkelstein 1995b). When the camel was domesticated and camel caravans began, it may have substantially changed the map of the Near East insofar as the all-important trade routes were concerned (Campagnoni and Tosi 1978). It was no longer necessary to travel only within regions that were watered by wells and goods could now be moved across the desert that stood between the people of Ancient Israel and their primary trading partners, the Egyptians (Bloch-Smith and Nakai 1999).

In general terms, the stories in Joshua and Judges reflect the agropastoralist, desert versus sown (see Chapter 3, this volume) themes of Biblical Early Israel as they relate to the specific regions allocated to each tribal group (Lemche 1985). In terms of the chronology of the stories, as they are presented by the Biblical writer, they begin with Judah and the Judges who were of this tribe. According to most Biblical scholars, though, references to the tribe of Judah and the possibility of a "king in Israel" were added later—perhaps to support the authority of a supposed United Monarchy (Alter 1981). The scholarly chronology of the most important narratives in Judges is considered to have actually begun with Deborah and Barak, from Joshua's tribe of Ephraim, and Jael, from the same tribe as Moses' father-in-law. Second in that chronology are the stories of Gideon and Abimelech, who came from the tribe of Manasseh. Third in chronological order is the story of Ehud from the tribe of Judah and Samson, whose story takes place in Judah (although Samson is from the tribe of Dan) (Malamat 1970).

Both stories associated with Judah speak of singular warriors who act on their own to destroy an enemy. In the case of the first story, the enemy is Moab, which the Israelites fought at the beginning of their sojourn in the land.

The story of Samson presages the coming conflict between the Israelites and the Philistines (see Chapter 5, this volume). The early Ephraim stories take place in a wild land that has not yet been tamed and which is subject to constant wars with the Canaanites. The Manasseh stories speak of a sedentary farming population threatened by nomadic predations and the third seems to be stories of flawed heroes living in fairly close proximity to urban centers and enjoying the benefits of surrounding civilizations while having occasional bellicose relations with them (Scham 2002). By and large, it is a warlike society on the verge of nationhood but also a rugged one constantly plagued with violence both within and without.

The writers of the Bible mythologized what they perceived of as their "shepherd history," although it is not clear that such a past ever truly existed (Halpern 1983). The special status accorded to nomads in the Bible has led many scholars to assume that they made a significant contribution to the ancient cultures of the Levant (Davies 1992; Finkelstein and Silberman 2002). In reality, the fluidity of early economies encouraged alternating processes of "nomadization" and "sedentarization" in mixed farming and herding pre-state cultures (LaBianca 1990). These terms usually refer to the responses of agropastoralists to environmental or other changes, following which they may emphasize either mobile herding or, alternatively, sedentary agriculture, but the responses may also be a result of political pressures from outside of, and within, the community. The parallels with the modern disaffected youth of the West Bank settlements are many. Brought up in an atmosphere of constant conflict, at odds with their own societies, seeking autonomy and a closer relationship to nature, they "lift up their eyes" unto the very hills in which the narratives of Early Israel, their supposed ancestors, were formed (Shafran 2002).

The archaeology of the Early Iron Age peoples of Palestine indicates a society of small hamlets inhabited by people in control of their environment (Dever 1992; Finkelstein 1988). No longer forced to take to higher ground with their flocks in the event of crop failure, they had found enough land and water to sustain the lifestyle of small farmers. They had found a way to balance the raising of crops and animals and increase the profitability of both; and it is indeed possible that these people had managed to achieve a level of independence and self-sufficiency not known elsewhere in the Near East (Feliks 1962). Without the redistributive economy that is associated with large urban centers or central sanctuaries, they were the controllers of both of their own labor and the products of their labor. It was a hard life, but truly disastrous events were few in number. Through the mobilization of all members of society, including men, women and children, success at consistently providing the necessary food supplies could be achieved.

In the Bible, Ephraim and Manasseh were sons of Joseph who received the blessing of their grandfather, Jacob, alongside Jacob's sons, who were ancestors of the other ten tribes. Although allotted different (adjacent) territories, they maintained close tribal ties, supporting each other when the northern tribes of Israel broke off from the southern tribes after Solomon's death. The name Ephraim refers to a "fruitful vine," a fitting name for a son who grew up amidst the splendors of New Kingdom Egypt (Kitchen 1995). In addition to being the name of Joseph's son, Manasseh was the name of a later "evil" king of the Tribe of Judah—a bad son of a good father, in this case, Hezekiah. The Hebrew root of the name Manasseh suggests that it is a person who "causes forgetfulness," perhaps referring to the fact that Manasseh settled mostly east of the Jordan River and, in effect, constituted a "thirteenth tribe." Judah, the name meaning "praised," was Jacob's fourth son. His father thought that Judah would be the ancestor of Israel's kings ("the sceptre shall not depart from Judah … and unto him shall the gathering of the people be," Genesis 49:10 KJV). Benjamin was the youngest of Jacob's sons and his name and was, as his name implies, the much-favored son of Jacob's "right hand." The etymologies are culturally significant as each, in some way, defines the physical and political attributes of the tribes and their members.

Without texts, other than the Bible, to indicate what their beliefs were, the only evidence of the ideology of Early Iron Age peoples comes from their geography and their material culture. The territory allotted to the tribe of Ephraim in biblical tradition is steep and mountainous, with few cultivable valleys but is, nevertheless, a highly productive area for some crops, particularly grapes. The wine of Ephraim was, according to the Bible, of the best quality and the men and women of the most stalwart character. Archaeological surveys of the region show that there were several large towns in the northeast portion in the Iron Age, even though there were few settlements there in the Late Bronze Age. There were also a number of smaller new settlements, most of them small hamlets at relatively high elevations. About a quarter of them had agricultural terraces (Gibson 2001) and almost all of the new Iron Age hamlets were close to larger villages. Bethel and Shiloh, both in the West Bank, were two of the sites that were Late Bronze Age towns rebuilt in the Iron Age with new plans (Finkelstein 1995a). Among the other Iron Age settlements built on previous Bronze Age foundations, were three where the inhabitants specialized in specific crafts—the metal (bronze and iron) working site of Khirbet Raddana, the bronze workshop at Ai (Khirbet et-Tell) and the central storage "silo" sites of Izbet Sartah (Finkelstein 1993).

To adjust to a harsher and less peopled environment, the people who lived in the hamlets allotted to Ephraim developed agricultural expertise in dry terrace farming. Tree crops in the territory of Ephraim were perhaps less important to the subsistence economy than elsewhere, given the limited number of olive oil installations found here. Villagers at the larger sites dug cisterns to store water, kept sizable flocks of sheep and goats and processed their grain on stone querns. Mostly, in the hill country of Palestine, figurines and depictions of nature provided the most evidence about the symbols they considered to be significant to their lives and their ideals (Douglas 2005; Hodder 1982).

Specific finds from excavations at Shiloh are depictions of the natural world that provide some insight into the ideology of these settlers, including a cult stand, featuring a leopard attacking a deer, a lioness and a ram's head. A famous vessel from Khirbet Raddana is a multi-handled krater with two bull's heads on the inside rim. Other pottery has been found at Ephraimite sites depicting ibex and ibex flanking trees. For the most part, the animal images dating to the Iron Age in this region demonstrate continuity with prior periods. The "bull" krater has cognates in Hittite material culture—bull imagery, in particular, is difficult to interpret because it is ubiquitous throughout the eastern Mediterranean in almost every period of antiquity. Similarly, rams were popular animals in Levantine art since at least the Chalcolithic period, and the lioness motif is known from both Canaanite and Philistine contexts. The ibex motif, especially the ibex with a palm tree, is more restricted in use to the Syro-Phoenician region (Bloch 1995). Further, its popularity in the Levant can be traced to the Late Bronze Age when these images started to appear in greater numbers. The design features native flora and fauna and is interpreted as representing male gods or personages with a female goddess represented by the palm (Scham 2002). This is one of the territories where the figure of the Israelite god Yahweh is most associated with goddess/consort Asherah (Dever 2005).

The archaeological evidence suggests that the people of Ephraim were expert at a number of urban crafts, notably metalworking, even while their primary economic base was the labor-intensive production of grain in small villages. The settlement pattern in Ephraim is one of the very large towns with numerous satellite settlements in close proximity usually without fortifications. For the most part, Ephraimites traded infrequently with their neighbors and with cultures further afield such as Phoenicia and Cyprus. They depended upon domesticated animals and may have attached some sacred role to at least two types, the bull and the ram, which were also revered elsewhere in the Near East. They produced numerous depictions of wild animals, particularly the ibex, which can be considered as, more or less, a symbol native to the region.

Their material culture speaks of a coexistence between agricultural and urban crafts as well as wild and domesticated animal exploitation. Symbolism also indicates certain aesthetic and cultic interest in the aspects and behavior of wild animals. A native narrative of post-conquest Ephraim, the story of Deborah, Barak and Jael (Judg. 4–5) takes place in a world that is, as yet, untamed. Beginning with the names of the protagonists, we find that the first hero of the story (Deborah means honeybee) is associated with a much sought-after serendipitous find. Honey was found in forests during this time period, as there is no evidence for the domestication of bees in Palestine prior to the Hellenistic Period. The land of milk and honey reference in earlier Biblical narratives is meant to suggest an empty land—a place where sheep can graze and where forests that have wild honey are abundant (Gottwald 1979, 1985). Nonetheless, the name Deborah suggests more than sweetness.

The bee is known in all cultures, for both its sugary product and its sting. Wild bees are often described in biblical texts as dangerous swarms. Consequently, it could be argued that the name Deborah might also encompasses a "waspish" warrior aspect. The implications of Barak's name—"lightning"—for a military leader must be viewed as positive but endowing Barak with the characteristics of lightning seems slightly derisive considering his part in this story. He may be swift in answering Deborah's call (Judg. 4:6–7) but his reluctance to do battle without her (4:8) implies an indecisive and recalcitrant personality that belies the quick impulsiveness that his name suggests.

Although the Biblical text makes clear that Deborah will not do battle, she will nonetheless accompany Barak at his request. Whether because of his dependence on her or for other reasons, her celebratory Song of Deborah does not grant to Barak, who won the battle, the full measure of credit for this victory. Rather, Deborah attributes it to the actions of another woman—Jael, the ibex. Jael is a "woman in the tent" who lured Sisera, the commander of the Canaanites, with milk and butter and then drove a tent peg through his skull. The Kenites, Jael's tribe, are prominent in Israelite lore. Jethro, the father of Moses' wife, was said to have been a Kenite (among the Midianites). Jael's name, like Deborah's, evokes a wild animal—an undomesticated cousin of the goats that were the primary herd animals raised in Palestine. The ibex continued to be hunted by the people of the central hills into the later Iron Age. Finally, it is notable that the image of the ibex and palm-tree is here effectively translated into the juxtaposed characters of Deborah and Jael. Deborah, the "mother in Israel," is introduced to us as habitually sitting beneath the palm-tree. Like the stories in Exodus, nomads in this story are characterized as heroic.

The territory identified in the Bible as that of Manasseh was one of fertile valleys and dense forests—a rich and prosperous land. This region was conveniently located for access both to the Transjordan and the sea. Its proximity to the Jezreel and Beth Shean Valleys made it a significant conduit to the large international cities of Megiddo and Beth Shean and smaller sites of Tel Jokneam, Tel Qiri, Tel el-Hammah and Tel Qashish. Abundant springs, soft limestone and reliable rainwater led to a density of settlement in Manasseh not known in other areas. Most of the important Late Bronze Age sites seem to have continued into the Early Iron Age but a number of new sites have also been identified from the latter period.

The city of Shechem (Tel el Balata near Nablus in the West Bank) was an important cult center in the Early Iron Age, as was Taanach (Tel Ti'inik also in the West Bank) (Campbell 1991). The well-known "cultic stands" found in two excavations at Taanach feature lions and winged sphinxes, ibex with trees and a rare human image of a youth strangling a serpent (Glock 1993). The town of Tell el-Far'ah (North), which has been variously identified as the Biblical Ophrah (de Miroschedji 1993) or Beth Barah, both of them mentioned in the story of Gideon, and the biblical Tirzah, gives evidence of having been planned villages of large houses with many items of material culture suggesting prosperity from an agricultural economy. Tirzah is both a place and a person in the Bible. She was an early Jewish feminist icon—one of the five daughters of a tribal elder who was allowed to own land in her own name even though women were forbidden from doing so as a general matter. Tirzah is also a name that resonated with the radical settler movement that preceded the Hilltop Youth (Neidle 2013). Tirzah Porat was the first person to be killed by Palestinians in the West Bank during the first intifada (Washington Post 1988).

The primary sites of Manasseh were occupied before the Iron Age, but the open air "Bull Site," with statuettes of bulls and standing stones and the controversial site of Mt Ebal, where bull figurines were found, along with bones of bulls, sheep, goats and male fallow deer, were not. The biblical account strongly suggests that Manasseh was a populous and culturally diverse region and it is likely that the concepts of divination, bull sacrifice and monarchy that feature in the Gideon story stems from this cultural diversity. Gideon, after all, was the son of a priest of Baal. Because of the heterogeneous population and the strong element of cultural continuity at the sites in the territory identified with Manasseh, it is difficult to say whether the rapid development of this region in the Iron Age might be looked upon as the consequence of one culture's actions or that of a collaboration of cultures.

The account of Gideon's leadership (Judg. 6.11–8.35), and that of his sons (Judg. 9–10), expresses a view of complete comfort with a well-developed and long-established agropastoralist way of life. Gideon's name, which roughly translates as "hacker," has often been taken as indicative of his action of cutting down the sacred Baal–Asherah grove. Joshua told Gideon's tribe Manasseh, along with Ephraim, to cut down the forests in order to make their homes (Josh. 14.17–18). We see Gideon at the beginning of the story threshing wheat by the winepress (Judg. 6.11). This is taking place notwithstanding the fact that elsewhere in the land, the sons of Ishmael are despoiling fields and driving people into caves.

The nomads themselves include the group from which Jael and her husband came—the Midianites. No longer allies, these individuals have developed an economic way of life based on camel pastoralism, that is presumed in this story to be at odds with settled agriculture. While in the Ephraimite story of Deborah, Barak and Jael, the "close to nature" Israelites, are contrasted favorably with the urbanized Canaanite enemy, in the Manassite story of Gideon, the heroes represent the more "civilized" world of agropastoralism in contrast to the peoples of the desert (Finkelstein 1992). Gideon's weapons are also of the "civilized" kind. He gathers a small army of men (Judg. 7:1–8) who may or may not be fit for battle. Regardless, it seems that they are never to actually do battle but instead frighten the enemy away with pitchers and lamps (7.20–21). The brave Bedouin celebrated in Deborah's song become, in this story, a crowd of fearful barbarians. The mythic nomadic past is but a dim memory. Such was the superiority of the fighting farmers of Manasseh that the camel pastoralists, although as numerous as grasshoppers, could be defeated with a mere clamor, while their tents could be overturned with "moldy barley bread."

Given these clear indications that this culture was so well established and prosperous, it is hardly extraordinary that they wished to adopt a more complex form of government. While Gideon refused to take this next obvious step, his son, Abimelech, saw the value in unified leadership (Judg. 9:2). We are told that he was predisposed to seek such a leadership role as indicated by his name (my father is king)—an appellation usually reserved for foreign rulers in the Bible. Nevertheless, his method of obtaining popularity, that is, slaying all other contenders and hiring mercenaries to subdue the people, may have been something the Middle East was not ready for at the time. Before Abimelech's reign begins, we know it is ill-fated, both because of his own actions and because of the nature of "Jotham's fable" (9:8–15).

It has been proposed that this fragment was written separately from the story of Abimelech, as it seems, on the surface, to have little connection with it. Insofar as the natural imagery of the Gideon-Abimelech story is concerned, it is of a piece. Jotham shares with Jephthah the distinction of having a name relating to Yahwistic religion within a composition that is otherwise lacking them. Thus, announcing his appearance on the side of good, the biblical account places in his mouth a curious literary aside about the trees' search for a king. The olive, the fig and the grape vine all refuse the honor, pointing to their distinctive positions in the repertoire of plants that are useful to humans. Only the bramble accedes to the requests and threatens, if it is not dealt with fairly by the other trees, to destroy all of them (Lindara 1973).

While on the surface it is easy to read the intent in this fable, to point out the inferiority of the tree that is willing to assume leadership and, by implication, Abimelech's inferiority, the story has another meaning. The cultivated plants that both extol their virtues and refuse, thereby, to take on any seemingly greater role are contrasted with the uncultivated bramble that is also not without its uses to humans. The perceived threat in this fable is the return to the wilderness, an enemy that in the Gideon account is personified by the Midianites and in the Abimelech account by young hooligans who devastate crops and cut down trees in order to torch the homes of their enemies (Judg. 9:48) like today's ruthless hill country pioneers. The recognition that this way of life was within the power of human beings to destroy as well as build is a vital element of the story that has particular significance for understanding the Hilltop Youth. The young revolutionary, Abimelech, demonstrates his power by destroying the crops and animals of the people of Shechem (Nablus) and rendering their soil infertile. Fire and untamed nature—entities that were used to beneficial purpose in the Deborah and Barak story—become a highly destructive force here.

Given this scenario, it is highly significant that Abimelech is killed with a millstone. The instrument of his death has numerous other meanings attached to it as well, for the Hebrew word used for the instrument of Abimelech's death specifically designates it as the upper, softer millstone but also refers to a branch of a tree used for grafting and a war chariot (in which form the word appears in the Song of Deborah). All of these meanings for this term can be applied to Abimelech's defeat. The good tree (of which he was a bad graft), the war chariots (which here represent the "forces" of civilization) and a soft, weak millstone wielded by a woman all kill him. Thus, it is cultivation, in both senses of the term, and stability that kill Abimelech—a rather neat turnaround of the threat in Jotham's Fable.

Although, throughout the Judges period, "there was no king in Israel," Abimelech's sad bid for a throne was later to be taken up, as the Bible records, by the men of the territories of Benjamin and Judah. Somewhat sparsely populated, the isolated settlements of the south were less prosperous than those of Ephraim and Manasseh. At the same time, the Judahites and Benjaminites found themselves among or close to the "other" peoples of the land—those of the coast and the Transjordan. They depended, for the most part, on limited cereal cultivation. The flocks of sheep and goats appear to have been more sizable at these sites, suggesting a larger pastoral economic base. Both cereals and caprid products would likely have been popular trade items with their urban neighbors and it is perhaps this particular mechanism of contact that eventually contributed to an earlier development of social stratification in this region. Sites closer to other cultural (and tribal) areas may have served as trading centers. Tell en-Nasbeh, for example, has numerous stone lined silos—more than would have been required by the village itself.

Bronze spear points, inscribed with their owners' names and appropriate warlike epithets and horse and rider figurines are characteristic of the unique material culture of Benjamin and Judah. The south Hill Country is known principally as a region of fortifications, large villages on the eastern fringes, smaller ones on the western side and a material culture that is either greatly mixed with or virtually indistinguishable from "Canaanite" Bronze Age sites. This was the territory of Ehud, the left-handed favorite son of the "Sons of the Right (Hand)," Benjamin. In the short and humorous description of Ehud's "campaign," we see him assassinating, while on a diplomatic mission, Eglon, the King of Moab, who has repossessed the city of palm trees which we presume to be Jericho (3.12–31). The palms of Ehud are, however, less benign than the palms of Deborah for they shelter not a honey bee but a fatted calf led to slaughter (the name Eglon roughly translates to heifer) more by an utterly trusting stupidity than by the cleverness of his adversary (Brettler 1995).

It should be clear that if there is anything consistent about the Judges narratives, it is that they do not really exalt legendary conflicts between human protagonists as many have supposed. There are no lasting gains for individuals or groups, no conquests and no changes in government as a result of heroic actions. The population of Early Iron Age Palestine, living mostly in small hamlets with a few more developed sites, *was* a "frontier" culture. The fact that both virtues and dangers are attendant to this is not an unusual concept for people who believe that they have come to a purportedly "empty" land to make their homes. Wilderness represents both attraction and threat. The attraction is what brings the settlers to the area and the threat is what they are determined to eradicate. Once it is eliminated, however, they find, like true frontier people, that the slow and steady advance of civilization imbues them with a certain longing for the simple past. Both Gideon's and Abimelech's stories suggest a society that looked upon the supreme control of their environment and the subjugation of their people as an achievable goal.

From the territories of Benjamin and Judah, we have evidence of a plot that is neither that of the frontier nor the city but instead has elements of both. With a vigorous militant outlook and a demeanor that could best be characterized as "me against the world," the heroes Ehud and Samson act from the fringes of society. Less leaders than incendiaries, they epitomize the fortified towns and Spartan living conditions of their tribal territories (Finkelstein and Silberman 2006). With them, we have a view of nature that can be described as casually exploitative. In these stories, human beings, collectively and individually, are both at the center of the natural world and at the pinnacle of it. The Hilltop Youth ideal of getting closer to the land recalls these early stories of taming the wilderness and defeating its hostile natives and represent romantically emplotted narratives. Although it seems strange to characterize the story of people who would engage in the kind of actions that displace families, destroy homes and murder children as romance, it should be remembered that the ideology associated with romance narratives is anarchy—the conviction that the state is corrupt and must be destroyed to make way for a new community. The Biblical Judges stories portray battles but they also speak of the dangers of lacking religious faith as the Early Israelites are constantly being set against each other and "sold" by God into the hands of enemies for their apostasy. This is perhaps the real "price tag" that may result from Hilltop Youth aggression—not only political but religious division in the land of Israel. Until then, as far as they are concerned there is no king in Israel and everyone will "do that which is right in their own eyes" (Judg. 21:25).

The stories of Judges, together with the archaeological evidence, demonstrates a trajectory that might be expected of any frontier culture progressing from subduing the wild to exploiting the land to its full capacity, and ending with the casual abuse of nature, which is concomitant with a more organized form of government. The comfortable and modern living conditions of the older settlements, which enabled their parents to effectively bypass the first phases of frontier development, to the Hilltop Youth signal that they really did very little to earn their place in the land God gave to them. The possibility of living for a higher purpose is thus squandered by evenings spent watching television and days spent working in offices or studying in Yeshivot. Neither is an active investment in what they believe is their true calling.

In a recent article, a writer explained his view that the Hilltop Youth hearkened back to the days of European Romanticism, concluding:

> The world of laws and rules, the world of settled folk, is perfectly reasonable and safeguards us from evil. However, its reasonableness is also its weakness. It's average, ordinary, logical. It is incapable of soaring. And, as such, it destroys in people any real contact with nature – which is to say that it destroys the place of truth within us.
>
> (Persico 2016)

Memorably, the author quotes one member of the Hilltop Youth who explained the following:

> I grew up in the groves of the religious-Zionist movement, but I was scornful of it and of its key figures … disconnected from the new way of life that included working the land and tending sheep, a deep connection to the earth, making do with little and displaying esprit de corps.
>
> (Persico 2016)

Reading this one might well come to the conclusion that these people are idealists who want to live peacefully and simply restore the land. They do not follow rules because they see a whole new world, one of humility and closeness with nature. More specifically, it is a domain without a history, without a government and most significantly, without Arabs.

In truth, theirs is not the open world of the visionary but rather the closed world of the fanatic. It is, in fact, the fortress world in which they grew up. The Hilltop Youth are simply a more active manifestation of the religious beliefs of their pious settler parents (Hass 2015). The settlement movement began, symbolically, with a reenactment of the Nation of Israel's "rite of passage." A Passover Seder was held in 1968 by a large group of religious Jews who rented rooms in an Arab hotel in Hebron and then refused to leave. Later, with the state's cooperation, they built Kiryat Arba, the settlement that spawned mass murderer Baruch Goldstein (Goldberg 2004). These were the events and rituals the Hilltop Youth grew up with—and they well remember the Seders that they experienced as children during which death is promised to the nations who do not believe in the Jewish God.

As the cup of wine was poured out for Elijah and the door was opened to receive him, the Hilltop Youth were trained to recite forcefully:

> Pour out thy wrath upon the nations that know thee not and upon the kingdoms that call not upon thy name; for they have consumed Jacob and laid waste his habitation. Pour out thy rage upon them and let thy fury overtake them. Pursue them in anger and destroy them from under the heavens of the eternal.

Nothing about the annual re-enactment of this ritual could have been lost upon them. Having avoided the contamination of contacts with "the other" as much as possible, they greet Elijah as the traditional herald of the Jewish Messiah (Mashiach), who will come at the End of Days to redeem them and destroy their unbelieving neighbors. These are the moments when vigilance becomes violence.

The Hilltop Youth narrative has its own logic but, at present, it is the logic of apocalyptic vision and, while waiting for the End of Days, they will make Elijah's work easier for him. Like the constant provocations of the people surrounding the Biblical Early Israelites that allegedly justified total war and mayhem, including the sacrifice of their children and suicide attacks, they believe that extremism in defense of vision is no vice. When the end of the world comes and the Messiah appears, the members of the movement imagine themselves standing alone on the summits of the hills where Israel was born, having rejected the towns and cities of their youth and brutally expelled "the other inhabitants of the land."

The Talmudic term *"shev ve'al ta'aseh"* was used scornfully in a blogpost by Hilltop Youth musical favorite Dov Shurin. It means that, if one is unsure of a particular course, sit and wait for Elijah the Prophet to arrive to tell you what to do (Shurin 2014), and it is clear this is something he does not approve of. Iconic nationalist Israeli songwriter Naomi Shemer wrote the song "Lu Yehi" that he references in the title of his post or, more correctly, she wrote new lyrics using the music to the Beatles song "Let It Be" (Lennon and McCartney 1970). Shemer, who died in 2004 as the Hilltop Youth movement was gaining momentum, made a habit of borrowing melodies from a variety of sources but she always maintained that the music for "Jerusalem of Gold," her anthem for the Six Day War, was original. It was actually based upon a Basque song—which she finally admitted shortly before her death (Avrahami and Wurgraft 2012).

But Shemer's lyrics have never been questioned as anything but her own. In Hebrew, they tie the themes of nature and nativism together profoundly—and perhaps insidiously, as her appeal in Israel is very broad and her songs are sung at even left-wing gatherings. She wrote an extremely popular song, beloved by Jews in the United States as well as Israel, that subtly recalls the stories in the Book of Judges, while also extolling that peculiar combination of enduring conflict, religion and nature that permeates Israeli culture and informs the "ideals" of the Hilltop Youth:

> Over all these things, over all these things
> Please stand guard for me my good God
> Over the honey and the stinger
> Over the bitter and the sweet
> Don't uproot a sapling
> Don't forget the hope
> May you return me, and may I return
> To the good land.

(Shemer 1982)

Bibliography

Ackerman, S. 1999. *Warrior, Dancer, Seductress, Queen: Women in Judges and Biblical Israel.* New York: Doubleday.

Aharoni, Y. 1976. Nothing Early and Nothing Late: Rewriting Israel's Conquest. *Biblical Archaeologist* 39: 55–62.

Al-Hadi, M. 1997. Palestine: From the Negotiations in Madrid to the Post-Hebron Agreement Period. Jerusalem: Palestine Academic Society for the Study of International Affairs.

Alter, R. 1981. *The Art of Biblical Narrative.* New York: Basic Books.

Arutz Sheva Staff. 2016. Yet Another Fire in Duma One Year After Deadly Arson: Not for the First Time, Fire Guts Home of Member of Dawabshe Clan, One Year After Three Killed in Arson Blamed on Jewish Extremists. *Arutz Sheva* 7, July 20, 2016. Retrieved from: www.israelnationalnews.com/News/News.aspx/215265.

Ascherman, A. 2017. The Hilltop Youth—The Inevitable Result of 50 years of "Occupation." *The Jerusalem Post*, April 29, 2017. Retrieved from: www.jpost.com/printarticle.aspx?id=489324.

Avrahami, I. and N. Wurgraft. 2012. Naomi Shemer Had No Reason to Feel Bad, Says Basque Singer. *Haaretz*, May 6, 2005. Retrieved from: www.haaretz.com/news/naomi-shemer-had-no-reason-to-feel-bad-says-basque-singer-1.157926.

B'Tselem. 2010. Background on Violence by Settlers. Jerusalem: The Israeli Information Center for Human Rights in the Occupied Territories.

Baumgarten, J. 1992. Urbanization in the Late Bronze Age in *The Architecture of Ancient Israel From the Prehistoric to the Persian Periods* (A. Kempinski and R. Reich, eds.), pp. 143–150. Jerusalem: Israel Exploration Society.

Beaumont, P. 2014. Palestinian Boy Mohammed Abu Khdeir Was Burned Alive, Says Official. *The Guardian*, July 5, 2014. Retrieved from: www.theguardian.com/world/2014/jul/05/palestinian-boy-mohammed-abu-khdeir-burned-alive.

Benvenisti, M. 2002. *Sacred Landscape: The Buried History of the Holy Land Since 1948.* Oakland, CA: University of California Press.

Bloch-Smith, E. and B. Nakai. 1999. A Landscape Comes to Life: The Iron Age I. *Near Eastern Archaeology* 62/2: 62–129.

Bloch, M. 1995. The Cedar and the Palm Tree: A Paired Male/Female Symbol in Hebrew and Aramaic in *Solving Riddles and Untying Knots: Biblical Epigraphic and Semitic Studies in Honor of Jonas Greenfield* (Z. Zevit, S. Gitin and M. Sokoloff, eds.), pp. 13–17. Winona Lake, IN: Eisenbrauns,

Boling, R. 1975. *Judges.* New York: Doubleday.

Borowski, O. 1998. *Every Living Thing: Daily Use of Animals in Ancient Israel.* London: Altamira.

Borowski, O. 2002. *Agriculture in Iron Age Israel.* Winona Lake IN: Eisenbrauns.

Brettler, M. 1989. The Book of Judges: Literature as Politics. *Journal of Biblical Literature* 108: 395–418.

Brettler, M. 1995. The Ehud Story as Satire in *The Creation of History in Ancient Israel*, pp. 188–203. London: Routledge.

Bunimovitz, S. 1994. Socio-Political Transformations in the Central Hill Country in the Late Bronze–Iron I Transition in *From Nomadism to Monarchy: Archaeological and Historical Aspects of Early Israel* (I. Finkelstein and N. Na'aman, eds.), pp. 179–202. Jerusalem: Israel Exploration Society.

Byman, D. 2011. *A High Price: The Triumphs and Failures of Israeli Counterterrorism.* Oxford: Oxford University Press.

Byman, D. and N. Sachs 2012. The Rise of Settler Terrorism. *Foreign Affairs*, September/October 2012. Retrieved from: www.foreignaffairs.com/articles/israel/2012-08-18/rise-settler-terrorism.

Campagnoni, E. and M. Tosi. 1978. The Camel: Its Distribution and State of Domestication in the Middle East During the Third Millennium B.C. in Light of Finds from Shahr-I Sokhta in *Approaches to Faunal Analysis in the Middle East* (M. Zeder and R.H. Meadow, eds.), pp. 91–104. Cambridge MA: Harvard University Press.

Campbell, E. 1991. *Shechem: Portrait of a Hill Country Vale; The Shechem Regional Survey.* Atlanta, GA: Scholars Press.

Caspit, B. 2015. Who Are Israel's Hilltop Youth? Israel Pulse. *Al-Monitor*, December 9, 2015. Retrieved from: www.al-monitor.com/pulse/originals/2015/12/hilltop-youth-douma-murder-dawabsha.html#ixzz4g2W2JxAN.

Caton, E. 2011. *Unsettling the Settlement: The Ideology of Israel's Hilltop Youth.* Unpublished Thesis. Haverford, PA: Haverford College, Department of Religion.

Davies, P. 1992. *In Search of "Ancient Israel."* Sheffield: Sheffield Academic Press.

de Miroschedji, P. 1993. Far'ah, Tell el-(North) in *The New Encyclopedia of Archaeological Excavations, II* (E. Stern, ed.), pp. 433–438. Jerusalem: Israel Exploration Society.

Dever, W. 1990. The Israelite Settlement in Canaan: New Archaeological Models in *Recent Archaeological Discoveries and Biblical Research* (H. Shanks, ed.), pp. 1–51. Seattle, WA: University of Washington Press.

Dever, W. 1992. How to Tell a Canaanite from an Israelite in *The Rise of Early Israel* (H. Shanks, ed.), pp. 27–60. Washington, DC: Biblical Archaeology Society.

Dever, W. 1998. Israelite Origins and the Nomadic Idea: Can Archaeology Separate Fact from Fiction? in *Mediterranean Peoples in Transition: Thirteenth to Early Tenth Centuries BCE* (S. Gitin, A. Mazar and E. Stern, eds.), pp. 220–237. Jerusalem: Israel Exploration Society.

Dever, W. 2003. *Who Were the Early Israelites and Where Did They Come From?* Grand Rapids, MI.: William B. Eerdmans Publishing Company.

Dever, W. 2005. *Did God Have a Wife? Archaeology and Folk Religion in Ancient Israel.* Grand Rapids, MI.: William B. Eerdmans Publishing Company.

Dotan, S. 2016. *The Settlers.* (Hebrew), Producers, E. Fialon, J. Aroch, P. Cadieux and S. Dotan. Produced in Co-Production with Yes.docu, ARTE, NDR, HR, BR, Radio Canada.

Douglas, M. 2005. The Pangolin Revisited in *Signifying Animals* (H. Willis, ed.), pp. 25–36. London: Routledge.

Ettinger, Y. 2003. God and Love and Rock 'n' Roll. *Haaretz*, September 25, 2003. Retrieved from: www.haaretz.com/print-edition/business/god-and-love-and-rock-n-roll-1.101191.

Faust, A. 2000. The Rural Community in Ancient Israel during the Iron Age II. *Bulletin of the American Schools of Oriental Research* 317: 17–40.

Feige, M. 2009. *Settling in the Hearts.* Detroit, MI: Wayne State University Press.

Feliks, Y. 1962. *The Animal World of the Bible.* Tel Aviv: Sinai Press.

Finkelstein, I. 1988. *The Archaeology of the Israelite Settlement.* Jerusalem: Israel Exploration Society.

Finkelstein, I. 1992. Pastoralism in the Highlands of Canaan in the Third and Second Millennia B.C.E. in *Pastoralism in the Levant Archaeological Materials in Anthropological Perspectives.* O. Bar-Yosef and A. Khazanov eds. Pp. 122-14.2 Monographs in World Prehistory No. 10. Madison, WI: Prehistory Press.

Finkelstein, I. 1993. Izbet Sartah in *The New Encyclopedia of Archaeological Excavations in the Holy Land* (E. Stern, ed.), pp. 652–654. Jerusalem: Israel Exploration Society.

Finkelstein, I. 1995a. *Shiloh: The Archaeology of a Biblical Site.* Tel Aviv: Tel Aviv University Press.

Finkelstein, I. 1995b. The Great Transformation: The "Conquest" of the Highlands Frontiers and the Rise of the Territorial States in *The Archaeology of Society in the Holy Land* T.E. Levy ed. Pp. 349–365. New York: Facts on File.

Finkelstein, I. and N. Silberman. 2002. *The Bible Unearthed: Archaeology's New Vision of Ancient Isreal and the Origin of Sacred Texts.* New York: The Free Press.

Finkelstein, I. and N. Silberman. 2006. *David and Solomon: In Search of the Bible's Sacred Kings and the Roots of the Western Tradition*. New York: The Free Press.

Friedman, R. 1990. *The False Prophet: Rabbi Meir Kahane – From FBI Informant to Knesset Member*. Chicago IL: Lawrence Hill.

Gibson, S. 2001. Agricultural Terraces and Settlement Expansion in the Highlands of Early Iron Age Palestine: Is There Any Correlation Between the Two? in *Studies in the Archaeology of the Iron Age in Israel and Jordan. Journal for the Study of the Old Testament Supp. Series* 331 (A. Mazar, ed.), pp. 113–146. Sheffield: Sheffield Academic Press.

Gilbert, M. 2008. *Israel: A History*. London: Black Swan.

Glanz, W. 2016. A Window into the West Bank's "Wildest, Most Violent" Areas. *New York Times,* May 23, 2016. Retrieved from: www.nytimes.com/2016/05/24/world/middleeast/a-window-into-west-banks-wildest-most-violent-areas.html.

Glock, A. 1993.Taanach in *The New Encyclopedia of Archaeological Excavations IV* (E. Stern, ed.), pp. 1428–1433. Jerusalem: Israel Exploration Society.

Goldberg, J. 2004. Among the Settlers. Will They Destroy Israel? *The New Yorker,* May 31, 2004. Retrieved from: www.newyorker.com/magazine/2004/05/31/among-the-settlers.

Gottwald, N. 1979. *The Tribes of Yahweh: A Sociology of the Religion of Liberated Israel*. Maryknoll, NY: Orbis Books.

Gottwald, N. 1985. The Israelite Settlement as a Social Revolutionary Movement in *Biblical Archaeology Today Proceedings of the International Congress on Biblical Archaeology, Jerusalem* (J. Amitai, ed.), pp. 34–46. Jerusalem: Israel Exploration Society.

Grigson, C. 1995. Plough and Pasture in the Early Economy of the Southern Levant in *The Archaeology of Society in the Holy Land* (T.E. Levy, ed.), pp. 245–268. New York: Facts on File.

Guest, P. 1998. Can Judges Survive Without Sources? Challenging the Consensus. *Journal for the Study of the Old Testament* 78: 43–61.

Gurr, T. 1970. *Why Men Rebel*. Princeton, NJ: Princeton University Press.

Halevi, Y. 1995. *Memoirs of a Jewish Extremist: An American Story*. New York: Little, Brown and Co.

Halevi, Y. 2014. *Like Dreamers: The Story of the Israeli Paratroopers Who Reunited Jerusalem and Divided a Nation*. New York: Harper-Collins.

Halpern, B. 1983. *The Emergence of Israel in Canaan*. Chico, CA: Scholars Press.

Harel, A. 2017. Beyond Gush Emunim: On Contemporary Forms of Messianism among Religiously Motivated Settlers in the West Bank in *Normalizing Occupation: The Politics of Everyday Life in the West Bank Settlements* (A. Harel, M. Allegra and D. Maggor, eds.), pp. 128–150. Bloomington IN: Indiana University Press.

Hareuveni, N. 1980. *Nature in Our Biblical Heritage*. Jerusalem: Neot Kedumim.

Hass, A. 2015. Why Are Israelis So Shocked by the "Wedding of Hate" Video? *Haaretz*. December 28, 2015. Retrieved from: www.haaretz.com/opinion/.premium-1.694136.

Hirschhorn, S. 2017. *City on a Hilltop: American Jews and the Israeli Settler Movement*. Cambridge, MA: Harvard University Press.

Hodder, I. 1982. *Symbols in Action: Ethnoarchaeological Studies of Material Culture*. Cambridge: Cambridge University Press.

Hopkins, D. 1985. *The Highlands of Canaan: Agricultural Life in the Early Iron Age. Social World of Biblical Antiquity, 3*. Sheffield: Almond Press.

Izenberg, D. 2006. Katsav and Ramon Defend Arutz 7 Pardons. *The Jerusalem Post*, May 31, 2006. Retrieved from: www.jpost.com/Israel/Katsav-and-Ramon-defend-Arutz-7-pardons.

Jones, C. 2013. Israel's Insurgent Citizens: Contesting the State, Demanding the Land in *Islamist Radicalisation in Europe and the Middle East. Reassessing the Causes of Terrorism* (G. Joffe, ed.), pp. 200–213. London: I. B. Tauris.

Kershner, I. 2014. *Barrier: The Seam of the Israeli-Palestinian Conflict.* New York: Palgrave MacMillan.

Killebrew, A. 2005. *Biblical Peoples and Ethnicity.* Atlanta, GA: Society for Biblical Literature.

Kitchen, K. 1995. Egyptians and Hebrews: From Ra'amses to Jericho in *The Origin of Early Israel Biblical, Historical and Archaeological Perspectives* (S. Ahituv and E. Oren, eds.), pp. 65–79. London: University College London Press.

Kraft, D. 2007. *Counter Violent Extremism. Lessons from Abrahamic Faiths.* East West Institution.

LaBianca, O. 1990. *Sedentarization and Nomadization: Food Systems and Cycles at Hesban and Vicinity in Transjordan, Hesban, I.* Berrien Springs, MI: Andrews University Press.

Lemche, N. 1985. *Early Israel: Anthropological and Historical Studies on the Israelite Society Before the Monarchy.* Leiden: Brill.

Lindars, N. 1973. Jotham's Fable: A New Form Critical Analysis. *Journal of Theological Studies* 24: 355–366.

Malamat, A. 1970. The Danite Migration and the Pan-Israelite Exodus-Conquest: A Biblical Narrative Pattern. *Biblical Studies* 51: 1–16.

Margalith, O. 1990. On the Origin and Antiquity of the Name "Israel." *Zeitschrift für die Alttestamentliche Wissenschaft* 102: 225–237.

Mayes, A. 1974. *Israel in the Period of the Judges.* London: SCM Press.

McCorriston, J. and F. Hole. 1991. The Ecology of Seasonal Stress and the Origins of Agriculture in the Near East. *American Anthropologist* 93: 46–69.

Mitchell, C. and J. Stahl. 2011. Jewish Roots Lead Deep into the "West Bank." *Christian Broadcast Network News*, November 25, 2011. Retrieved from: www.cbn.com/cbnnews/insideisrael/2011/august/jewish-roots-lead-deep-into-the-west-bank/.

Neidle, J. 2013. Locating the Power of the Settler Movement. *Journal of Politics and International Studies* 9/Summer: 481–519.

Nibbi, A. 1989. *Canaan and Canaanite in Ancient Egypt. Discussions in Egyptology.* Oxford: Oxford University Press.

Pedahzur, A. 2012. *The Triumph of Israel's Radical Right.* Oxford: Oxford University Press.

Pedahzur, A. and A. Perliger. 2009. *Jewish Terrorism in Israel.* New York: Columbia University Press.

Persico, T. 2016. What's Driving Israel's Radical Settler Youth to Rebel? *Haaretz*, January 31, 2016. Retrieved from: www.haaretz.com/israel-news/1.700089.

Rainey, A. 2001. Israel in Merneptah's Inscription and Reliefs. *Israel Exploration Journal* 51: 57–75.

Reinl, J. 2016. Palestinians Sue Pro-Israel Tycoons For $34.5bn. *AlJazeera*, March 7, 2016. Retrieved from: www.aljazeera.com/news/2016/03/palestinians-sue-pro-israel-tycoons-345bn-160307191923877.html.

Remnick, D. 2013. The Party Faithful. The Settlers Move to Annex the West Bank and Israeli Politics. *The New Yorker*, January 21, 2013. Retrieved from: /www.newyorker.com/magazine/2013/01/21/the-party-faithful.

Rivlin, P. 2010. *The Israeli Economy from the Foundation of the State through the 21st Century.* Cambridge: Cambridge University Press.

Scham, S. 2002. The Days of the Judges When Men and Women Were Animals and Trees Were Kings. *Journal for the Study of the Old Testament* 26/3: 37–64.

Scham, S. 2006. Colony or Conflict Zone? *Archaeological Dialogues* 13/2: 205–207.

Scham, S. 2005. The Lost Goddess of Israel. *Archaeology* 58/2. Retrieved from: http://archive.archaeology.org/0503/abstracts/israel.html.

Shafran, D. 2002. We the Youth of the Hills. *Nekuda* 257/1: 18–27.

Shemer, N. 1982. *Number Three (Sefer Gimel)*. Jerusalem: Lulav.

Sherratt, A. 1981. Plough and Pastoralism: Aspects of the Secondary Products Revolution in *Patterns of the Past: Studies in Honour of David Clarke* (I. Hodder, G. Isaac and N. Hammond, eds.), pp. 261–305. Cambridge: Cambridge University Press.

Shurin, D. 2014. Ruby Rivlin's Victory: "Lu Yehi" Defeats "Let it Be." *The Jewish Press*, June 18, 2014. Retrieved from: www.jewishpress.com/indepth/columns/dov-shurin-columns/ruby-rivlins-victory-lu-yehi-defeats-let-it-be/2014/06/18/0/?print.

Sprinzak, E. 1991. *The Ascendance of Israel's Radical Right*. Oxford: Oxford University Press.

Stek, I. 1986. The Bee and the Mountain Goat: A Literary Reading of Judges in *A Tribute to Gleason Archer* (W. Kaiser and R. Youngblood, eds.), pp. 53–86. Chicago, IL: Moody Press.

Taub, G. 2010. *The Settlers and the Struggle over the Meaning of Zionism*. New Haven, CT: Yale University Press.

Thompson, T. 1999. *The Mythic Past: Biblical Archaeology and the Myth of Israel*. New York: Random House.

Tranas, H. 2012. *The Wild Wild West Bank. Investigating Causes of Increased Settler Violence 2006–2011*. Master's Thesis. Oslo: Oslo University.

Tucker, B. 2015. Hilltop Youth Cannot Stay Silent as State Allows Terror: Founder of Samaria Town Urges State to Stop Persecuting Hilltop Youth and Help Them Instead, Noting They Face Bloodshed Daily. *Arutz Sheva*, December 18, 2015. Retrieved from: www.israelnationalnews.com/News/News.aspx/205120.

Whitelam, K. 1996. *The Invention of "Ancient Israel": The Silencing of Palestinian History*. London: Routledge.

Willis, P. 2005. Introduction in *Signifying Animals: Human Meaning in the Natural World*, pp. 1–24. New York: Routledge,

Zeveloff, N. 2017. The Teenagers Pushing Israel to the Right. *The Atlantic*, February 7, 2017. Retrieved from: www.theatlantic.com/international/archive/2017/02/settlers-amona-teenagers-israel/515904/.

Zohary, D., D. Speigel-Roy and P. Speigel-Roy. 1975. Beginnings of Fruit Growing in the Old World. *Science* 187: 319–327.

7 "Realm like his was never won by mortal king"

Huthis, Himyarites and hard-lines

> Ours the realm of Dhu'l-Qarnayn the glorious,
> Realm like his was never won by mortal king.
> Followed he the sun to view its setting
> When it sank into the sombre ocean-spring
>
> (Seventh-century poet Hassan bin Thabit quoted in
> Van Donzel and Schmidt 2014)

> The hurdle facing negotiations and dialogue is that the other party wants to achieve
> through the talks what it wanted to achieve through war, not understanding that
> the path of dialogue and peace is different to the path of war.
>
> (Interview with Abdel-Malek al-Huthi by
> Ghobari and El-Dahan 2016)

While working on a research project in Yemen about eight years ago, I interviewed American army officers about their "civilian" activities in the country—most of which seemed to involve youth media and theater. I was somewhat taken aback by the incongruity of the military entering the entertainment business, but the youthful soldiers assured me that they were not unacquainted with the academic literature that was relevant to their work. "We operate on a 'clash of civilizations' model," they said. I am still not certain what type of global conflict is ameliorated by youth radio and children's theater, but they were quite earnest in their belief in what they were doing. They were part of Special Operations in Yemen, soldiers that the *New York Times* described as "war's elite tough guys" (Shanker and Oppel 2014), specifically a group once called PSYOPS. In recognition of the fact that this term was getting a somewhat tainted reputation, the United States Army relabeled these activities. By the time I started to interview them, PSYOPS In Yemen had become Military Information Support Operations (MISO). The individuals I was interviewing were its "Civil-Military Support Element" (CMSE).

In addition to instilling in them the rather diverting habit of calling any female over the age of 25 "ma'am," the training that my informants had received clearly focused upon the very perspectives that Edward Said so cogently criticized in Orientalism (Said 1978)—in particular, those of Bernard Lewis, erstwhile supporter of the American misadventure in Iraq. The rigid historicism of Lewis and his like-minded colleagues have had little appeal in the social sciences where Said's multidisciplinary explorations have been more influential. Anthropological archaeologists have, similarly, embraced many of Said's ideas as the, by now, conventional discussions in the field on nationalist uses of the past, world heritage politics and the significance of cultural property, offer testament. It impressed me then, and continues to do so, that postcolonial views, which may constitute an academic turning point in the scholar's understanding of the East, have failed to penetrate in the slightest degree the thinking of the American foreign policy and defense establishment. Their strategic approach, which consisted of generously funding a whole host of education and culture projects while simultaneously engaging in drone strikes, was based upon the collected works of Samuel Huntington (2002) and other purveyors (Lewis 1990) of the history of conflict and deterioration that they believe characterizes Islamic civilization.

This has provided the framework within which American policy makers can express deep appreciation for the heritage (read "past") of the Middle East, while justifying military incursions in the present. This was in 2009 and, since that time, I have had cause to think about the remarks of those sincere young men. Perhaps my response should have been—"really, and how is that working for you?" as it was clear even at that time that Yemen was on the brink of chaos that no puppet show could possibly stem. To be fair, the United States has finally recognized the futility of its programs in Yemen and has changed its strategy. They eliminated the education and culture projects. Drone attacks continue.

Today, there seems to be little left in Yemen that has not been destroyed in what seems to be a free-for-all struggle enmeshing the United States, Iran and, most of all, Saudi Arabia (Gause 1990). When I was in Yemen, I noted that Yemeni attitudes toward the Saudis could best be described as wary. The authors of one tome on the subject, a decade before the current mass devastation wrought by Yemen's giant predatory neighbor to the north, blatantly declared that "[t]he history of Saudi Arabian-Yemeni relations for many is a chronicle of antagonism, conflicts and border disputes" (Al-Rasheed and Vitalis 2004: 2).

Even for someone who has spent as much time as I have in the Middle East, Yemen was quite a revelation. I was used to the Ottoman architecture of Jerusalem, Jordan and southeastern Turkey, but the buildings of Sana'a, made of stucco rather than stone, were of a markedly different, and far more intricate, style. The tenth-century Persian explorer and geographer, Ibn Rustah, wrote about the symmetrical beautifully adorned brick and stone houses of Sana'a (Lamprakos 2016). Taller than the traditional buildings of the Levant, they looked to my untrained eye to be Moorish in style—reminiscent of the architecture of Al-Andalus. An addition to its fascinating historic architecture was the distinctive nature of Yemeni dress.

The women I encountered in the street were either completely black clad or veiled by a very colorful sitara, a long loose covering. Every man appearing on the streets of the Old City seemed to be wearing a thoob (white robe), dark Western style jacket and, most intriguingly, an out-sized, highly decorated, dagger (jambiyya) stuck in his belt. They have a formidable appearance but the men of northern Yemen (and the women as well) are known for their friendliness to strangers. I encountered few who spoke English, and no one there understood my very inadequate Palestinian Arabic but people were invariably obliging anyway. When I was lost and unable to give a taxi driver proper directions, he visited a number of stores to find a person who spoke English and then refused to allow me to pay him for the cab ride because it had been so much trouble (for me).

My colleagues and I visited a shop selling antique jewelry in the middle of the souq where the owner brought out an assemblage of granulated and filigreed silver pieces, most of which, he assured me, had been "made by Jews." I knew something about the Jewish community in Yemen and the fact that they were the preeminent silversmiths in the country. Yemen has, without a doubt, had a Jewish population for at least 1,700 years. Many people point to the Himyarite Kingdom of the fourth to sixth centuries as the first historical manifestation of Jews in Yemen but the Yemenite Jews claim that their community is much older. In fact, the Jews of Sana'a have a tradition that they arrived in the region before the destruction of Solomon's Temple.

Yemen's Jews over the centuries became involved in a number of different trades that their Muslim neighbors shunned. Silversmiths, blacksmiths, potters, masons, carpenters, shoemakers and tailors, Jews were the craft economic backbone of the country. Over the centuries, the relationship between Jews and Muslims became a fixed economic and social division of labor. While farming and herding were considered Muslim occupations, Jews supplied finished tools and vital services.

It was not a history that was free from persecution, although Yemenite Jews did receive a security of sorts in return for their labor and expertise from the Yemeni Imamate. For example, when Saudi Arabia took over the ancient city of Najran in 1934, its 600 Jews were given one day to leave and most of them fled for their lives to the Yemeni city of Sa'ada. The Saudi king later demanded that they be returned, to what fate it is not clear, but the Imam refused because he had declared that the refugees were "Yemenite Jews" and, therefore, under his protection (Ahroni 2001).

The task set for me and for my colleagues in Yemen was an attempt to understand the history and culture of the country within a few weeks (although one of our group was more knowledgeable on Yemen than the rest of us). We concentrated on the north of the country because Sa'ada was then in open revolt against the central government and had been for years. Few of us really knew much about the nature of the conflict outside of the rather general view that it was primarily tribal and, secondarily, religious. The term "Huthi" was mentioned several times but we had little opportunity to investigate the causes of Huthi rebellion. At the same time as we were planning the "stabilization" of the North, mostly by throwing money at it on behalf of the international aid community, the central Yemeni government was moving tanks and fighter aircraft into Sa'ada to launch an offensive against the Huthis. The name that the Yemeni Military chose for these activities, "Operation Scorched Earth," says it all (Day 2012).

Hundreds of thousands were removed from or fled their homes and hundreds were killed, most of them non-combatants. The Saudis joined in the carnage because the Huthis have had a particularly troubled history with Saudi Arabia, dating from the participation of Saudis in the national unification process of the 1990s that ended the 1,000-year rule of the religious group the Huthis belong to—the Zaydis (Terrill 2011). Saudi Arabia, claiming a violation of their borders, was eager to participate. They had not invaded Yemen for almost 20 years, showing rather unusual restraint, but they have been bombarding it off and on for years, whenever they were able to claim that their borders have been breached.

Today, Saudi Arabia is again attacking Yemen, with able assistance from the United States. More than 10,000 people have been killed since the bombing campaign began two years ago and *The New York Times* has reported that the Trump administration has approved the resumption of sales of precision-guided munitions to Saudi Arabia (Shear and Baker 2017). Despite the absurd asymmetries of power in this conflict, a lot of censorious Middle East news analysis continues to be focused on the Huthis and their takeover of the Yemeni capital of Sana'a. Huthi combatants, sometimes referring to themselves as Ansar Allah (helpers or supporters of God), have not yet found their way onto the United Nations terrorist list despite the best efforts of Yemen's President in exile, Abd Rabbuh Mansour Hadi (*Al-Arabiya English* 2017), and they do not necessarily fit the typical extremist profile. They appear to have no hegemonic aspirations beyond self-rule and, according to several news reports, while the Huthis adopted the ubiquitous slogan "Death to America, Death to Israel, Curse the Jews," they have thus far been the only Middle East extremist group to apologize to the United States for it (Hadi Habtoor 2016). It is not to be expected that apologies to Israel will be forthcoming.

There is little doubt that Aansar Allah fits within the general theme of violent rebellion in the Middle East—but the Saudis have, permanently it seems, taken the prize for terrorism in Yemen. In the midst of all of these disruptions, Aansar Allah continues to issue such disturbingly violent tweets as "Mr. Abdulmalek Badr Al-Din Al-Huthi urges the exploitation of the next planting season. As long as the aggression continues our steadfastness continues" and "Fifth activation of the document of tribal honor signed by a large segment of the Yemeni people" (Ansar Allah Alyemen @AansarAllah March 25, 2017), while the international press accuses them of fighting a "proxy war" on behalf of Iran (Salmoni et al. 2010). The United States Department of State confirmed their belief that the link between the Huthis and Iran justified a military operation to pry them out of their entrenched position in the north of the country. This despite the fact that Huthi cultural and religious roots in the Arabian Peninsula go back much further than those of the House of Saud, relative newcomers in the Peninsula dating from the eighteenth century (Al-Rasheed 2010).

The Huthis are adherents of a religious group known as Zaydis who ruled the highlands of Yemen off and on from around 890 CE to 1962 (CE), when a military coup deposed the last Imam and established the Yemen Arab Republic (Bidwell 1983). The Zaydis were, according to tradition, founded by the eponymous Zayd ibn 'Ali (d. 740 CE), a fourth-generation descendant of the Prophet (Kennedy 2016). The background of Huthis in Yemen goes deeper than the ninth century CE, however (Adra 1985). Although the Huthis disavow having a specific (Brandt 2014) identity, the group looks to the tribes of the northern Bakil federation for support. The Bakil and the other largest tribal federation, the Hashids, can trace their lineages back thousands of years, beginning centuries before Islam. They have been either allies or enemies throughout their histories. Both of these tribes have acted as mediators between empires, states and kingdoms on the one hand and tribes people on the other. Both have been Zaydis since the ninth century but their interests do not always overlap in other respects (Carapico and Myntti 1981).

The Bakil Federation joined together with the Hashids during the Byzantine period and gave their allegiance to the Himyarite Kingdom that had overcome the Kingdom of Saba in the second century BCE. The ancient Himyarite kings of Yemen appear to have adopted monotheism around the second or third century CE. Like so many religious conversions in the ancient world, this rejection of polytheism may have been prompted by the increasing threats posed by three great imperial powers—the Aksumites in what is today Ethiopia to the south, the Byzantines in the west and the Sassanians in the east. Wedged between powerful exponents of the Christian faith and the zealots of Persian Zurvanism (a form of Zoroastrianism). Thus, it may have been a conversion of convenience. As they are today, the Arabs of Yemen had a keen interest in maintaining their independence—and so the Himyarites, as a nation, turned to Judaism.

It was a decision from the top and the motives of the Himyarite kings for embracing one of the world's oldest monotheist religions is subject to much debate. During this pre-Islamic period, Jews and polytheists were identified as the chief religious antagonists to Christians. In the space of less than a century, they had expelled Jews from Jerusalem, torn down or transformed Roman temples and taken over every bit of territory in the Middle East that was not claimed by the Sassanians (Loreto 2012). In the early years of Christian empires, the goal of the hegemons was conversion and, thereafter, submission. The Sassanians had begun to reverse their policy of religious tolerance in conquered territories and started to push Zurvanism on their populations, perhaps as a reaction to the Christian menace. The Sassanian Empire at its height was never able to maintain control over Arabia, but the Byzantines had been having some success there (Potts 2010). Despite this, one important economic prize remained un-grasped by any of these empires. The Himyarites stood between the Byzantines and the ancient fabled port of Aden. Aden was a city of great age and symbolic importance. Many Yemenis say that the history of the city goes back to the beginning of humanity and aver that the graves of Cain and Abel can be found there. In addition, it was a major trade conduit between India and the West and, thus, coveted by several ancient empires (Markovitz 2004).

In the face of the solid threat of these empires of the faithful, the indigenous religion of Arabia could not be described as a unified, or more importantly unifying, religion. Rather, it represented an "almost unlimited variety of beliefs and practices" (Aslan 2011: 6)—not precisely a creed to inspire national cohesion. Speculating on the Himyarite conversion, at least one scholar suggests that it was the proximity of the newly militant, highly organized Christian Aksumite Dynasty that might have inspired such a move. Not long after their adoption of Christianity, Aksumite rulers, which up to that point had been a "trading empire," began to seek an expansion of their territory (Bowersock 2013). Conversion to Christianity, no doubt, was seen by the fiercely independent Himyarites as a road to conquest either by the Byzantines or the Aksumites. Aksum had managed to maintain a large measure of self-rule in northern Ethiopia because of an early strategic alliance with the Byzantine Empire and the fact that its lands extended deep into southern Africa where even the long arm of the Byzantines could not practically reach. Himyar would be offered no such autonomy. Conversion to the Persian religion and incorporation into the Sassanian Empire was unthinkable given the new stringency of Sassanian governance. Like the Huthis, the Jewish Himyarites took a decidedly confrontational stance in the face of the great powers of their day.

Himyarite origins, as recovered from contemporary sources and archaeological evidence are, like those of many Arabian peoples, somewhat obscure. It appears that Arabia at the end of the second century was dominated by four states, Himyar (a relatively new polity), Saba, Hadhramaut and Qataban. Around the end of the second and beginning of the third centuries CE, Hadhramaut annexed Qataban and Saba attempted to subjugate Himyar by allying themselves with Aksum. The Aksumite Kingdom, then known as a mercantile realm was primarily interested in breaking Himyarite control over commerce in the Red Sea region. An inscription celebrating the Sabaean treaty with Aksum declares that, "they agreed together that their war and their peace should be in unison, against anyone that might rise up against them, and that in safety and in security there should be allied" (Munro-Hay 1991: 72). The intrusion of the Aksumites into South Arabian politics, however, created a prolongation of the conflicts between Saba and Himyar—a situation that did not completely resolve itself until the conquest of both kingdoms by the Sassanians in the sixth century (Hoyland 2001).

The first of the Jewish Himyarite kings, according to later Muslim historians of this period, was Abu Karab As'ad, who is reputed to have converted after a decisive encounter at Yathrib (Medina in Saudi Arabia). Abu Karab later became a hero to early Muslims and his story is enshrined in the work of Ibn Ishaq, revered biographer of Mohammed who is credited with compiling all of the traditions relating to Islam from its earliest days. Writing less than 100 years after the Prophet's death, Ibn Ishaq describes a conflict between the Himyarites and the people of Yathrib that resulted in the King's conversion. According to his account, Abu Karab had left his son in Yathrib and the people of the city treacherously killed him. Intent on exacting retribution, the king went to Yathrib to exterminate its residents and "cut down the palms" (Peters 1994: 49). On entering the city, he was approached by two members of the Banu Qurayza tribe, a group of Jews who had fled Syria and the Christian Ghassanid Kingdom. They were religious leaders of the tribe who had been sent to Abu Karab to ask him to spare the city because it was to be the future home of the great prophet. Apparently convinced, Abu Karab acceded to their request and summarily converted to Judaism. Subsequently, he took the "rabbis" with him to Mecca where, according to Ibn Ashaq, they authenticated the Ka'ba as the "Temple of their father Abraham." The newly devout Abu Karab, also according to this tradition, initiated the custom of covering of the Ka'ba with the Kiswa (Peters 1994: 50).

Upon Abu Karab's return to Yemen, he greeted his irate people who had heard of his rejection of their religious traditions and agreed that his rabbi companions would go through an ordeal by fire in order to convince his subjects to convert to Judaism as well. In a religious showdown reminiscent of the Biblical story of Elijah and the prophets of Baal, fire consumed the polytheist priests and their holy objects and spared the adherents of what became the Himyarites new religion. Ibn Ishaq's account is the most complete source for Muslim traditions about these events and it speaks of what was once a clear respect by early Muslims for the "other monotheism." Writing many years after the Islamic conquest of Arabia, Ibn Ishaq could afford to be gracious to the legendary first Jewish Himyarite king as the struggle to convert the people of Yemen was decades past. The historical record suggests that the people of Himyar, then living under the Sassanians, who eventually conquered them, fought aggressively against the proponents of yet another hegemonic religious power (Bosworth 1999).

Ibn Ishaq further tells us that Abu Karab died under mysterious circumstances leaving three very young sons and the throne was left open to be seized by an unbeliever. Dhu Shanatir was a ruler whom the historian condemns as an evil pedophile who attempted to ravish and kill the last of Abu Karab's line, one Dhu Nuwas, after having done likewise with his older brothers. The young man and legendary king fought together until Dhu Shanatir succumbed and the young Dhu Nuwas cut off his head and displayed it in the window of the palace. The kingdom thus resumed the religious practices of his forefather and Dhu Nuwas commenced his rule with all of the zeal of someone reborn. The Himyarite Kingdom returned to Judaism—with a vengeance (Zeev 2000).

At this point, we start to find highly diverging accounts of the Himyarites from Muslim and Christian sources. The mother of Dhu Nuwas may have been a Jew from Mesopotamia, according to one Syriac source. If that was in fact the case, she would have lived at least part of her life under Sassanian rule

(Power 2012). Some see this as a possible explanation for the king's violent persecution of Christians under his mandate as not only an expression of his confrontational Jewish faith, but also as a policy meant to curry favor with the Sassanians. The Christians of Arabia had often been aligned with the interests of the Byzantine Empire, which was the perpetual enemy of the Sassanids. The city of Najran, where the Himyarite ruler had erected an enormous synagogue, rebelled against him by burning it down. Dhu Nuwas sent an immense army to besiege the city—which lasted over six months and ended with the city sacked and burned and its inhabitants massacred. Oddly, these events took place in the month of Tishri, when the most important holidays of the Jewish year, Rosh Hashanah and Yom Kippur, occur. The death toll in this account is said to have reached about 2,000. Their churches were set on fire, including one where hundreds had taken sanctuary.

The unintended consequences of these horrific acts were that Najran later became a major pilgrimage center where Christian rulers built a new and even larger church rivaling the Kaba, and the religious leader of the Najran Christians was canonized as Saint Aretas. Najran later came to represent the beginning of the end of Dhu Nuwas, who died in battle not long after the Najran events. Himyar had already begun to divide along religious lines and the factional conflict that ensued made it easier for the Aksumites, who were already enraged by the massacre and persecution of their co-religionists, to conquer it. The army of Aksum crossed the Red Sea and marched against the Himyarite capital. According to most historians, the enemy killed Dhu Nuwas after taking his city, his family and his treasury. Legend has it, however, that to avoid being captured or suffering an ignominious death at the hands of the Christian infidels, Dhu Nuwas rode into the sea and was drowned (Newby 2000). The last Himyarite king, Ma'adikarib Ya'fur, was a Christian who won the throne, against several Jewish rivals, with the help of Aksum.

Eventually, a Christian Aksumite governor by the name Abraha became ruler of the Himyarites. While Islamic tradition admires the Jewish Himyarites, it decidedly disapproves of Abraha, who waged a scurrilous military campaign against the holy city of Mecca around 570 CE, the year in which Mohammed was born. Ibn Kathir, writing in the fourteenth century, states that Abraha was assailed with stones from the heavens descending like a black cloud and further declares that "[t]here never fell a stone on a soldier except it dissolved his flesh and burst it into pieces" (Ibn Kathir 1422, trans. Al Halawani 2001). It is also told that his elephants refused to take the men into the precincts of the city. Later Islamic historians came to call this time the "year of the elephant" in commemoration of these events coinciding with the birth of the Prophet. Abraha also marched through Bir Hima, now in Saudi Arabia, leaving on the stones a depiction of an elephant that led his army (Robin 2012). An inscription found elsewhere in Arabia, states that, while he failed to take Mecca, he conquered Yathrib (Medina). This event, for Muslim chroniclers, officially marks the end of the Jewish Himyarite kings in the place where it began—the desert oasis where Abu Karab was convinced by two rabbis not to destroy their city because a great prophet would arise there (Ibn Kathir 1422, trans. Al Halawani 2001: 144).

For many years, scholars have doubted that the Himyarites' religion was anything other than a localized form of monotheism appropriating language and features from Jews with whom they came into contact. A coherent record of their reign has been difficult to piece together because historical accounts of the Himyarites are strikingly divided along sectarian lines. They are vilified by Christian writers, admired by Muslim ones and, curiously, ignored by Jews. Rabbinic sources contemporary with the Himyarites make no mention of them and medieval Jewish scholars, even Maimonides, who were very aware of Yemenite Jewish history, overlook their contribution to it. Later Jewish writers either were uninterested in this history or failed to reach a consensus on it even after numerous Sabaean-Himyarite inscriptions were translated.

Notably, Judah Halevy, the German Biblical scholar, after many years of travelling in the Yemen desert in the company of Jewish guides, simply refused to believe that King Yusuf (Dhu Nuwas) was really Jewish, while his colleague, Arabist Eduard Glaser, who visited Arabia dressed as, and in the company of, Arabs, disagreed. Today, there is a rapt audience for the Himyarite narrative among Israeli scholars who, unlike Halevy, are not put off by their record of violence against their Christian subjects. Himyarites are also a popular subject on anti-Zionist blog posts where contributors condemn their violence or, alternatively, suggest that Yemen, not Palestine, is the true Jewish homeland.

The extent and length of their adherence to Judaism still remains in doubt, as Robin (2010) has observed and, also, the numbers of their subjects who converted. The Himyarites began as a tribal kingdom, a form of governance that implies that their leaders would have been given deference during their lifetimes but might not leave a lasting legacy. Only two very strong rulers have emerged from the historical record but their influence may have been enough to sustain the Jewish nature of the kingdom for some time. Tubba Abu Karab As'ad. known from archaeology, was a celebrated military leader but no definite references to Judaism have emerged from the translations of the texts from his reign. Archaeological investigations have more or less confirmed the Judaism of Dhu Nuwas based upon the translation of a famous inscription found at the Saudi Arabian site of Bir Hima praising his victories and imploring "God who owns the heavens and the earth" to "bless king Yusuf Asar Yathar, king of all nations."

Yusuf Asar Yathar was the official name of Dhu Nuwas. The latter was a sobriquet given to him because of his curly hair (sometimes characterized as sidelocks—see below). Another text related to this king gives the details of his spoils of the war against the people of Najran as amounting to 12,500 war trophies, 11,000 captives and 290,000 camels, cows and sheep—a recounting that bears a striking resemblance to the Biblical account of the Conquest of Ai in the book of Joshua. A more recent inscription has emerged from the Himyarite capital of Zafar—a text referring to a thitherto unknown king, Shurahbiil Yafur. It recounts the renovation of the old Hargab palace in the

Himyarite capital but contains no reference to religion. Very few Himyarite inscriptions, in fact, speak explicitly of Jewish religious beliefs but one example was found at Bayt al-Ashwal and dates from the first half of the fifth century. The text, describing one Yehudah Yakkaf, says in Hebrew that it was "written by Yehudah, the well-remembered, amen shalom, amen," and, in Sabaean, "by the power and grace of his lord, who created his soul, lord of life and death, lord of heaven and earth, who created all things, and with the financial help of his people Israel and the empowerment of his lord."

Since these inscriptions have surfaced, archaeologists have begun to explore sites with more confidence about their designation as Himyarite, including Qaryat al-Faw of the Kinda (al-Ansary 1981) and Najran (Zarins 1983), but Zafar, with its substantial ruins that are attributable mostly to the Himyarites (270–523), has yielded the most information (Yule 2008). Excavations have shed considerable light on the nature of the capital and the material culture of the Himyar. In addition, several other possible indicators of Jewish culture have been discovered there. The excavator of Zafar has written about a ring found a few years before his project began that depicts a Torah shrine. The name Yishaq bar Hanina is engraved on it—the first name shown in Hebrew. Another striking find at Zafar was a stepped chamber that bears some resemblance to ritual baths uncovered at Jewish sites. Locals believed the chamber to be the remains of a church but there was no evidence that one ever stood in that location. Finally, a more enigmatic piece of evidence is a unique depiction of a male face, thought by some to be that of Dhu Nuwas, showing distinct sidelocks, which have been posited by some (Goitein 1951) to have originated in Yemen rather than eastern Europe.

The Sassanian Empire annexed parts of Yemen in the late sixth century CE but left most of the region to enjoy autonomy with the exception of the two major cities of Sana'a and Aden. This event effectively severed the ties between Yemen and Ethiopia and may have changed the course of Christianity in Arabia (Bowersock 2013). Thereafter, Yemen became one of the first regions to be converted to Islam and, for the most part, joined the early Muslim community without much conflict. Although Himyar did not leave much of a trace insofar as their Jewish traditions, its real impact was on the development of Islamic culture in Yemen. The conflagrations that began with the Najran Massacre profoundly changed the politics of the Arabian Peninsula, eventually shifting the Himyarites into the Persian sphere of influence and placing polytheists at a decided disadvantage, especially in the oasis cities of Nejd and Hijaz, where Islam was quickly established.

Robin goes even further than Bowersock in arguing for a connection between Himyar and Islam, claiming that Mohammed faced the same challenge as the kings of Himyar—how to unify a fractious, polytheistic, tribal society and, presumably knowing Himyarite history, ripped a page from their book (Robin 2012). In addition, Abu Karab, and his descendant Dhu Nuwas, were accorded the status of being acknowledged precursors of Islamic monotheism. Certainly, Yemeni Islamic culture has also co-opted this history as well as popular legends, especially the well-known epic *The Adventures of Sayf Ben Dhi Yazan*, a Himyarite King credited with dethroning Abraha with the assistance of the Persian Empire. Presumably, Dhi Yazan was neither Christian nor Zurvan, which would clearly suggest that he was Jewish but no contemporary historical or archaeological records relating to him have been found. Both of these kings also figure in Yemeni traditions about the end of days (Jayyusi 1999). Dhi Yazan's descendants are believed to be the group from which the Aden-Abyan army of the apocalypse is prophesied to come (Al-Umqi 2010). Dhu Nuwas is considered to be one of the Himyarite kings who, according to popular legend, will return.

Despite its importance in later Muslim culture, Himyar was, according to Arabic sources, reluctant to embrace the new religion and did not do so until after the Prophet's death. The powerful tribal kingdom did not join in the wars against apostasy or support the Muslims against the Sassanians (Power 2012). The Umayyad Dynasty took over Sana'a and Najran in 660 CE and appointed governors in Yemen but the Umayyads never controlled the entirety of Yemen. Still, there were few outright rebellions against the caliphate during this time. After the Abbasids overthrew the Umayyad caliphs, they continued the Umayyad regime of decentralized, if watchful, governance. In the course of the ninth century the power of the Abbasids over various fringe areas waned. Local Yemeni dynasties emerged, which, at times, both challenged and allied with the major power.

Principal among the historical challengers to the control of the caliphates in Yemen were the followers of al-Hadi ila'l-Haqq Yahya (d. 911 CE), called Zaydis after the great grandson of the Prophet, Zayd Ibn Ali (d. 740 CE). Yahya's ambition on entering Yemen from Hijaz was to try to build a power base for the Zaydiyyah Movement and reform what he considered to be heterodox Islamic practices. Zaydiyyah spread among the highland tribes (Swagman 1988) but, while Zaydi rule in Yemen is usually seen as extending for almost a millennium, there were many episodes in which their authority was challenged. The Ismaili Sulayhid dynasty ruled Yemen for more than 100 years in the eleventh and twelfth centuries, earning the undying enmity of the Zaydis. Europeans and Ottomans vied for control of the Red Sea trade. For a short period of time, the port of Aden came under British control (Gingrich 2014).

The Ottoman Empire claimed all of Yemen in 1539 but they were pushed out less than a century later by Al-Mansur al-Qasim (d. 1620), the first Imam of the Qasimi Dynasty. Mansur sought to restore Yemen as a Muslim nation free of the contamination of Sufism, which had become especially popular in the Middle East, beginning in the ninth century CE and was gaining followers in Yemen. Initially, the Ottomans recognized in the Yemeni Sufis potential allies whose universalist outlook could fit in well with the Turkish Muslim empire. Zaydis and Sufis had a generally antagonistic relationship, even though some notable Yemeni Imams had tolerated their presence (Haykel 2002). Beginning with Mansur, the Imamate began attacking Sufis and Sufism ostensibly because they supported the Ottomans in Yemen, although, given the Sufi inclination for avoiding politics, such "support" probably amounted to nothing more than passive acceptance (Daftary 2013).

Mansur's descendant, al-Mutawakkil, faced a more overt challenge when Sulayman Jamal, the leader of Yemen's Jewish community, proclaimed himself as a messiah in 1670 CE. He made this declaration in front of the Governor's Palace in Sana'a where, clothed all in white—the color associated with martyrdom in Yemeni Islamic religion—he prophesied that Jews would displace Muslims as rulers. Taking upon himself the attributes of a Mahdi seeking to restore a "purer" form of Islam, he acted with great force against Jamal and his Jewish followers. Jews were declared to be no longer dhimmis under the covenant of protection and were thereafter subjected to persecution. Al-Mudawakkil actually eased up on some of these strictures during his lifetime but inexplicably on his deathbed ordered the expulsion of the Jews from Yemen just as his grandfather had expelled the Ottomans (Klorman 1993). The Qasimis were the last of the Zaydi dynasties to control Yemen and their rule was uninterrupted (Serjeant 1992).

In the eighteenth and nineteenth centuries, the Imamate's power declined as European interest in Yemen increased. As the state bureaucracy grew, the imams became more and more detached from their people and their tribal connections (Alaini 2004) and adopted the style of Middle East monarchies, becoming increasingly distant figures. The country was thus left open to another Ottoman invasion in 1848, which failed to re-establish Turkish rule. The Ottomans were driven out yet again by a leader called Al-Mutawakkil, a side branch of the Qasimis and the Mutawakkilite Kingdom of Yemen was declared. Two powerful imams, al-Mutawakkil Yahya Muhammad Hamid ad-Din and his son Ahmad bin Yahya, ruled Yemen as a small kingdom for the next 44 years. Imam Yahya was assassinated but after a brief period of instability, he was succeeded by his son, Ahmad bin Yahya, who was succeeded, in turn, by his son Muhammad al-Badr, whose very brief reign ended with the establishment of the Yemen Arab Republic.

A history of messianism in Yemen, both Jewish and Muslim, has interested a number of scholars—in fact, the last Jewish messianic movements since the beginning of the nineteenth century occurred in Yemen and attracted Muslims as well as Jews (Klorman 1990). Hathaway has suggested that Yemeni messianism has converged around the history and region of the Himyarites, whose history primarily came to represent for prototypes of Yemen's first "convert or die" kingdom. This proved to have more appeal to the majority Muslim population than to the Jewish one whose power was much more limited (Hathaway 2003). Even the aforementioned Sulayman Jamal did not overtly reference the rule of the Himyarites when he announced an imminent Jewish takeover of Yemen and his appeal may have been intended to persuade more Muslims to his cause than Jews who were by then a minority. By Sulayman's time, conversion in doctrinaire Judaism was discouraged. In any event, Jewish messianic expectations in Yemen ended with the mass migration of Yemeni Jews to Israel beginning in 1949, and today, most of them fail to claim this storied history as their own asserting, instead, that they are an old community that pre-dates the Himyarite Kingdom (which is probably true).

They further dispel any notion that they are descended from converts, although, given their concentration in the former Himyarite regions of Yemen, many of them undoubtedly are. In Muslim messianic movements, in contrast, the Himyarite past, entrenched as it is in the highlands of Yemen, has figured in a number of different ways. Both Dhu Nuwas and Dhi Yazan have come down in Yemeni Islamic tradition as "forerunners," which is clearly a messianic role. One Muslim pretender to Mahdism arose at the end of the Sulayhid period (twelfth century CE) and ironically adopted the title of "al-Himyari" in order to pose as a Himyarite descendant, even while forcing mass conversions of Jews to Islam.

Although Yemen has seen its share of messianic movements in which Himyar history was meaningful, today, it arises in quite unexpected religious contexts (Haykel 1995). A contributor to the Wikileaks documents informs us, or more correctly, the United States Department of State, that Anwar al-Awlaki, the American-born Yemeni cleric who was assassinated by the United States, was a member of the powerful Alaliq tribe, who consider themselves as the sole heirs of Dhi Yazan. He continues to explain to his audience that the stronghold of the Himyarite kingdom, Kawr al Awaliq, is one of the most rugged regions in the country and it is from here that the Yemeni army of the apocalypse is prophesied to originate. While al-Awlaki's Al Qaeda connections have never been proven to the satisfaction of Yemenis, it seems clear that the organization's affiliate in Yemen is interested in using this region and its history to establish its local authority (Al Umqi 2010).

The Zaydi revival movement begun by Hussein Al Huthi has not made use of this history and the reason for this seems more socioeconomic than theological (Barron 2008). While Klorman (1990) suggests that the political Zaydism that culminated in the Imamate in the ninth century CE might very well have been influenced by messianic eschatology prompted by Jewish messianism, Zaydi revivalism of the twentieth and twenty-first centuries is primarily a reaction to local ideological challenges (Adams 1986). The so-called democratic "youth bulge" in Yemen and other developing Arab countries has destabilized the region and challenged traditional social hierarchies of the old division between sayyids, traditional Yemeni elites descended from the Prophet, and young Yemenis, more educated than their forebears, who see no reason to continue this religious distinction. Taking advantage of this situation, the Huthi revival began with a youth movement (Vom Bruck 1999a and 1999b).

Claiming that the Zaydism of the twentieth and twenty-first centuries had become corrupted, Huthis have, as a basic premise, the view that one is obligated to rise up against an unjust ruler—what they deemed the President of the Yemen Republic, Ali Abdullah Saleh al-Sanhani al-Humairi, to be—that is, until the Saudis began to meddle. Saleh and the Huthis discovered some mutual interests and formed an alliance against their giant aggressive neighbor. Since then, it has proved to be a marriage of inconvenience and parted with the assassination of Saleh in 2017. In some ways, it is the old story of the Bakil against the Hashid, which was Saleh's tribe—sometimes allies, more often, foes (Dresch 1989 and 1991). Nevertheless, for all that the movement is named after its leaders, the Huthis actually have a dispersed structure that helps them to generate the support of many diverse elements in Yemen, including the powerful Hamdan tribe, making their coalition one of the first to unite leaders from all three traditional tribal federations.

A chief target of Huthi indignation has been Saudi Salafism (Haykel 2002), which they perceive as a threat to Yemen and its tribal culture. They are perhaps less intent upon their hatred of the United States than their purloined battle cry indicates but, nonetheless, they see our activities in Yemen (perhaps rightly) as insidiously supporting Saudi interests (Clark 2010). If the United States knew the Middle East better, they might adopt the reasoning that the enemy of their enemy (Al Qaeda) should be their friend, but it is the fear of Iran that casts a dangerous shadow over the Huthi rebellion as far as Western nations are concerned. As I write, it has become clear that the Huthis, who have been battling the government on one front or another for well over two decades (1989), may now represent the most stable political movement in the country. Were it not for the fact that non-Yemeni governments are colluding to unseat them, with the likely result of plunging the country into internal chaos, they may just develop the ability to form a government (an outcome that they have never aspired to) (Blumi 2010).

There is no certain way of estimating the extent of the influence of Iran amidst all of the unfounded indictments emanating from the political establishment of the United States and the government of Yemen recognized by the West (Zaidi 2016). These accusations betray a profound ignorance of the differences between Huthi Zaydism and Iranian Shi'ism. The Huthi Zaydis do not self-identify as a Shi'a sect. The religion that the Huthis are attempting to revive is very different from the Iranian version of Shi'ism (Twelver Shi'ism), both in doctrine and practice. Zaydis do not believe in a last Imam who lives in occultation and will reappear as Mahdi at the end of days. Also, they encourage a personal relationship with God that precludes the kind of passion plays, celebrations and pilgrimages to shrines that are typical of Iranian religion. Religious Huthis also reject mysticism and esoteric knowledge and aver that learning is theoretically open to all. In addition, the obligation to spread Islam throughout the world, very significant in Iranian religion, does not figure in the Huthi's Zaydi theology.

They have displayed no interest in proselytizing nor do they ascribe to the theory of an Islamic State such as that which is espoused in Iran. Even though they had a political imamate, Huthis have never proposed a post-war political order based on Zaydism. Although the Zaydi political imamates have some meaning in informing their notions of the injustices visited upon them by the Sunni majority, they have expressed no desire to re-establish it. The Huthis have moved away from the imam as proper ruler of Yemen and are not subordinate to a clerical hierarchy or its jurists. If the Huthis are intent on remaining true to their religious identity, and there is every indication that they are, their loyalty to the Islamic Republic of Iran could hardly run very deep (Salmoni et al. 2010). Although Huthis abjure making pilgrimages to Muslim shrines, they do ascribe a religious significance to their historical territory of Sa'ada, a once beautiful medieval city that has been all but destroyed by the Saudi onslaught (Heiss 2014).

It is telling, according to the Huthis' narrative, that it was through those mountains that the Saudis entered and began to lay waste to their native land. While the Saudis still seem to deny that they have ever crossed over into Yemeni territory on the ground, the Huthis charge them with setting up a base on Jabal Dukhan in Saudi Arabia, very close to the border with Yemen on the west side. Huthi units in retaliation entered into Saudi territory and engaged in a skirmish that took the lives of two Saudi border guards. As a result, Saudis considered this as provocation enough to enter the fray in Yemen, ostensibly to fight on the side of Yemen's "legitimate" President Abdrabbuh Mansour Hadi. As the sole candidate running, Hadi was "elected" in 2012. He subsequently resigned in 2015, retreating to Aden, and then rescinded his resignation a few months later while he was mysteriously making his way to Riyadh, Saudi Arabia.

Religion for the Huthis is bound up with the highland regions of the mountainous north. Polytheist, Christian, Jewish and Muslim have called this region home. North Yemenis never seem to have been nomadic or even semi-nomadic but have been characterized from ancient times as farmers. An old proverb from the Yemeni highlands asserts that "the pride of a qabila [tribes-person] is in his land." While Yemenis consider the lands north of Sana'a to be the home of the Hashid and Bakil Confederations, Sa'ada has a unique mix of different tribal groups (Salmoni, Loidolt and Wells 2010). Huthi Zaydism is a strategically designed theology meant to adjust to the demands of the modern world in which the heroes of the past such as Dhi Yazan have no place. Nevertheless, Saudi sponsored news sites invoke this hero's name as a warning to Yemenis not to become too closely allied with Persians (although it was because of the Persians that the Yemenis were able to throw off the yoke of the Christian Ethiopians). As the story in Saudi Arabia goes, Dhi Yazan was successful in ridding Yemen of the hated Aksumite Christians but was later executed by his Sassanid allies. In the Yemeni story, he is assassinated by Ethiopian servants after being installed as king by the Sassanians.

The Huthi websites *Al-Menpar* and *Sada Online*, along with YouTube, are the main media sources for the Huthi narrative. In addition, the Yemeni Zaydi-connected website *New Omma* is cautiously supportive of the Huthi cause. The reports and images on these sites consist of different kinds of information, ranging from biographical details on the Huthi family, pro-Huthi editorials, speeches by Husayn al-Huthi and Abd al-Malik al-Huthi and videos demonstrating the group's military strength and determination. The ideology reflected on the internet is one of solidarity and victimization. Much of the material on the Huthis in Arabic speaks of Islamic revivalism in general and the conflict as a fight between good and evil specifically (Caton, 2005). These platforms also feature a number of locally composed poems, traditionally called *qasa'id* (Taminian 1999; Rodionov 1996), containing laudatory praises for the martyred Husayn al-Huthi and other fallen Huthi heroes. The lectures and speeches delivered by Husayn al-Huthi decry the lack of religious consciousness among Zaydis, while others deride American foreign policy and the United States support of the Yemeni president in exile and the Saudis. Yemen *qasa* is a long-held means of delivering cultural propaganda in northern Yemen and has proven quite effective in the past (Dresch 1981 and 1984).

Gaining a unitary narrative from these sources is difficult, especially given the barriers to obtaining information about daily events in Yemen. The aspect of solid unyielding resistance to empire is inherent in most Huthi sponsored reports. Northern Yemen managed to resist the Ottomans and the British Empire and has remained remarkably autonomous throughout its long history. Saudi Arabia has represented a kind of covert imperialism over the years, seeking to control political events in Yemen without engaging in full-scale intervention, until today. Very little written material in English has appeared on the conflict that tells the story from the Huthi perspective but one notable recent exception are the reports of Shakdam, whose recent book, *A Tale of Grand Resistance* (2016), is a compendium of her reports on the conflict in Yemen, most of which read like the Huthi sponsored websites.

In rather poetic fashion, reminiscent of *The Adventures of Sayf Ben Dhi Yazan,* her reports on the victories of "the sons of Hamdan who are defiantly reclaiming their history, their land, their nation" warn that

> [t]he real war for Yemen will be ultimately fought in its Highlands, a land which no conqueror could ever tame to its will. And though many tried: from the Romans to the Ottomans, the sons of Hamdan never could be made to submit. This time again, Yemen northern tribes could prove too much of a challenge, even before the combined might of Riyadh's wealth and America's military power. Yemen, history remembers, does not look kindly on invaders!
>
> (Shakdam 2016)

There is no way of discerning for sure whether Dhi Yazan's "suspicious Judaism" would preclude any references to him by the Huthis, who are known to be fairly intolerant of other religions. The movement, in fact, originally seems to have been obsessed by putative crimes against Islam committed by Jews all over the world as evidenced in the speeches of Hussein al-Huthi. The organization has evolved, though, in many ways since the death of its founder. The recent speeches of Abdel Malik al-Huthi in comparison to those of his deceased brother are telling in terms of what seems to be the growing politicization of Huthi ideology. Abdel Malik's speeches convey the idea that the Huthis now represent not a movement but a government under siege. Several values emphasized by his brother still remain in his rhetoric, such as faith, adherence to tribe and identity, honor and shame and, most of all, strength.

In other cases, the frequency of terms used shows a number of differences. Variations of the terms "occupy" and "resistance" appear throughout his speeches, while they are absent in those of his deceased brother. Saudi Arabia, the United States and Israel are the obsession of Abdel Malik, often mentioned together ("US is the head of the aggression, Israel is its heart and KSA-UAE with their mercenaries are its hands") while references to Jews do not appear at all (except in the aforementioned slogan). As Sa'ada was one of the main Jewish places of residence in Yemen, the Huthi family would be unlikely not to have come into contact with them at some time or other but today they are no longer a feature in the Yemeni political landscape. After Hussein Al Huthi's death in 2004, the already small number of Jews that remained in Yemen was reduced by over 90 percent.

Any Himyarite effect on relations between Jews and Muslims in Yemen during the beginning of Islamic tradition has long dissipated and left behind only legends of "proto-Muslim heroes" and apocalyptic myths. The Jewish Himyarite kingdom lasted for just over a century—but it was some 1,500 years ago when it ended. There are a very few traces of Himyarite effects upon the Jews of Sa'ada recorded, but traces of the romantically emplotted past of the Himyarites remained into the nineteenth century. A diplomatic visitor to Yemen in 1874 described groups of "warrior Jews" living in the vicinity of Sa'ada (Parfitt 1996). The Huthis are in many ways a product of this past, although they would scarcely acknowledge it. Members of the movement were doubtless exposed to the "Muslim" hero Dhi Yazan and perhaps even Dhu Nuwas. They are also the products of centuries of messianic movements, both Muslim and Jewish, emanating from northern Yemen that were forged in the fire of the religio-tribal contests of the pre-Islamic period. In terms of the main connection between the historical tribe and the modern, it does not matter what religion Dhi Yazan really espoused or, indeed, whether he even existed. He was a folk hero, revered by both Sunnis and Zaydis in Yemen as the man who defeated the Westernized Christian kingdoms of the Middle East and North Africa with the help of Persians (Vom Bruck 1999b).

Out of resistance to the incursions of Western Christians and Persian Zurvans, the Himyarites formed a militant religious state that was as dedicated to attacking Christians as it was to the observance of Jewish law. The records of their reigns have been preserved in Greek and Syriac accounts that condemn Dhu Nuwas as a monster and in Arabic sources that portray Dhu Nuwas as an almost messianic figure. In fact, Imru' al-Qais, a sixth-century poet and one of the last of the Kindite kings, provided the basis for later comparisons of Dhu Nuwas with the Quranic Dhul-Qarnayn (commemorated in the poem which appears at the beginning of this chapter), who was given the power to raise a wall between mankind and the denizens of chaos, Gog and Magog, entities that, in Jewish tradition, were to be defeated by the Messiah at the end of days (Van Donzel and Schmidt 2014).

Sixth-century poet Imru' al-Qais is still esteemed today as one of the finest poets in the Arabic language. His long poem, "Let us stop and weep," is prized as one of the best examples of pre-Islamic Arabian verse. As a friend and ally, he was deeply affected by the demise of Dhu Nuwas. In his honor, he penned the following lines:

Art thou not saddened how fate has become an ugly beast,
The betrayer of its generation, he that swalloweth up people?
It has removed Dhū Nuwās from the fortresses
Who once ruled in the strongholds and over men
An armored knight, who hurriedly broke the ends of the earth
And led his hordes of horse unto her uttermost parts
And has shut up a dam in the place of the sunrise
For Gog and Magog that are (as tall as) mountains!

(Imrū al-Qais 1998)

Bibliography

Adams, M. 1986. One Yemen or Two? in *Arabia and the Gulf: From Traditional Society to Modern States: Essays in Honour of M.A. Shaban's 60th Birthday* (I.R. Nettod, ed.), pp. 120–131. London: Croom Helm Ltd.

Adra, N. 1985. The Tribal Concept in the Central Highlands of the Yemen Arab Republic in *Arab Society: Social Science Perspectives* (N.S. Hopkins, ed.), pp. 275–285. Cairo: The American University in Cairo Press.

Ahroni, R. 2001. *Jewish Emigration from the Yemen 1951–98: Carpet Without Magic*. London: Routledge.

Al-Ansari, A. 1981. *Qaryat al-Faw: A Portrait of Pre-Islamic Civilisation in Saudi Arabia*. Riyadh: University of Riyadh.

Al-Arabiya English. 2017. Yemen Requests UN to Designate Huthis as "Terrorists." *Al-Arabiya English*, February 19, 2017. Retrieved from: http://english.alarabiya.net/en/News/gulf/2017/02/19/Yemen-requests-UN-to-designate-Huthis-as-terrorists-.html.

Al-Rasheed, M. 2010. *A History of Saudi Arabia*. Cambridge: Cambridge University Press.

Al-Rasheed, M. and R. Vitalis. 2004. Introduction in *Counter-Narratives History, Contemporary Society, and Politics in Saudi Arabia and Yemen* (M. Al-Rasheed and R. Vitalis, eds.), pp. 1–10. New York: Palgrave Macmillan: 1-10.

Al-Umqi, U. 2010. Al-Masdar Online Looks into Al-Qa'ida's New Strategy in Southern Yemen; Taking Control Over Kawr Al-Awaliq Operating Under the Popular Army. Wikileaks GMP20101006155001.

Alaini, M. 2004. *Fifty Years in Shifting Sands: Personal Experience in the Building of a Modern State in Yemen*. Trans. by H. al-Haifi. Beirut: Dar An-Nahar.

Ansar Allah Alyemen @AansarAllah, March 25, 2017.

Aslan, R. 2011. *No god but God (Updated Edition): The Origins, Evolution, and Future of Islam*. New York: Random House.

Barron, O. 2008. Things Fall Apart: Violence and Poverty in Yemen. *Harvard International Review* 30: 12–13.

Beeston, A. 1985. Two Bi'r Ḥimā Inscriptions Re-Examined. *Bulletin of the School of Oriental and African Studies, University of London*, 48/1: 42–52.

Bidwell, R. 1983. *The Two Yemens*. Boulder, CO: Westview Press.

Blumi, I. 2010. *Chaos in Yemen: Societal Collapse and the New Authoritarianism*. London: Routledge.

Bosworth, C. 1999. *The History of Al-Tabari: The Sasanids, the Lakhmids, and Yemen.* Albany, NY: State University of New York Press.

Bowersock, G. 2013. *The Throne of Adulis: Red Sea Wars on the Eve of Islam.* Oxford: Oxford University Press.

Brandt, M. 2014. Inhabiting Tribal Structures: Leadership Hierarchies in Tribal Upper Yemen in *Southwest Arabia across History: Essays to the Memory of Walter Dostal* (A. Gingrich and S. Haas, eds.), pp. 91–116. Vienna: Austrian Academy of Sciences Press.

Carapico, S. and C. Myntti, 1981. A Tale of Two Families: Change in North Yemen 1977–1989. *Middle East Report* 170/21: 24–29.

Caton, S. 2005. *Yemen Chronicle: An Anthropology of War and Mediation.* New York: Hill and Wang.

Clark, V. 2010. *Yemen: Dancing on the Heads of Snakes.* New Haven, CT: Yale University Press.

Daftary, F. 2013. *Geographies of Peace: New Approaches to Boundaries, Diplomacy and Conflict Resolution.* New York: I.B. Tauris.

Day, S. 2012. *Regionalism and Rebellion in Yemen: A Troubled National Union.* Cambridge: Cambridge University Press.

Dresch, P. 1981. *The Northern Tribes of Yemen: Their Origins and Their Place in the Yemen Arab Republic.* Dissertation. Oxford: Oxford University.

Dresch, P. 1984. The Position of Shaykhs Among the Northern Tribes of Yemen, Man. *New Series* 19/1: 31–49.

Dresch, P. 1989. *Tribes, Government and History in Yemen.* New York: Oxford University Press.

Dresch, P. 1991. The Tribes of Hashid-wa-Bakil as Historical and Geographical Entities in *Arabicus Felix, Luminosus Britannicus: Essays in Honour of A. F. L. Beeston on His Eightieth Birthday* (A. Jones, ed.), pp. 8–24. Ithaca, NY: Ithaca Press.

Gause, F. 1990. *Saudi-Yemeni Relations: Domestic Structure and Foreign Influence.* New York: Columbia University Press, 1990.

Ghobari, M. and M. El-Dahan. 2016. Yemen's Huthi Leader Says U.S. Provides Political Cover for Saudi Strikes. *World News*, September 2, 2016. Retrieved from: www.reuters.com/article/us-yemen-security-idUSKCN11818G.

Gingrich, A. 2014. Galactic Polities: Anthropological Insights for Understanding Yemen's Pre-Ottoman Past in *Southwest Arabia across History: Essays to the Memory of Walter Dostal* (A. Gingrich and S. Haas, eds.), pp. 117–124. Vienna: Austrian Academy of Sciences Press.

Goitein, S. D. 1951. Al-Peot v'al Simanim. *Haaretz*, 18 January 1951 [in Hebrew]. (Republished in Yosef Tobi, The Sidelocks of the Jews of Yemen. *Arabia* 3 2005/6.)

Hadi Habtoor, A. 2016. Houthis Apologize for "Death to America" Slogans. *Asjarq al-Awsat* (English Edition), June 29, 2016. Retrieved from: http://english.aawsat.com/abdul-hadi-habtoor/news-middle-east/houthis-apologize-death-america-slogans.

Hathaway, J. 2003. *A Tale of Two Factions: Myth, Memory, and Identity in Ottoman Egypt and Yemen.* Binghamton NY: State University of New York Press.

Hathaway, J. 2005. The Mawza Exile at the Juncture of Zaydi and Ottoman Messianism. *AJS Review* 29/1: 111–128.

Haykel, B. (1995). A Zaydi Revival? *Yemen Update* 36: 20–21.

Haykel, B. 2002. The Salafis in Yemen at a Crossroads: An Obituary of Shaykh Muqbil al-Wâdi'î of Dammâj (d. 1422/2001). *Yemen Report*, October 2002, pp. 28–31.

Haykel, B. 2009. A Zaydi Revival? Yemen Update 36, 1995. Retrieved from: www.aiys. org/webdate/hayk.html.

Heiss, J. 2014. Sa'da Revisited in *Southwest Arabia across History:Essays to the Memory of Walter Dostal* (A. Gingrich and S. Haas, eds.), pp. 79–90. Vienna: Austrian Academy of Sciences Press.

Hoyland, R. 2001. *Arabia and the Arabs from the Bronze Age to the Coming of Islam*. London: Routledge.

Huntington, S. 2002. *The Clash of Civilizations and the Remaking of World Order* (The Free Press ed.). London: Simon & Schuster.

Ibn Kathir. 1422. (2001). Stories from the Qu'ran. Trans. by A. As-Sayed Al-Halawani. Cairo: Dar al Manarah.

Imru al-Qais. 1998. *Dīwān imrī al-qays* (Yāsīn al-Ayyūbī, ed.). Beirut.

Jayyusi, L. 1999. *The Adventures of Sayf Ben Dhi Yazan: An Arab Folk Epic*. Bloomington, IN: Indiana University Press.

Kennedy, H. 2016. *Caliphate: The History of an Idea*. New York: Basic Books.

Klorman, B. 1990. Conversion to Islam among Yemeni Jews under Zaydi Rule [in Hebrew], *Pe'amim* 42: 105–126.

Klorman, B. 1993. *The Jews of Yemen in the Nineteenth Century: A Portrait of a Messianic Community*. Leiden: Brill.

Klorman, B. 2009. Yemen: Religion, Magic, and Jews. *Proceedings of the Seminar for Arabian Studies*, Vol. 39. Papers from the Forty-Second Meeting of the Seminar for Arabian Studies held in London, July 24–26, 2008, pp. 125–134.

Lamprakos, M. 2016. *Building a World Heritage City: Sanaa, Yemen*. London: Routledge.

Lewis, B. 1990. The Roots of Muslim Rage. *The Atlantic Monthly*, September 1990.

Loreto, R. 2012. Recent studies in pre-Islamic Yemen. An Overview. *Rassegna di Studi Etiopici, Nuova Serie* 4/2012: 239–266.

Markovits, C. 2004. *The Global World of Indian Merchants, 1750–1947*. Cambridge: Cambridge University Press.

Munro-Hay, S. 1991. *Aksum: An African Civilization of Late Antiquity*. Edinburgh: Edinburgh University Press.

Newby, S. 2000. *Judaism and Islam: Boundaries, Communications, and Interaction*. Leiden: Brill.

Parfitt, T. 1996. *The Road to Redemption: The Jews of the Yemen, 1900–1950*. Leiden: Brill.

Peters, E. 1994. *Muhammad and the Origins of Islam*. Binghamton, NY: State University of New York Press.

Potts, D. 2010. *The Story of the Origins in Roads to Arabia: Archaeology and History of the Kingdom of Saudi Arabia*. Catalogue of the exhibition Roads of Arabia: Archaeology and History of the Kingdom of Saudi Arabia. Musée du Louvre, Paris, July 14–September 27, 2010, pp.70–79.

Power, T. 2012. *The Red Sea from Byzantium to the Caliphate: AD 500–1000*. Cairo: American University in Cairo Press.

Robin, C. 2010. *Antiquity*. Catalogue of the exhibition *Roads of Arabia: Archaeology and History of the Kingdom of Saudi Arabia*. Catalogue of the exhibition Roads of Arabia: Archaeology and History of the Kingdom of Saudi Arabia. Musée du Louvre, Paris, July 14–September 27, 2010, pp. 80–99.

Robin, C. 2012. Les Rois de Kinda in *Arabia, Greece and Byzantium. Cultural Contacts in Ancient* and *Medieval Times, Volume II* (A. Al-Helabi, D. Letsios, M. Al-Moraekhi and A. Al- Abduljabbar, eds.), pp. 59–130. Proceedings of the International Symposium on the Historical Relations between Arabia the Greek and Byzantine World (5th century BC–10th century AD), December 6–10, 2010. Riyadh: King Saud University.

Rodionov, M. 1996. Poetry and Power in Hadramawt. *New Arabian Studies* 3/1996: 118–133.

Said, E. 1978. *Orientalism*. New York: Pantheon.

Salmoni, B., B. Loidolt and M. Wells. 2010. *Regime and Periphery in Northern Yemen: The Huthi Phenomenon*. Santa Monica, CA: RAND.

Serjeant, R. 1992. The Zaydī Tribes of the Yemen: A New Field Study. *Bulletin of the School of Oriental and African Studies* 55/1: 16–21.

Shakdam, C. 2016. The Battle for Sanaa: A Tale of Grand Resistance. *RT News Op-Edge*, August 28, 2015. Retrieved from: www.rt.com/op-edge/313717-sanaa-yemen-saudi-houthis/.

Shanker, T. and R. Oppel. 2014. War's Elite Tough Guys, Hesitant to Seek Healing. *New York Times*, June 5, 2014. Retrieved from: www.nytimes.com/2014/06/06/us/politics/wars-elite-tough-guys-hesitant-to-seek-healing.html?_r=0.

Shear, M. and P. Baker. 2017. Saudis Welcome Trump's Rebuff of Obama's Mideast Views. *The New York Times*, May 20, 2017. Retrieved from: www.nytimes.com/2017/05/20/world/middleeast/donald-trump-saudi-arabia.html.

Swagman, C. 1988. Tribe and Politics: An Example from Highland Yemen. *Journal of Anthropological Research* 44/3: 251–261.

Taminian, L. 1999. Persuading the Monarchs: Poetry and Politics in Yemen, 1920–50 in *Le Yemen Contemporain* (R. Leveau, F. Mermier, and U. Steinbach, eds.). Paris: Editions Karthala.

Terril, W. 2011. *The Conflicts in Yemen and U.S. National Security*. Carlisle, PA: Strategic Studies Institute.

Van Donzel, E.J. and S. Schmidt. 2014. *Gog and Magog in Early Eastern Christian and Islamic Sources: Sallam's Quest for Alexander's Well*. Leiden: Brill.

Vom Bruck, G. 1999a. The Zaydi Sadah of the Yemen: The Temporalities of a Religious Tradition. *Oriente Moderno, Nuova serie*, 18(79)/2: 393–411.

Vom Bruck, G. 1999b. Being a Zaydi in the Absence of an Imam: Doctrinal Revisions, Religious Instruction, and the (Re-) Invention of Ritual in *Le Yemen Contemporain* (R. Leveau, F. Mermier, and U. Steinbach, eds.), pp. 169–192. Paris: Karthala Editions.

Yule, P. (ed.) 2008. *Late Antique Arabia Ẓafār, Capital of Ḥimyar*. Abhandlungen der Deutschen Orient-Gesellschaft Herausgegeben von der Deutschen Orient-Gesellschaft. Band 29.

Zaidi, H. 2016. Huthi Politics, *South Asia*, December 2016: 44–46.

Zarins, Kabawi. 1983. Preliminary report on the Najran/Ukhdud survey and excavations 1982/1402 AH. *Atlal* 7: 22–40.

Zeev, R. 2000. Judaism and Rahmanite Monotheism in the Himyarite Kingdom in the Fifth Century in *Israel and Ishmael: Studies in Muslim-Jewish Relations* (T. Parfitt, ed.), pp. 32–35. New York: Saint Martins Press.

8 "Our place here is but a deception"
Al-Andalus in modern Islamic ideology

O people of Al-Andalus, spur your mounts, for our place here is but a deception.
The fabric of the peninsula is unraveling from the edges, and the cloth even unravels from the center.
We are in the midst of enemies we cannot get rid of. What kind of life is this, living in a basket of vipers?

(Ibn Ghazal, trans. Ruggles 2003: 140)

Life is like unto a piece of carrion!
God gave it the semblance of a gazelle grazing on the mountain slope;
Down into the plain the hunter pursues her,
And when his time is come, Fate whisks him away!

(Middle Atlas Berber poem, Peyron 1995: 99)

"In 2009 and 2010, you know, Spain was really suffering economically from the [global] crisis. Spanish business people began to move here—more and more coming to set up businesses and live." My Moroccan colleague told me this to demonstrate that Spain and Morocco, in spite of their painful past, were staunch allies. Indeed, the relationship seemed to be on a good footing at the time of my visit after a number of trials in the past two decades. Several Moroccan citizens, including a business owner in Madrid, were found to be responsible for terrorist acts in Spain in 2004 and, a few years later, the newly installed Spanish king, Juan Carlos, and his queen, Sofia, made a trip to Ceuta and Melilla on the north coast of Africa—cities that Morocco has claimed since 1974. After that visit, King Mohammed VI promptly withdrew his country's ambassador to Spain in protest (Abend 2007) but all was forgiven by 2011 when the number of Spaniards registered as residents in Morocco quadrupled (de Haas 2012).

Spain had long since come to terms with its Muslim heritage but that does not necessarily translate into an enthusiasm for it and there are many Spanish detractors of a Spanish-Moroccan cultural rapprochement. At least one prominent Spanish scholar has dedicated his life's work to exploding the myth of Al-Andalus as a pluralistic society (Fanjul 2004) and decries cultural celebrations of Spain's Islamic history as a sop to Muslim immigrants and Arab trading partners. He pointedly criticizes events such as the "Andalusí Evenings" held at the historic Niebla Castle, which are described as "[s]eeking to reproduce and recreate the Islamic culture that dominated the Iberian Peninsula for eight centuries" with a "dinner program that features musical entertainment, dance, and theater from al-Andalus" (Fanjul 2009: 230). Of course, at least two of these activities would have been unlikely entertainment in the real Al-Andalus but the purpose of these kinds of Andalusian heritage presentations has little to do with real Islamic culture or government attempts to pacify Muslims both within and outside of the country. Rather, it has everything to do with the fact that the main tourist sites of the region are Islamic.

Later, on the same day as my conversation with my colleague in Morocco, I thought about this as I visited the remarkable site of Chellah in Rabat. A Phoenician and Roman city, called Sala originally, Chellah is an amalgam of ancient and medieval architecture flourishing on the periphery of Al Andalus. Strictly speaking, the Maghrib was part of the "Islamic West" but Al-Andalus specifically refers to the Iberian Peninsula under Islamic rule (Gomez-Rivas 2015). The Almoravids and the Almohads brought Al-Andalus and the Maghrib together after decisively defeating the armies of Castile and Aragon. At Chellah, the Almoravids, with the spoils of their conquest of the Iberian Peninsula, established a royal burial ground and rebuilt the Great Mosque on the site of the Arab Umayyad mosque. The successors of the Almoravids, the Almohads, also used the site as a royal burial ground.

Later, one of the last of the Maghrib dynasties to rule over Al-Andalus (for a very short time), the Marinids made the site into their holy necropolis. The Banu Marin built a complex that included an elaborate mosque with an early example of a typical Moroccan tall square tower—a design borrowed by the Spanish and Italians for sacred buildings erected during the Renaissance. The tall minaret of the now-ruined mosque was built of stone and zellige tilework, and still stands (Buresi et al. 2012). Storks nest on the top of the tower undisturbed by the restoration work. The guard told me that Muslims revere storks because they make an annual pilgrimage to Mecca during their migrations (see also Sax 2001: 153).

While all of the Maghreb dynasties came into power by defeating the previous dynasty, they had one thing in common with each other that they did not have with the Arab caliphates. They were Muslim, to be sure, but they followed their own specific revivalist forms of Islam, born in the Maghrib. Further, and more importantly, their native language was not Arabic. They were Berbers and spoke a native tongue that probably predates Arabic by as much as 2,000 years (Ilihiane 2017).

The more restored site of Kasbah of the Oudayas, which I had visited before Chellah, is in Rabat proper, right on the edge of the old medina. Chellah was, in former times, a city that was separated from Rabat. The latter owes its existence primarily to the Almohad Dynasty and the Kasbah is the best-known example of Almohad architecture in the city that they essentially built and which is, today, Morocco's capital. Moriscos (Muslims who had been forced to convert to Christianity) rebuilt the Kasbah, which was then in ruins, in the seventeenth century after one of several expulsions from Spain. They settled in Morocco and established an independent (Islamic) republic in Rabat for about half a century. What is left of the original Kasbah of the Oudayas is an upper story built by the Almohads. The Alaouites (the dynasty currently in power in Morocco) rebuilt the lower story. The Kasbah has a peaceful walled garden and the oldest standing mosque in Rabat. Built by the Almohads, it is enclosed within its impressive fortress-like walls. The minaret of the mosque was restored by Ahmad al-Inglizi, an Englishman who converted to Islam in the eighteenth century (Bargach 2008). Finding fame in the late eighteenth and early nineteenth centuries, the Kasbah was described by American novelist Edith Wharton, who wrote the following when she visited it during the final days of the First World War:

> Salé [Chellah] the white and Rabat the red frown at each other over the foaming bar of the Bou-Regreg [River], each walled, terraced, minareted, and presenting a singularly complete picture of the two types of Moroccan town, the snowy and the tawny. To the gates of both the Atlantic breakers roll in with the boom of northern seas, and under a misty northern sky.
>
> (Wharton 1920)

The Kasbah and Chellah are, like many historical sites in the Middle East, palimpsests. Medieval remains are superimposed on ancient sites and, in turn, are overlaid by more recent historical remnants (Maṭālsī 2000). They are also testament to the success of the Berber dynasties, in particular, the Almohads, in bringing Spain and North Africa together. Ironically, those scholars who, like Fanjul (2004: 2009), question the tolerance of Al-Andalus, often completely overlook the history of the regime that would serve to prove their point. Arab Al-Andalus may have been a period of coexistence, Berber Al-Andalus, at least under the Almohad Caliphate, was not.

Although it does not fit into the myth of the "golden age" of Al-Andalus, increasing evidence is emerging that gives us a more complete picture of this period—one that suggests that the Almohads had a more lasting impact on the region than was previously supposed. The narrative of occupation of a diverse cosmopolitan Euro-Muslim society by an intolerant horde of fundamentalist jihadists from nowhere came to dominate historical literature about the Almoravids and Almohads, who have still not been fully recognized as significant participants in the historical fantasy of Al-Andalus. Nevertheless, Berbers were part of that picture from its very beginning. Fighting under the Arab Caliph of Damascus, Abd al-Malik ibn Marwan, the leader that Ibn Khaldun called "one of the greatest Arab and Muslim Caliphs," Berber warriors had made the conquest of Iberia by the Umayyads possible (Collins 1999).

Afterwards, the ruling Arab dynasties treated the Berbers with what amounted to contempt during most of their history in North Africa. The Berbers had become the first population in the region to convert to the new religion but were treated no differently than non-Muslims for all that. They were given a lesser share of the spoils of conquest after having undertaken a far greater share in the fighting. Most Arab governors in the Maghrib taxed the

Berbers as dhimmis in contravention of Islamic law. Radical Kharijite activists found an enthusiastic audience among the resentful Berbers by espousing a puritanical Islam, which was later to become a hallmark of the Almohads, and equality for Berbers. In the mid-eighth century, Berber revolts broke out all over North Africa. In the Maghrib, the combined Berber armies were victorious for a time but were finally defeated at Cordoba (Ilahiane 2017).

The Berber hold on Morocco and the central Maghrib continued and the Arab dynasties were never again to control that part of the world without the cooperation of the Berber population. The Arab Idrisid dynasty was the most significant of these regimes and ruled for two centuries in the Maghrib with Berber support, by embracing the Zaydi religion that came to be espoused by northern Yemeni tribes (see Chapter 7, this volume). Zaydism is distinguishable from Shi'ite religion in a number of ways. Chief among the beliefs specific to this version of Islam is the conviction that rulers must not only claim descent from Ali and Fatima but must also prove their worth by taking up arms against the unjust rule of Muslims who reject the rights of the Prophet's descendants (Kennedy 2016). Although religiously out of step with the Sunni Muslim rulers, who came after them, the Idrisids were primarily responsible for the rapid spread of Islam throughout the Maghrib and are considered to be the ancestors of the current royal family in Morocco (Larooui 1977).

After intermittent periods of caliphate rule, the best known and most successful Sunni Berber dynasties, the Almoravids (1040–1147) and the Almohads (1121–1269), rose up and, together, managed to wrest control of Al-Andalus from both Muslims and Christians and maintain the hegemony for over two centuries. The distinction that Al-Andalus was for at least half of its history not Arab at all but Berber may be lost on many non-Muslims but the indigenous people of North Africa have preserved their unique culture in face of successive waves of invasion from antiquity until modern times. Western historiography, heavily influenced by Arab historians, portrays the Almoravids and Almohads in particular as barbarians—the name "Berber" actually stems from the Greek word for unruly foreigners. Today, Amazigh is the preferred term for Berber ethnicity and Tamazight for their language. The use of these words historically is problematic because they have been designated as Berbers for centuries and the term has not become so pejorative that the Berbers themselves reject it. In fact, the French "Le berbérisme" (English Berberism) is still used by Amazigh activists (Ennaji 2005).

In any case, it is far more likely that the Almoravids and Almohads identified themselves using versions of these names that refer to their extended clans rather than as members of such a broad group. As a result of an alliance formed with the Arab Caliphate in 1086, in order to fight Alfonso VI, the Almoravids were the first Berber dynasty to cross over into Spain, defeat the Christians and subdue the Muslim emirs. By the year 1090, their empire included the western Sahara, Morocco, half of Algeria and all Muslim Spain, including Valencia, Granada, Cordoba, Seville and Lisbon. The Almoravid emir administered these cities from the newly constructed capital at Marrakech (Boone et al. 1990).

Like the Almohads that came after them, the Almoravids had begun as a religious reform movement sparked by a charismatic spiritual leader, Abd Allah Ibn Yassin, who espoused a version of Islam that rivaled the Almohad rulers in strictness. The Almoravids, however, were from the desert rather than the mountains and had made a prosperous living from grazing herds and raising crops in the fertile oases of the Moroccan lowlands and they were more exposed to the wider world. The rulers who followed Yassin became progressively more urbanized. This attitude proved to be a beneficial one for the non-Muslims who lived among them but fundamentalist Almohad leaders characterized the dynasty's last rulers as weak and ineffective partly for this reason (Bennison 2016).

Despite the extent of their power, the Almoravids were unable to quell the Almohad uprising and the leader of the insurgents, Ibn Tumart, established a small independent mountain kingdom, flouting Almoravid authority, in 1120 CE. About 27 years later, Ibn Tumart's Almohad successors had overthrown the Almoravids, conquered Marrakesh and declared themselves to be a new caliphate. They then extended their power over all of the Maghrib by 1159 and, soon, the Iberian Peninsula was in their hands. Almohads were a completely new class of rulers. They were, in effect, an Islamic messianic movement that had begun in the High Atlas Mountains.

Ibn Tumart, founder of the Almohad dynasty, was a firebrand preacher who had traveled the Muslim world before returning to his home in the Maghrib to spread the good word about the oneness of God and the threat of heresy. Upon his return, he began a religious reform program to purify Berber Islamic practices. This was the beginning of his campaign against the Almoravid rulers and their complex elitist Maliki school of law, with its emphasis upon rationalism and the power of the Arab caliphates. According to Almohad legend, Ibn Tumart was given a specific imprimatur by the famed twelfth-century philosopher al-Ghazali, who wrote of a form of Islam that did not disdain politics but, instead, authorized "commanding right and forbidding wrong" by imposing a duty to address injustices by rulers, states and even whole societies (Hathaway 2005).

Espousing his brand of political Islam, Ibn Tumart took to the road and, unsurprisingly, it was not long before the Almoravids began to hear of this new movement forming in the highlands of Morocco. Escaping from the authorities, Ibn Tumart found refuge among his native Masmuda Berbers. It was not long after that he proclaimed himself as Mahdi (messiah) and declared an independent state in the High Atlas.

During the month of Ramadan in 1121 CE, Ibn Tūmart stood up before his Berber followers in the mountains of Morocco and delivered a forceful sermon that might have been a turning point in the Almohad movement. He first entreated God to "bless our lord Moḥammed, the Messenger of God, the herald of the Imam-al-Mahdi [messiah], who will fill the earth with equity and justice, just as it had been filled with tyranny and oppression." Then, Ibn Tumart reminded his audience that "God sent him [the Mahdi] to abolish falsehood with the truth and to eradicate tyranny with justice" (Jones 2013: 81). According to an anonymous fourteenth-century Andalusian historian, ten of the men who had heard this came up to Ibn Tūmart declaring "O Sīdī [master], this description is found in no one but you. Therefore you are the Mahdi." They pledged their oath of loyalty to him then and there, "just as the Companions of the Messenger of God pledged their loyalty to him" (Jones 2013: 83).

Ibn Tumart did not live to see the extent of the Almohad regime that he had started. The Almoravids charged him with fomenting rebellion and he was brought before the emir to defend himself. Even though he claimed to be a simple scholar attempting to bring about reform (Hathaway 2005), the emir's advisors and the judges of Marrakech accused him of being an agitator and a heretic and recommended execution. The ruler had mercy, perhaps because he was impressed with Ibn Tumart's scholarship, and merely expelled him from the city after a flogging. He quickly returned to his old ways going about the country destroying wine jars, lecturing people in the street on their behavior or dress and engaging in vociferous debate prompting complaints from his neighbors. The emir again lost patience with him and had him arrested. He escaped this time as well and had many more skirmishes with the authorities but lived to fight, and be defeated by, the Almoravids, in a decisive battle in which he reportedly lost thousands of his followers.

This was a major setback, but the feisty Almohads did not go away after the death of their leader and proceeded to carry on with the project of conquest without him. Ibn Tumart's family took over where he left off with the help of a council of ten advisors and a wider group composed of the chiefs of the Masmuda Berber tribes. The first Almohad Caliph was Abd al-Mu'min who had been a follower of Ibn Tumart. He received the bay'a (oath of allegiance) from the Almohads in 1133 CE and immediately took the bold step of declaring himself *Amir al-Mu'minīn*. The Almohad rulers thought of themselves as true caliphs and legitimate inheritors of sovereignty over the land. For 13 years they continued to fight with the Almoravids, who had a formidable military, so Al-Mu'min began to concentrate on subjugating the highlands in the north and south of Morocco before descending to the open plains. Finally, he was able to subdue the Almoravids and bring about the fall of their capital at Marrakech. It was then that he was able to turn his attention to Al-Andalus.

He launched an expedition to cross the Straits of Gibraltar and captured Seville in 1147 CE and, afterwards, moved on to Cordoba, the crown jewel of Andalusia. In 1150 CE, all remaining Andalusian emirs came to Chellah to pledge their loyalty to Al-Mu'min. He next turned to the east to what is now the country of Algeria. The Arab tribes of the region had banded together to resist the Almohad conquerors because they were being treated well under the Berber Hammadid dynasty and were not sanguine in their beliefs that the Almohads would be similarly indulgent rulers. A highly unusual offer of assistance to the tribes came from the Normans who pledged to send several thousand men from Sicily. Probably to their detriment, the tribal chiefs proudly declined the offer because they did want to ally with a Christian power against their co-religionists. So, the Almohads won the day—and the property of the conquered tribes. Their families were also taken captive but later, after he was more assured of their loyalty, Al-Mu'min returned them to their homes with lavish gifts (Bennison 2016).

While he was magnanimous to his fellow Muslims, including his enemies, the same could not be said of the behavior of Al-Mu'min and his successors to Jews and Christians. Under Almohad rule, there was a mass exodus of Jewish scholars (Alfonso 2007). Among them was the famous scholar and poet Abraham Ibn Ezra, the "Rabbi Ben Ezra," who was the dramatis persona in Browning's famous poem. His lament for Al-Andalus was written in 1164 and is a testament to the painful transition from the acceptance of Jews by the Almoravids to the zealotry of the Almohads: "Woe for calamity has descended upon Al-Andalus from the heavens! My eyes, my eyes flow with water ... Without guilt, the Exile dwelled there untroubled, Undisturbed for one thousand and seventy years" (Decter 2005: 83). The Jewish community of Spain had been given the freedom to practice their religion since the Roman Period. Now it was the choice between conversion, death or exile.

Yusuf Yacoub Al-Mansur was the last great Almohad Caliph. An accomplished military leader, he was able to thwart the Christian Reconquista for a time. His reign was also a time of internationalism and learning that most Moroccans recall with pride. It was Al-Mansur who undertook the rebuilding of the Kasbah of Oudayas in the Rabat medina. Al-Mansur protected the Aristotelian philosopher Averroes (Ibn Rushd), who was an enemy of the followers of that same thinker, al-Ghazali, who encouraged Al-Mansur's forefather Ibn Tumart (Fromherz 2010). At the same time, his religious persecutions forced the Jewish philosopher Maimonides to leave Fez for a friendlier Muslim climate in Egypt. A Christian country seemed to have been out of the question because Moshe Ben Maimon only knew Hebrew and Arabic. Al-Mansur, like his predecessors, is often described in standard histories as a religious fanatic but from the perspective of Muslim history, his suspicions about Christians and Jews were based not just on religious belief but on what he might consider to be strategic grounds (Taieb-Carlen 2010).

There are those who question whether the Almohads had a systematic and official policy of persecution. One analysis of Cairo Ginizah documents found evidence that conversion by persuasion was practiced under the first Almohad Caliphate, following their conquest of areas where Jews lived (Bennison and Gallego 2007). While this hardly suggests that they were in any way accepting of members of other faiths, it should be considered in the context of a time in which they were engaged in a program of forcible conversion of other Muslims to their particular form of Islam. Seen from a modern perspective, the Almohads appear to have been a blot on the free exchange of ideas that constitutes our vision of Al-Andalus. But, it is probably true to say that Christians and Jews suffered daily injustices at the hands of *all* Muslim rulers of Al Andalus, both Arab and Berber (Wasserstein 1995).

Nevertheless, the Almohads could well have been excessively harsh because they were parochial rulers. The much-touted tolerance of Arab Al-Andalus might well have been a function of lack of attention by the caliphates centered in Damascus, Cairo and Baghdad to governance in Morocco and Spain, as well as the fact that the emirs on the periphery saw the pragmatism of continuing to engage in lucrative exchanges with non-Muslims. That does not constitute a policy of religious freedom. Indeed, it is easier to believe that toleration of other religious beliefs by anyone in the medieval world would be completely alien. Just a sampling of some of the events that occurred in Europe and the Middle East during the time that the Almohads were in power is illustrative. In the 56 years between 1148 and 1204, the French Monk Rodolphe inspired the massacre of Jews throughout Germany, a slaughter of 6,000 Shi'a was sanctioned by the new Sunni ruler of Damascus, Pope Lucius III began the Catholic Inquisitions and three crusades to the Holy Land had taken countless lives, including those of Christians and Jews (Rubies 2017).

The end of the Almohad dynasty came about as suddenly as the beginning. After about a century and a half of hegemony, the Arabized Berber Marinids challenged their rule. Approaching the walls of Marrakesh in 1269 CE, the Marinid cavalry was met by the person of the Almohad Caliph himself riding into battle and certain death. In a (by now) time-honored Near Eastern tradition, the Marinid Sultan sent the caliph's head to Fez, where it was stuck on the city gate. The Almohad Caliph's family escaped to the mountains as the founder of their dynasty had done so many years before but were hunted down and eliminated without mercy. Almohad power had been based upon the contention that its caliphs were descended from the Prophet but as their territory expanded that core of belief dissipated. Their power had begun to unravel long before their final defeat. It was the old story of imperial decline—civil wars and rebellions within their territories had weakened them and made them vulnerable to conquest. The Marinids enjoyed a reign of several hundred years before they were conquered themselves by their relatives, the Wattisids, whose rule was far shorter. The Iberian Peninsula had long since slipped from the control of the Moroccan dynasties by then. The height of Berber hegemony in Europe had been under the Almohads (Fancy 2013).

In general, archaeological exploration of the medieval period in the Maghrib is at a nascent stage of development (Boone and Benco 1999). Further, the nature of archaeological classification, based as it is on ceramic analysis, is conducive to economic but not necessarily to ideological inquiry, which is the focus of establishing narratives. As has been made clear by many studies, there was an unprecedented level of trade in agricultural products brought about by the Almohad unification of southern Spain, Morocco and western Algeria and the Almohads dominated trade networks throughout the western Mediterranean. Consequently, the towns and cities of Al-Andalus, particularly those with access to Atlantic ports, grew quickly. Seville, a town that had been overshadowed by Cordoba, grew in prominence as an Almohad capital and as a primary trade conduit because of its location at the most northerly navigable point on the Guadalquivir for deep draft vessels that enabled ocean going ships to come directly from the Atlantic and anchor there (Bridgman 2009).

Control over the sub-Saharan gold trade was perhaps even more responsible than centralized agricultural production for the establishment of a functioning Almohad state. The Almohads built on the establishment of the trade by the Almoravids. Occurring at a point in time when long distance trade had become an absolute necessity for establishing authority, their successful military campaigns and subsequent conquests put the Maghrib at the center of the lucrative gold trade. As a result, the Almohads were able to develop the interior of Morocco and establish closer economic links between cities and the hinterlands. As a dynasty that had its origins in the High Atlas Mountains, the Almohads were particularly well positioned, and well disposed, to do this. As a result, they were able to institute a relatively effective system of taxation throughout the empire. Their control in the Maghrib lasted for a sufficient amount of time to make these changes permanent and, significantly, they were able to extend their systems after the Marinid conquest via the Hafsids, a dynasty that ruled in Tunis that had declared their independence from the Almohads but continued to support Almohad doctrine and institutions (Fancy 2013).

Excavations of the quintessential African "City of Gold," Sijilmasa, have gone far in explaining Almoravid and Almohad ideology as well as economy. Described by historian and geographer Ibn Makri as "the last civilized place" before intrepid gold traders began their long march across the Sahara, it was seen by medieval writers as a place of great splendor. A ninth-century scholar, al-Ya'qubi, said of Sijilmasa that "[the gold] is found like plants and it is said that the wind blows it away" (Messier 2015: 17). The tenth-century scholar Al-Masudi, wrote that: "[a]ll that gold which the merchants obtain is minted in the town of Sijilmasa" (Messier 2015: 18). Sijilmassa was the first Almoravid conquest and it was taken with the full support of its elders who were wearied by over six decades of rule by the Algerian Maghrawa Berbers. Al-Bakri wrote in the eleventh century that they got more than they bargained for with the firebrand Ibn Yassin, who followed a strict interpretation of Islam, later to be relaxed somewhat by his descendants (Messier 2015). He went about the city destroying musical instruments and wine shops. The city did rebel against the Almoravids on several occasions but it stayed within their hands until their kingdom was overtaken by the Almohads. The Almohads took the city in the mid-twelfth century and it was responsible, in large part, for their ability to expand the Saharan gold trade. The Jews of Sijilmasa were to greatly regret the loss of Almoravid rule, which they had found strict and rigid, when the far more violent Almohads slaughtered many of them after offering conversion at the point of a sword (Messier 2010).

Located near the modern town of Rissani, the backdrop for Sijilmassa's ruins is a barren landscape interspersed with lush date palm oases and agricultural fields. The ancient city is on a small hill over the plain of the River Ziz. The ruins are a mass of mounds, some of them rising ten meters above the plain. There are remnants of a large mosque built in the seventeenth to eighteenth centuries, which tourists assume are a part of the ancient medieval city that consists mainly of plains of pot sherds and ruined mud brick walls. After initial explorations, archaeologists concluded that it was long narrow city along the river Ziz with a short wall around the oasis and a taller wall around the heart of the city.

Sijilmassa, according to archaeologists, expanded during the Almoravid and Almohad periods due to its progressive expansion of water resources. Al-Bakri reported in the eleventh century that, "[t]he water in the town is brackish as it is in all the wells of Sijilmassa" (Al-Bakri, quoted in Hopkins and Levtzion 1981: 65). Given that Al-Bakri was writing about one decade after the Almoravid conquest of Sijilmassa, archaeologists have concluded that engineering changes in the Ziz followed the Almoravid conquest. Thus, Sijilmassa was able to retain its significance and continued to grow during the Almohad period (1148–1255). With the redirection of the river, the oasis population also increased its agricultural output exponentially. The city's role as the main conduit for the Saharan gold trade was exploited far more profligately after the end of the Almohad period and, as imperial authority vanished from the Moroccan scene, Sijilmassa gradually was replaced by small independent towns and villages (Lightfoot and Miller 1996).

Archaeologists know the name of the Grand Mosque in Sijilmasa at the time of the Almoravids from historical sources and they have managed to locate its remains just beneath the surface. The building was almost square and divided into five aisles, four of equal width and a wider center aisle facing the mihrab. Archaeological evidence also indicates that when the Almohads arrived in the city, they changed the orientation of the Almoravid Grand Mosque. Historical records state that when the Almohads took Marrakech, Al-Mu'min refused to enter the city because, according to his religious advisors, "the mosques of your city are not exactly facing the true qibla." They corrected the orientation of the mosques of that city and the first mosque that they rebuilt in Marrakech faced five degrees farther south. Archaeologists believe that the same thing was done in the grand mosque of Sijilmassa, which was reoriented and expanded in the middle of the twelfth century. A section of a column, a column capital in the area of the mihrab and another slender column with a floral motif on its capital, just like the ones flanking the mihrab of an Almohad mosque built in their home territory of the High Atlas, are clear indications of Almohad rebuilding (Messier and Miller 2015).

Rectification of Almoravid mosques was commonly done by the Almohads even though their orientation was not a true correction and faced even further to the south of Mecca than the Almoravid mosques. There are several theories and a considerable literature on the subject of mosque orientation, but there are no definitive answers about these activities by the Almohads, whose strict adherence to Islamic law would indicate a more punctilious attention to directing their prayers toward Mecca. Many of the steps they took to abrogate Almoravid rule were highly symbolic, such as the choice of white as their emblematic color and the reorientation of the mosques. In each case, the theme is one of purification—the reconstruction of Islam as a simpler antinomian belief.

The expansion of the mosque to twice its size indicates that the population expanded rapidly and prospered after the Almohad conquest, although as noted previously, the Jewish population dwindled. Wealthy neighborhoods were found in Sijilmasa from the Almohad period, indicating that the merchant class survived the conquest and even flourished. Houses with adobe walls on stone foundations were richly decorated with geometric patterns and stylized floral patterns. It also appears that, despite the outright rejection by the Almohads of the Maliki School of Islamic jurisprudence, the Grand Mosque of Sijilmasa continued to attract scholars from all over, including several local students who became distinguished Sufi scholars (Lightfoot and Miller 1996).

The long-term effect of the changes brought about by the fundamentalist Almohad regime was that North Africa became a unified and powerful civilization that left a substantial legacy. For the first time, a ruling dynasty was able to control the High Atlas, which had been a den of rebellion—in point of fact, of their own rebellion. Even the Roman Empire had been unable to secure this region and there are many doubts that the modern state of Morocco has effectively done this. A number of important river systems originate in the High Atlas that form the basis for large cities and towns in the north. The Almohads used this region as a refuge and a natural fortress. They had first undertaken to subdue all of the Atlas Mountain Berber tribes before launching their conquest of the lowlands and of southern Spain and was the first political power to establish this kind of confederation. The combination of a new religion that focused on fundamental concepts rather than complex legal formulations and supra-tribal solidarity was formidable (Bennison 2016).

The Reconquista by Christians was a process of many centuries culminating in 1492 when the Spaniards conquered Granada, the last Muslim stronghold in Europe. Spain was reclaimed by Christians to never again to be part of the Umma and the theme of a lost utopia permeated Arabic literature in the West. Near the beginning of the Reconquista, a Muslim general led his troops into battle with Aragon with the battle cry "Are you going to flee from paradise?" From the sixteenth to the nineteenth centuries, Seville, Cordoba, Valencia and Granada were spoken of by Muslims with reverence and the prayer, "May God restore it to Islam" (Ruggles 1993: 175). The loss of a Muslim foothold in the West essentially meant that the legacy of Al-Andalus would be blotted out of Western history for many generations.

Only 65 kilometers across the Strait of Gibraltar, the Maghrib stayed Muslim, independent and, notwithstanding the Arabization project of some previous caliphates, Berber. Most Moroccans may acknowledge their Berber descent but the overwhelming majority speak Arabic and French and do not have many Anazigh cultural traits. After the Wattisid dynasty, there was a turning point in the sixteenth century when the Maghrib was taken over by successive Sharifian dynasties that claimed no historical or cultural relationship to Al-Andalus.

The Saadis were native to the Maghrib, but made the claim (probably fictitious) that they had Arabian origins. They ruled for a little over a century and were finally displaced by the Alaouites, who claimed a similar lineage, although they also were from the region, and they continue to rule Morocco to this day. The Saadis and the Alaouites introduced a new element to Moroccan leadership. Their claim of descent directly from the Prophet Mohammed evolved into the practice of the monarch assuming the title of Emir al-Mumineen (Commander of the Faithful)—a practice that is now embedded in the Moroccan constitution (Geertz 1971). It was also during these periods that Islam in Morocco became heavily influenced by Sufism, which came to the region during the fifteenth century and took hold during the time of chaos at the end of the Banu Marin. The faith instilled by zawiyas (Sufi institutions) thereafter played an important role in Moroccan religion (Munson 1993).

With these intervening governments, any true memory of Al Andalus in Morocco has been lost. In traditional Moroccan culture, Al-Andalus seems to have taken on the aspect of a fantasy but Muslims outside of the region see it quite differently. The media arm of Al Qaeda in the Islamic Maghrib (AQIM) is named for Al-Andalus and deceased founder of the group, Osama bin Laden, famously lamented the loss of Al-Andalus in a number of statements comparing the Reconquista to the "American supported" takeover of Jerusalem by Israel. Bin Laden spoke of raising "the unique flag of Allah on all stolen Islamic land, from Palestine to Andalus" (Louayene 2011:35). The Islamic State magazine, *Dabiq*, speaks of Al-Andalus as "[a] victorious frontier of victory until the arrival of the Hour" in which it will be taken again after the final battle (Dabiq 2012).

Nonetheless, Al-Andalus represents more of a reverie than a clarion call, and Moroccans for the most part ascribe to the notion of a "golden age" (Menocal 2002). "It was nothing like they [Al Qaeda and Islamic State] say—it was a peaceful time, a time of learning," my colleague told me. Extremist groups and Moroccans, of course, are not the only ones to yearn for it—Muslim rule over a large piece of southern Europe is similarly spoken of elsewhere. A highly placed member of the Royal House of Saud, Prince Turki Al-Faisal, recently told a reporter, "The loss of Andalusia is like losing part of my body. The emptiness remains. I have a passion for Andalusia because it contributed not only to Muslims but to humanity and human understanding. It contributed to the well-being of society, to its social harmony. This is missing nowadays" (Ahmed 2017). Considering that Saudi religious traditions have been responsible for inspiring the highest ranks of Al Qaeda and Islamic State, the latter seems to be empty rhetoric.

Among Muslim nations, Morocco has the most supportable claim over the legacy of Al-Andalus, although most people in the country would be quick to disavow the kind of extremism practiced by the Almohad messianists. Morocco has historically resisted efforts to make it part of an Arab or Muslim confederation and is like Egypt in this respect. Pan-Arabism, which reached the height of its popularity in the 1950s and 1960s, failed to sufficiently engage Moroccans and Egyptians who, after a short-lived experiment, rejected the idea of a unified multinational Arab state (Segalla 2009). In both cases, a certain sense of historical and cultural exceptionalism pervades their relationship with others in the Middle East and North Africa and, interestingly, both Egyptian and Moroccan dialects are known for being almost unintelligible to other Arabic speakers.

The unique character of religion and politics in Morocco, where a number of groups espouse radical change while the government attempts to counter it with its own religious rhetoric, is, in many ways, a product of the country's extraordinary place in the history of the Islamic World. Yet, despite many efforts that receive the continued support of the United States and Europe, Morocco is not free from the ravages of extremism and extremists. Men of Moroccan origin carried out the first major attack in Europe after the advent of the new millennium. The Madrid train bombings of March 11, 2004, killed almost 200 people. Al Qaeda claimed responsibility for the attack but it appears that they operated in this instance more as publicist than planner. The organization characterized the attack as "part of settling old accounts with Spain, the crusader, and America's ally in its war against Islam" (Lowney 2005: 1). The Spanish president tried to use this reference in order to avoid the political ramifications of his decision to back the disastrous United States invasion of Iraq and so sought to bury any modern implications of the attack as soon as he could, digging even deeper into the past for an explanation:

> The problem Spain has with Al Qaeda and Islamic terrorism did not begin with the Iraq Crisis. In fact, it has nothing to do with government decisions. You must go back no less than 1,300 years, to the early 8th century, when a Spain recently invaded by the Moors refused to become just another piece in the Islamic world and began a long battle to recover its identity.
>
> (Tremlett 2008, xvii)

This deft resort to nativism, religious discrimination and history did not serve the president well at the time and controversy over the incident persists. The Madrid bombings exposed deep political and social rifts in Spanish politics, standing in sharp contrast to the response to attacks elsewhere in Europe that stimulated unity rather than discord. As for Morocco, in addition to dealing with the growing perspective in Spain that it was exporting terrorists, it had its own series of attacks to deal with in Casablanca. As a consequence, the government has cast suspicion on religious authorities that seem to espouse what they consider radical ideologies. One such individual was someone who had been under scrutiny for many years, Sheikh Abdessalam Yassine, the deceased founder of one of the most influential Islamic organizations in Morocco, who was long targeted by the government for anti-monarchist views.

Widely considered to be the country's leading dissident during his lifetime, Yassine is seen by some in government as an incendiary influence like Said Qutb in Egypt. Yassine, however, did not ascribe to Qutb's notion of overthrowing modern Muslim societies because they have strayed from the true path. Rather, Yassine suggests that "[e]ven though there are those among us and among our leaders who are apostates, our ummah is still that of our master Mohammed, its core Islamic beliefs are intact and Jahili beliefs cannot penetrate it" (Dadaaoui 2011: 130–131). As a Muslim cleric, Yassine was an exemplar of Morocco's religion and history. The son of a poor Amazigh farmer who claimed descent from the Prophet, his unique combination of Islamic purism, Berber and Sharifian origins and membership in a Sufi order covered all of Morocco's cultural and religious bases. He was widely respected and widely mourned when he died in 2012.

Speaking truth to power was a habit of almost 40 years duration for Yassine, beginning with his 1974 letter admonishing King Hassan II, the father of the current monarch. The famous missive was entitled "Al-Islam aw al-tufan" or "Islam or the Deluge"—a title simultaneously recalling the flood story of Noah and Louis XV's legendary prediction about the demise of the French monarchy. Regardless of the implications of the title, made all the clearer when he translated the document into French, Yassine did not, as is popularly believed, call upon the king to step down. Instead, he characterized him as a potentially devout man who had strayed from the right path. It was only later that his message, and that of the movement he established, took on an anti-monarchical tone.

Even though Yassine was not a proponent of the kind of violence attributed to Islamic State and Al Qaeda, his messianic message signaled the rise of a new political rhetoric within the formerly narrow confines of the relationship between religion and the state in Morocco. At a time when the discourse of democracy espoused by secular political organizations was being repressed, Yassine's appeal for a godly monarchy posited a scenario that, he believed, would lead to the establishment of a new caliphate under a repentant (and preferably Moroccan) leader (Zeghal 2009). Yassine's arguments for Al Adl Wa Al Ihssane (Justice and Spirituality) became the hallmark of his critique of the Moroccan government—and later the name of the opposition party he founded that has been declared illegal but is not overtly banned.

The Moroccan version of the Arab Spring took off during the second half of February 2011 with demonstrations across the kingdom. Made up of a variety of composite elements, it brought together students, the unemployed, the left and Shaykh Yassine's organization. Their complaints were similar to those of neighboring Tunisia—that is, the economy, high youth unemployment even among educated young people and the elite monopoly of political power. The king responded with a campaign of vilification and harassment against the leaders of the movement, followed by what seemed to be an accession to some of their demands. Mohammed VI announced constitutional revisions, which transferred some powers from the king to parliament, followed by a popular referendum, the resignation of the sitting government and elections in which the Justice and Development Party, a reform oriented Islamic organization inspired by Yassin, was enfolded in the government after receiving the majority of votes (Daadaoui 2011).

In Morocco today, the distinction between Arab and Amazigh is not sharply drawn, but being Amazigh is essentially a matter of self-identification and consistent use of the language. Thus, even though the Moroccan population is almost completely Amazigh in origin (Gómez-Casado et al. 2000), only a minority of Moroccans speak Tamazigt (the name for the language). The loss of Tamazight through urbanization and Arabization policies has meant that over time, more Moroccans identify as Arab, even if their parents or grandparents were Berbers. Yassine readily acknowledged his Amazigh identity and spoke Tamazight but his position with respect to Berberism was problematical to Berber activists. In the early years of both Yassine's religious movement and the Berber culture movement, the Government of Morocco tended to conflate the two because one of the early intellectual Amazigh leaders, Mohammed Chafik, was a friend of Yassine's. Nevertheless, while Yassine and his movement were most concerned with the secularization of Morocco, the Amazigh fight has been against the progressive Arabization.

Both Yassine's movement and the Amazigh movement are opposed to Western modernity, the one for religious and the other for cultural reasons, but outside of that they have not found much common ground. In Yassine's *Dialogue with an Amazigh Friend*, he "urges the Imazighen [the Amazigh people] to abandon their interest in the Amazigh language and popular culture" (El Ednani 2007: 49). Within a predominantly Muslim society, the Amazigh movement for cultural and linguistic rights has always been more secular than religious and activists even cite secularism as an important value in their culture. This is primarily due to the fact that Islamization in modern Moroccan society is now linked to post-independence Arabization. Before the seventh century CE Arab invasions, Berber culture was religiously diverse and had significant numbers of both Christians and Jews. Although the Berbers held on to their cultural majority in the face of successive waves of Arabs, the culture changed irrevocably with the conversion of the population to Islam. Yassine as a claimant of Sharifian heritage privileged Arabic as the language of Allah over his childhood tongue.

Combatting Salafism, as opposed to cultural revival movements, has proven to be a greater challenge for the Moroccan Government. One of its chief strategies has been to support a resurgence of Sufism. Donations from the royal family are now being funneled into zawiyas (Sufi learning institutions) and their promotion of Sufism in the media has produced television shows dedicated to broadcasting Sufi dhikr (remembrance) featuring devotional dancing, recitation and meditation ceremonies and a series of lectures and seminars. By familiarizing Moroccans with their Sufi heritage and the non-political philosophy behind its practices, those who are underwriting this effort hope that it will provide the religiosity that might otherwise be sought in extremist camps, while discouraging participation in politics and public affairs (Bouasria 2015).

Elsewhere, putting Sufi religion in the spotlight of the War on Terror has tragically backfired. The United States has successfully recruited Sufi organizations into its counter-terrorism campaign—and has encouraged European and Muslim majority nations in Africa and Asia to do likewise, but a chief ally of Western nations, Saudi Arabia, practices a form of Islam that Sufis consider their principal ideological adversary. Rather than alienate a crucial ally, Western nations have attempted to ensnare Sufis in the politics of governments that are targeted by extremist organizations, and as a consequence, Sufi shrines and historic sites in Syria, Iraq, Mali and elsewhere have been destroyed (Muedini 2015).

Sufism, while decidedly older, is not the only indigenous Muslim religious tradition in Morocco. The rise of militant Islam in Morocco should be considered within the broader historical context of political and cultural resistance that has developed in certain areas over time (Pargeter 2009). Salafism has been a part of the Moroccan religious scene since the late nineteenth and early twentieth century and resulted in a convergence of Eastern Arab trends imported and reinterpreted within the Moroccan context with Moroccan reform movements. The most important feature of this religious reformist movement in Morocco was, at first, a strong critique of the Sufi practice of worshipping at the shrines of saints. Morocco's native Salafi movement was appropriated by Moroccan nationalism as a driving force in the Moroccan struggle for independence from French colonial rule.

Morocco's native Salafism is thus not the attraction for extremists in the country today. To the extent that extremism has taken hold in Morocco, its appeal has followed the pattern seen in many other countries. Young people whose families moved into the cities in recent decades and who have low education levels see Morocco's urban Westernized economy as promulgating a lifestyle that they cannot afford (Runciman 1966). In addition, there is the powerlessness that comes with the widely held perception in Morocco that the country's polity and economy are still firmly in the grip of the same small elite who make up the core of the makhzen (powers). It is true that rapid urbanization has created shanty towns that are neither part of the old society nor integrated into the new one and people living in them are attracted to a discourse that promotes personal piety, one of the few factors that is within the control of the poor people living in these limbo settlements. Because they reject the West, and what they see as the selective and opportunistic manner in which Europe and the United States apply democratic principles, these disaffected individuals are easily influenced by promises of a better life based upon their religious traditions. Further, their outrage is also based upon a belief that is specific to North Africa, which is the fear of takeover by Europe, based upon the historic treatment of Algeria and Western support for dictators in Egypt and Tunisia (Clancy-Smith 2001).

Not surprisingly, given its history, there are clearly geographical influences on the development of extremism in Morocco centered on the less accessible (to the government) parts of the country. In Moroccan culture, there is a divide between the bled al-siba (land of dissidence), where inhabitants formerly refused to pay taxes to the central authority, and bled al-Mahkzen (land of government). The bled al-siba has always been the areas where the Amazigh live, such as the Moroccan Rif, which has been called "the heartland of global terrorism" because the plotters of the Madrid bombing seemed to have had links to the region. Tetouan and Tangier, the cities of the Rif, are thought to be bases for networks that send people to fight in the Middle East and the region has long been associated with rebellion, especially remembered for its fierce resistance to Spanish colonial forces (Jacinto 2016).

There is a deep resentment in the Rif against the monarchy in general. The residents of Tetouan have not forgotten that the former king, King Hassan, had called them savages after the army killed a number of people during bread riots in the city. Nor have they forgotten how the king razed a popular public square in the center of the city in order to extend his Tetouan palace, which he never used (Willis 2014). Morocco's leading designated terrorist group, the Moroccan Islamic Combatant Group (GICM), began in the Rif. The group was probably formed in the 1990s and is supposedly closely affiliated with Al Qaeda (Coolsaet 2005). While the GICM includes Amazigh members and flourished in some Amazigh areas, they are in no way considered as Berber movements and there is clear evidence that they did not persuade the local Amazigh population to support them. The arrest of many of the GICM's members in Tetouan was a major blow to the organization and was, no doubt, enabled by local informants (Stanford University 2012).

A wily politician, King Mohammed VI has managed to co-opt or thwart most of the social movements in his country at every turn. In 2011, the Amazigh movement won a very significant reform—official recognition of their language and culture in a new constitution. It followed months of Arab Spring-inspired protests by the 20 February Movement, a broad coalition in which Amazigh activists played a key role. This, of course, is not a resolution of their concerns, as many have pointed out that there are vestiges of discrimination against them everywhere, including in the highest levels of government. Prime Minister Abdelilah Benkirane, who took office in late 2011, made no secret of his views on the Amazigh movement. He has described the Imazighen as a "simple people who eat little and spend their time dancing and singing" and compared the letters of the Amazigh alphabet to Chinese. Nevertheless, the king is widely recognized as a supporter of Amazigh rights and was the first ruler to acknowledge the Amazigh element of the country's identity (Raymond 2014).

But with its current emphasis on being a model Muslim nation in the War on Terror, Morocco has neglected some of the concerns of its traditional Amazigh population. Although they have been chided by Morocco's Minister of Higher Education as fighting against the Arabic language and Islam, Amazigh activists have concentrated on their own cultural issues and avoided religious doctrine (Jabrane 2016). The last thing that the government of Morocco would want to encourage is making the Amazigh culture movement more religious given the Berber history of religious zealotry—even though it is some centuries back.

It is Morocco's unique and sometimes volatile mixture of Arab and Amazigh cultures, as represented by Al-Andalus, that has been a chief contribution to its prominence and stability among Middle Eastern and North African nations.

For Spain, Al-Andalus has simply become a foreign interlude evidenced by fascinating tourist sites that they are perfectly happy to maintain and promote. Spain has not been hit as hard by attacks from Islamic State or Al Qaeda as other countries in Europe but there has, nonetheless, been a stepped-up effort on the part of both aimed at "taking back" the Iberian Peninsula. A social media and public advertising campaign aimed at generating support for ISIS features images of famous Spanish landmarks and monuments emblazoned with Arabic slogans praising Islamic State. One of these images shows the medieval Islamic Aljafería Palace in the Spanish city of Zaragoza with the Islamic State flag photoshopped on top.

More surprising was Islamic State graffiti on a statue of Jesus in a Basque beach city (Tomlinson 2017). Ironically, the Basques themselves have spawned a group (the Euskadi Ta Askatasuna or ETA) that has carried out more violent attacks against targets in Spain than any groups tied to Islam so they can certainly tough out a propaganda campaign promoting other forms of extremism. Even more to the point, the Basque country was never Islamic. These poster campaigns are accompanied by videos in which the Islamic Caliphate vows to "liberate" Al-Andalus from non-Muslims. The video shows an ISIS member delivering a speech in Spanish which, in translation, says:

> I say to the entire world as a warning: We are living under the Islamic flag, the Islamic caliphate. We will die for it until we liberate those occupied lands ... and I declare: Spain is the land of our forefathers and we are going to take it back with the power of Allah.
>
> (Brandon 2015)

Part of this campaign has been spurred by the fact that Spain and Portugal, in recognition of their roles in the tragic history of Jews in the Iberian Peninsula, have offered Sephardic Jews a right to return as of 2014. Groups that had set their sights on recapturing Spain did not fail to notice. They demanded a similar right for Muslims—an action that would plainly bring many more Muslims than Jews into the region. "Persecution of Jews was just that, while what happened with the Arabs was part of a conflict," according to one Portuguese lawmaker who sponsored the bill. Spanish officials did not hesitate to remind Muslims that they had come to the Peninsula as conquerors who subjugated the native populations, while Jews had lived peacefully in Iberia for centuries before Christianity arrived.

The Muslim groups have not seen this distinction and claim that they were forced to convert to Christianity and expelled from areas conquered by Christians just as Jews had been. In fact, Muslims were expelled from Spain and Portugal on a number of occasions—even those who had converted to Catholicism were not immune. In the sixteenth and seventeenth centuries, Christian rulers, suspicious of the converts and, convinced that they would rise up to take back lands that were once Muslim, forced them out. Most of them came to Morocco—and left their mark on the Kasbah of the Oudayas in

Rabat as noted previously. One Spanish journalist descendant of Muslim converts expressed his complete outrage over the decision not to allow a "right of return" to Muslims:

> [The] decision to grant Spanish citizenship to the grandchildren of the Hebrews in Spain in the fifteenth and sixteenth centuries, while ignoring the Moriscos, the grandsons of the Muslims, is without doubt, flagrant segregation and unquestionable discrimination, as both communities suffered equally in Spain at that time. The decision could also be considered by the international community to be an historic act of absolute immorality and injustice…[t]his decision is absolutely disgraceful and dishonorable.
>
> (Arbaoui 2014)

The writer then asked, "[i]s Spain aware of what might be assumed when it makes peace with some and not with others? Is Spain aware of what this decision could cost? Has Spain considered that it could jeopardize the massive investments that Muslims have made on its territory?" (Arbaoui 2014). In the meantime, those cities that caused so much bad feeling between Spain and Morocco in 2004, Ceuta and Melilla, are now functioning as a conduit to Europe for Muslims that want to see a Muslim Al-Andalus become a reality— from neighboring North African countries from which people can officially enter Europe without ever having to cross a body of water.

Al-Andalus seems perpetually doomed to exist as conflicting religious and cultural visions—Muslim versus Christian, Jewish versus Muslim, Christian versus Jewish, Berber versus Arab, tolerant versus intolerant and, most significantly, East versus West. Historically, the Arab state that was a model of cosmopolitanism and the Berber state that was the picture of militant provincialism, were, in the first instance, a place and time of worldly sophistication and, in the second instance, a powerful Muslim state that triumphed over the West. It seems disingenuous to say, but these two visions actually coexisted throughout the period and, if we look more closely, we will find that the seemingly fanatical Almohads were an integral part of both. So it is not awkward to consider the Almohad history, to be, at its height, romantically emplotted.

Founded by a reformer from the mountains who had the courage of his convictions and the ability to establish a kingdom and organize an insuperable military, the Almohad dynasty maintained its core principles better than any other Andalusian power. The roots of romance itself can be found in European encounters with Islam, both peaceful and confrontational. The Almohads, representing as they did a decided break with previous traditions, provided much of the drama in those encounters. They were, most of all, rulers who were part of the land they governed. In that sense, they were rooted extremists who had grown up under the thumb of their increasingly decadent and corrupted urban lowland cousins and who sought to overthrow them and establish a true Islamic state based not on law but on belief—and for all that, their cultural milieu inspired some of the greatest Islamic scholars ever known.

If not for the Almohads, European culture would be quite different today. Ibn Rushd (known in European literature as Averroes) was a valued member of the Almohad Caliph's court and was protected by its ruler from the fundamentalist Muslim clerics of the time, among them Ibn Ghazali, whose fear-filled verse began this chapter. A proponent of Aristotelian philosophy, which was considered heretical, Ibn Rushd was largely responsible for the acceptance and popularity of Aristotle among later European scholars, who translated Averroes work on Aristotle into Latin. The eminent historian Ibn Khaldun emigrated to the Moroccan city of Fez during the final years of the Almohad/Hafsid Kingdom. Ultimately, it was his close association with, and understanding of, the Almohads that had the greatest impact on the development of his historical theories. Ibn Khaldun, like Ibn Rushd, found both welcome and support from Almohad rulers.

Further, the religion of all the Abrahamic faiths would have also been quite different without the Almohads. The message of God's incorporeality that they purveyed resonated throughout the medieval world. There is much evidence that even Maimonides, who was forced to flee from the Almohad lands, was strongly influenced by their religious teachings while he was living and working among them (Fraenkel 2010). Further, their mystical inclinations and emphasis upon faith in the oneness of god made Almohad Al-Andalus a conducive atmosphere for the message of Sufism. Muhyyeddin Ibn Arabi, another renowned thinker supported by the Almohads, is still acknowledged as a great master and even a saint of the Sufi tradition. Growing up as the son of a military advisor to the second Almohad Caliph, Ibn Arabi became a mystic, philosopher, poet and sage, and is regarded as one of the world's great spiritual teachers.

Ibn Arabi's works indicate that he had developed his own interpretation of the core beliefs of his masters. His mystical vision of God was accepting of the idea that each person has a unique path to the truth, which unites all paths. He believed in the unity of all religions having said that "[t]here is no knowledge except that taken from God, for He alone is the Knower... the prophets, in spite of their great number and the long periods of time which separate them, had no disagreement in knowledge of God, since they took it from God" (Chittick 2014: 169).

Accordingly, although he was closely linked with what was supposed to have been one of the most fanatical and violent regimes in Andalusian history, his poems are messages of love, peace, the healing beauty of nature and, in many ways, perfectly encapsulate the different sides of Al-Andalus that he experienced during his life and tried to reconcile:

> My heart has become capable of every form: it is a pasture for gazelles and a convent for Christian monks,
>   And a temple for idols, and the pilgrim's Ka'ba, and the tables of the Tora and the book of the Koran.

I follow the religion of Love, whichever way his camels take. My religion and my faith is the true religion.

(Muhyyeddin Ibn Arabi as quoted
in Said 2009: 182)

Bibliography

Abend, L. 2007. Spain, Morocco Tensions Rising. *Time*, November 6, 2007.

Ahmed, A. 2017. What Andalusia Can Teach Us Today About Muslims and Non-Muslims Living Together. *Huffington Post*. Retrieved from: www.huffingtonpost.com/akbar-ahmed/andalusia-muslims-non-muslims-living_b_7088320.html.

Alfonso, E. 2007. *Islamic Culture Through Jewish Eyes: Al-Andalus From the Tenth to Twelfth Century*. New York: Routledge.

Arbaoui, L. 2014. Descendants of Moorish Muslims Demand the Right of Return to Spain. *Morocco World News,* February 23, 2014. Retrieved from: www.moroccoworldnews.com/2014/02/123374/descendants-of-moorish-muslims-demand-the-right-of-return-to-spain/.

Bargach, J. 2008. Rabat: From Capital to Global Metropolis in *The Evolving Arab City: Tradition, Modernity and Urban Development* (Y. Elsheshtawy, ed.), pp. 99–116. London: Routledge.

Bennison, A. 2016. *The Almoravid and Almohad Empires*. Edinburgh: Edinburgh University Press.

Bennison, A. and M. Gallego. 2007. Jewish Trading in Fes on the Eve of the Almohad Conquest. *Miscellanea de Estudios Arabes y Hebraicos, Sección Hebreo* 56: 33–51.

Boone, J. and N. Benco. 1999. Islamic Settlement in North Africa and the Iberian Peninsula. *Annual Reviews in Anthropology* 28:51–71.

Boone, J., J. Myers and C. Redman 1990. Archeological and Historical Approaches to Complex Societies: The Islamic States of Medieval Morocco. *American Anthropologist* 92/3: 630–646.

Bouasria, A. 2015. *Sufism and Politics in Morocco: Activism and Dissent.* London: Routledge.

Brandon, J. 2015. Spanish Islamic State Arrests Illustrate Continuing Recruitment. Jamestown Foundation, April 17, 2015. Retrieved from: www.refworld.org/docid/5538aecd4.html.

Bridgman, R. 2009. Contextualising Pottery Production in Al-Andalus during the Almohad Period: Implications for Understanding Economy in *Atti del IX CongressoInternazionalesulla Ceramica Medievalenel Mediterraneo Venezia, Scuola Grande dei Carmini Auditorium Santa Margherita* (S. Galici, ed.), pp. 95–100, November 23–27, 2009.

Buresi, P. and H. El Aallaoui. 2012. *Governing the Empire: Provincial Administration in the Almohad Caliphate (1224–1269)*. Trans. by T. Bruce. Leiden: Brill.

Chittick, W. 2014. *The Sufi Path of Knowledge: Ibn al-Arabi's Metaphysics of Imagination.* Albany, NY: State University of New York Press.

Clancy-Smith, J. 2001. *North Africa, Islam and the Mediterranean World: From the Almoravids to the Algerian War.* London: Routledge.

Collins, R. 1999. *The Arab Conquest of Spain*, 710–797. London: Blackwell.

Coolsaet, R. 2005. *Between Al-Andalus and a Failing Integration: Europe's Pursuit of a Long-Term Terrorism Strategy in the Post Al Qaeda Era.* Brussels: Royal Institute for International Relations.

Daadaoui, M. 2011. *Moroccan Monarchy and the Islamist Challenge: Maintaining Makhzen Power.* New York: Palgrave MacMillan.

Daadaoui, M. 2017. Book Review of "Young Islam: The New Politics of Religion in Morocco and the Arab world." *Cambridge Review of International Affairs*. Retrieved from: http://dx.doi.org/10.1080/09557571.2016.1271187.

Dabiq. 2012. Issue 2. Islamic State. Retrieved from: https://clarionproject.org/docs/isis-isil-islamic-state-magazine-Issue-2-the-flood.pdf.

Decter, J. 2007. *Iberian Jewish Literature: Between al-Andalus and Christian Europe*. Bloomington, IN: University of Indiana Press.

Ennaji, M. 2005. *Multilingualism, Cultural Identity, and Education in Morocco*. New York: Springer Books.

Fancy, H. 2013. The Last Almohads: Universal Sovereignty between North Africa and the Crown of Aragon. *Medieval Encounters* 19/1-2: 102–136.

Fanjul, S. 2004. *Al-Andalus contra España: la forja del mito [Al-Andalus Against Spain. The Forge of Myth]*. Madrid: Siglo XXI.

Fanjul, S. 2009. Uses of a Myth: Al-Andalus. *Studies in 20th and 21st Century Literature* 33/1: 1–21.

Fraenkel, C. 2010. Legislating Truth: Maimonides, the Almohads, and the Thirteenth Century Jewish Enlightenment in *Studies in the History of Culture and Science: A Tribute to Gad Freudenthal* (G. Veltri, ed.), pp. 209–232. Leiden: Brill.

Fromherz, A. 2010. *The Almohads: The Rise of An Islamic Empire*. London and New York: I.B. Tauris.

Geertz, C. 1971. *Islam Observed: Religious Development in Morocco and Indonesia*. Chicago, IL: University of Chicago Press.

Gomez-Rivas, C. 2015. *Law and the Islamization of Morocco under the Almoravids*. Leiden: Brill.

Hathaway, J. 2005. The Mawza 'Exile at the Juncture of Zaydi and Ottoman Messianism. *Association for Jewish Studies Review* 29/1: 111–128.

Ilahiane, H. 2017. *A Historical Dictionary of the Berbers (Imazighen)*. Lanham, MD: Rowman and Littlefield.

Jabrane, E. 2016. Moroccan Minister of Higher Education Calls for Fighting "Amazigh Extremists." *Morocco World News*, January 17, 2016. Retrieved from: www.moroccoworldnews.com/2016/01/177634/moroccan-minister-of-higher-education-calls-for-fighting-amazigh-extremists/.

Jones, L. 2013. The Preaching of the Almohads: Loyalty and Resistance across the Strait of Gibraltar. *Medieval Encounters* 19: 71–101.

Kennedy, H. 2016. *Caliphate: The History of an Idea*. New York: Basic Books.

Laroui, A. 1977. *The History of the Maghrib: An Interpretive Essay*. Trans. by R. Manheim. Princeton, NJ: Princeton University Press.

Lightfoot, D. and J. Miller. 1996. Sijilmassa: The Rise and Fall of a Walled Oasis in Medieval Morocco. *Annals of the Association of American Geographers* 86/1: 78–101.

Louayene, A. 2011. Pathologies of Moorishness: Al-Andalus, Narrative, and Worldly Humanism. *Journal of East-West Thought* 1/3: 31–44.

Maṭālsī, M. 2000. *The Imperial Cities of Morocco*. Paris: Terrail.

Menocal, M. 2002. *Ornament of the World: How Muslims, Jews, and Christians Created a Culture of Tolerance in Medieval Spain*. Boston, MA: Back Bay Books.

Messier, R. 2010. *The Almoravids and the Meanings of Jihad*. Santa Barbara, CA: Praeger.

Messier, R. and J. Miller. 2015. *The Last Civilized Place*. Austin, TX: University of Texas Press.

Muedini, F. 2015. *Sponsoring Sufism: How Governments Promote "Mystical Islam" in Their Domestic and Foreign Policies*. Evanston, IL: Northwestern University Press.

Munson, H. 1993. *Religion and Power in Morocco*. New Haven, CT: Yale University Press.

Pargeter, A. 2009. Localism and Radicalization in North Africa: Local Factors and the Development of Political Islam in Morocco, Tunisia and Libya. *International Affairs* 85/5: 1031–1044.

Peyron, M. 1995. Middle Atlas Berber Poetry. *The Alpine Journal* 10/344: 96–99.

Raymond, P. 2014. Morocco's Berbers Urge Broader Reforms. *Al-Jazeera English,* May 6, 2014. Retrieved from: www.aljazeera.com/indepth/features/2014/03/moroccos-berbers-urge-broader-reforms-2014357321228806.html.

Rubies, J. 2017. *Medieval Ethnographies: European Perceptions of the World Beyond*. London: Routledge.

Ruggles, D. 1993. Arabic Poetry and Architectural Memory in Al-Andalus. *Ars Orientalis* 23: 171–178.

Ruggles, D. 2004. Mothers of a Hybrid Dynasty: Race, Genealogy, and Acculturation in al-Andalus. *Journal of Medieval and Early Modern Studies* 34/1: 65–94.

Runciman, W. 1966. *Relative Deprivation and Social Justice: A Study of Attitudes to Social Inequality in Twentieth-Century England*. Oakland, CA: University of California Press.

Said, A. 2009. Educating for Global Citizenship: Perspectives from the Abrahamic Traditions in *The Meeting of Civilizations: Muslim, Christian, and Jewish* (M. Ma'oz, ed.), pp. 177–186. Eastbourne: Sussex Academic Press.

Sax, B. 2001. *The Mythical Zoo*. Oxford: ABC-CLIO.

Segalla, S. 2009. *Moroccan Soul: French Education, Colonial Ethnology, and Muslim Resistance, 1912–1956*. Lincoln, NE and London: University of Nebraska Press.

Stanford University. 2012. *Mapping Militant Organizations*. Moroccan Islamic Combatant Group. Retrieved from: http://web.stanford.edu/group/mappingmilitants/cgi-bin/groups/view/129.

Taieb-Carlen, S. 2010. *The Jews of North Africa: From Dido to De Gaulle*. Lanham, MD: University Press of America.

Tomlinson, S. 2017. We Will Recover Our Land From the Invaders: ISIS Issues Chilling Threat to Launch Terror Attacks in Spain to Reimpose Muslim Rule After 500 Years. *The Daily Mail*, May 20, 2017. Retrieved from: http://www.dailymail.co.uk/news/article-3412030/We-recover-land-invaders-ISIS-issues-chilling-threat-launch-terror-attacks-Spain-bid-expand-caliphate-Europe.html.

Wasserstein, D. 1995. Jewish Elites in Al-Andalus in *The Jews of Medieval Islam: Community, Society, and Identity* (D. Frank, ed.), pp. 101–110. Leiden: Brill.

Wharton, E. 1920. The Kasbah of the Oudayas. *In Morocco*. Republished online by the Literature Network. Retrieved from: www.online-literature.com/wharton/in-morocco/1/.

Willis, M. 2014. *Politics and Power in the Maghrib: Algeria, Tunisia and Morocco from Independence to the Arab Spring*. Oxford: Oxford University Press.

Zeghal, M. 2009. On the Politics of Sainthood: Resistance and Mimicry in Postcolonial Morocco. *Critical Inquiry* 35/3: 587–610.

Epilogue
"Those who do not remember history are condemned to retweet it"[1]

> My father left me some money (as a good father will) and I multiplied it many, many times to over $10 billion … I am the BEST builder, just look at what I've built. I am a great builder—I build great things and people come.
>
> (Trump 2016)

> When I was young, although the son of a nobody … Nabopolassar, King of Babylon, who pleases Nabu and Marduk, I, built for Imgur-Enlil—Babylon's great fortification wall; the original boundary-marker from antiquity; the solid border as ancient as time itself; the lofty mountain peak that rivals the heavens; the mighty shield that locks the entrance to the hostile lands … I had them use the hoe and imposed the basket of conscription on them. I moved its accumulated debris, surveyed and examined its old foundations, and laid its brickwork in the original place.
>
> (Al-Rawi 1985, trans. Nabopolassar Cylinder ca. 626 BCE)

The boast was a figure of speech that seems to have been absent for the most part from modern American politics. Nevertheless, when I first began to read statements on Twitter like those reproduced at the beginning of this chapter, I was immediately struck by their familiarity. It is a literary genre that is a standard feature of Ancient Near Eastern imperial inscriptions. As Liverani has pointed out:

> The exercise of comparing the boasts of ancient royal inscriptions with modern political speeches of Near Eastern countries has been carried out from time to time and quite recently as well. Another exercise could also be attempted, namely, comparing them with the speeches of our own modern Western countries; the result could be a surprise for many people.
>
> (Liverani 1996: 288)

As this book, hopefully, has demonstrated, I am (like Liverani) interested in these reverberations of the ancient past in the political present.

Sargon's description of his birth, Nabopolassar's declaration that "[the gods] made everything I did succeed" (Nabopolassar Cylinder ca. 626 BCE) and Hammurabi's avowal that "I am the wise ruler who bears the responsibility of government," have their twenty-first century incarnations in 140-character declarations that "my father Fred Trump left me a relatively small amount of money but vast amount of knowledge" and "the smart guy is what this country needs." The sense of Esarhaddon's declaration that "I am powerful. I am a hero, I am gigantic, I am colossal, I am honored, I am magnified, I am without an equal among all kings" is conveyed in a series of (only slightly subtler) assertions that "I am the only one who can fix this ... I am the strongest on economic issues by far! ... I am attracting the biggest crowds, by far ... I am the only one that knows how to build cities" (Trump 2016).

When I realized that, immediately after the election, millennials like those in my classroom were dazed and confused, I began to think that a "rooted" resistance narrative was forming in my own country—and much of it was in reaction to the belligerent online presence of a seemingly unhinged baby boomer. None of this odd behavior on the part of this president, positioned at the head of one of the most powerful nations on earth, would have struck anyone in the Ancient Near East as madness. There was certainly a great deal of insanity in the royal houses and ruling parties of the empires discussed in this book but censure from the population was usually reserved for those who engaged in the wanton murder of their close relatives or engaged in religious persecution. Braggadocio was not just excused—it was expected.

It was the fairly low-key demeanor of Trump's predecessor that paved the way for liberal shock and awe at the fact that this kind of behavior could be awarded with a high office. As Obama was clearly America's first cosmopolitan leader, young people who came of age during his administration might be excused for believing that the world was expanding and global problems were at the forefront of our concerns. Commenting on an early international trip by then President Obama, one writer exulted:

> He signaled what makes us wonderful without declaring that we're wonderful. Leaving business moguls and Americanists at home, he relied on an entourage of ideas ... Philosopher-prez in chief and cosmopolitan in chief. After all this time, you figure, we were entitled to one. It looks as if we've got him.
>
> (Romano 2009)

Then again, for every Marcus Aurelius, there is a Commodus waiting in the wings.

President Trump has a philosophy of sorts—one that I recognized immediately as (to my chagrin) akin to mine. It occurred to me, as well as to others, early in his campaign that Donald Trump could be the first postmodern President of the United States. All of my acceptance of alternative ideas, the death of objectivity and the demise of facts came to life in the person of a white male with dubious morals and a free-wheeling idea of what constitutes "truth." Certainly, Trump would be highly unlikely to believe that he is either post or pre-modern. He, doubtless, sees himself as the ultimate devotee of modernism—a believer in all things new and shiny. A profligate builder who is constantly moving on from success, from failure, from bankruptcy, from creditors, from businesses, from wives, from television and, now, from reality.

He may very well qualify as a modernist in his business life but, as a leader, his actions speak to a wholesale denunciation of rationality and a rejection of the grand narratives that have controlled American politics for generations. The belief in the benefits of being an immigrant nation, the idea that a wealthy country such as the United States has a responsibility to help poorer nations and the concept of the nation as a leader on the world stage have all fallen under the Trump onslaught of xenophobic braggadocio. Rashid Khalidi called former President's Bush's incursion into Iraq on several occasions "a faith-based, fact-free initiative." President Trump's own engagement with the Middle East has the "fact-free" down well enough but there can be no argument that his actions are not based upon faith, belief or philosophy. Rather, he is completely guided by a quality of leadership that is very ancient indeed—instinct.

Thus far in this volume, I have refrained from focusing much on individuals, except in the case of the Himyarites, whose story survives mostly as a result of later Muslim hagiographies of their rulers. It was, in part, the spirit of messianism inspired by the Himyarite stories that informed the resistance of the Huthis as a movement in Yemen today. Along with other peoples discussed here, their narratives have come down to us primarily as stories of a people and their rulers. It is a characteristic of these "rooted resistance narratives" that they are not dependent on the idea of a "savior" like Salahadin, the Kurd who has, strangely, taken a back seat to the little-known Medes in the narratives of the Kurdistan Worker's Party (PKK).

Western nations, whose resistance movements are long past, have made the mistake of assuming that they are dependent upon significant individuals. Therefore, their approach to countering violent extremism is based upon the belief that toppling charismatic leaders will naturally destroy the defiance of their supporters. The capacity of charismatic leaders to self-destruct is not to be underestimated and, with that in mind, we should accept that, regardless of how their leaders are removed, followers may simply carry on or elevate a new successor to assume the role. Leadership, whether charismatic or not, can easily become an ascribed status in many parts of the world. The millennia-old tradition of the warrior-ruler in Egypt, for example, has never been based upon the abilities of any one person and seemingly endures even without the skills of a Ramses the Great or a Gamal Abdel Nasser. The extravagant and over-indulgent ruler may or may not have his or her comeuppance but the extent to which such a reputation may be a source of pride is seldom considered as merely skimming Donald Trump's archive of supporter tweets suggests. Nothing succeeds like excess—at least insofar as revolutionary leadership is concerned.

Conversely, nothing fails like success—at least insofar as bureaucratic leadership is concerned. As has been pointed out in the foregoing chapters, many Ancient Near Eastern kingdoms were established by insurgencies and there is little indication that the transition from extremist leader to bureaucratized leader was an easy one. Some were more effective than others but there are spectacular catastrophes that stand out—the religious insurgencies of Akhenaten and Nabonidus, the political insurgencies of Bar Kokhba and Absalom and the economic insurgency of Judas of Galilee and his zealots. Like these resistors and others described in the previous chapters, some of the new American President's followers have been forming their own extremist narratives even though there is very little indication that Trump shares their (or any) ideology. Once insurgencies become official, leaders often develop a fear of the very outrage that propelled them into their positions and may readily betray their supporters in favor of stability.

Beyond the dangers of becoming what one had convinced one's own supporters to detest, there are other inherent dangers in store for those resistors who want to stay in their positions and who are not attentive to the lessons of history. One of the first issues that sovereigns who have bitterly fought their way to the throne encounter is the question of succession. Most such individuals want to place their children in a position to inherit their power regardless of whether such a practice is acceptable to their followers.

The Biblical succession narratives of the House of David show the dangers of over-dependence on one's progeny to successfully wield power. When King David grew old, according to this account, his eldest living son Adonijah made a play to take over the throne in his father's lifetime. A rival faction, consisting of the prophet Nathan, the priest Zadok and the leader of the royal guard, put Bathsheba's son forward. Through some stroke of luck for Solomon, David's other sons, Absalom and Amnon, had thoughtfully disqualified themselves by engaging in violent and unlawful behavior some years before. Solomon ascended to the throne and became a wise and celebrated ruler, as the Judahite Biblical historian tells us, whose kingdom upon his death fell apart due to the idiocy of his son and heir Rehoboam (Halbertal and Holmes 2017).

Over and above false promises, true double dealing with one's followers can be a dangerous thing. The first King of the Medes, Deioces, has many stories associated with him not the least of which was spun by the archetypal collector of oral traditions in the Near East, Herodotus (see also Chapter 3, this volume). Deioces plotted to gain ultimate power over the egalitarian Medes, who, at that time, were living in separated small cities and villages. He first established a reputation as an impartial judge in his own territory that spread to other townships. This was a time of chaos in Media and Deioces quickly became the law and order candidate for high office by refusing to continue in his much-vaunted role of dispensing justice until lawlessness reigned anew—even worse than before, so that the Medes assembled and at last resolved to elect him as their new king. When the ruse was discovered, his popularity quickly waned and he was forced to hide behind a series of strong walls within which he stayed, surrounded by bodyguards, receiving the reports of his "watchers and listeners." All of this was the "official narrative" of Deioces reign and, as such, is accepted by no historians of the ancient world today.

This story is possibly based on a true one involving one Daiukku who lived under the Assyrian Empire as a Mannean provincial governor. Unlike Deioces, his story demonstrates another issue with insurgent leadership—blatant nepotism. Those who achieve office by deceptions and false promises often feel uncomfortable with trusting anyone who is not a blood relative. Daiukku had put his son forward as his official representative when he was clearly not prepared to take office. He was taken hostage by the Urartians in order to extort the support of Daiukku in the Urartian battle against his own overlord. The Assyrian Emperor intervened on behalf of his vassal, captured Daiukku, and exiled him with his entire family to Syria.

The obvious thing that these stories have in common is that they represent "the morning after" in terms of what happened to the more extremist leaders of the Gutians, the Medes, the Israelites, the Himyarites and Berber Al-Andalus. The exceptions among the groups examined in this volume are the Philistines and the Bedouin—both in some ways "mobile" societies that attempted to adjust to being surrounded by sedentary people with an alien culture. What made the Philistines different was their acceptance of mercantilism as a means to maintain power rather than violence, a strategy that for decades was adopted by Palestinians. What made the Bedouin different was their insistence on maintaining autonomy and independence at all costs. This has succeeded in helping them to maintain their traditions but has also exposed them to the antagonism of empires and nation-states—and accusations of terrorism.

The pursuit of happiness through democracy has limited appeal, especially when it fails to move the social or economic needle very much for the disenfranchised. This may be why the default solution to Middle East intra-state conflicts is establishing a new state. This has been proposed, seriously, for Palestinians and Berbers and disingenuously for Israeli settlers, and it has been achieved to some degree by the Kurds and the Huthis. The Bedouin by all accounts do not seem to want a state—either their own or anyone else's and their wisdom in this is undervalued. While a new autonomous homogeneous state may be attractive to those who believe that they have suffered much at the hands of those in power, the prospect of governance once it is achieved, discourages and disappoints. The populist Trump uprising sailed him into office but once he took the helm, he began to complain that the job was much harder than he thought. The New Yorkism "who knew…?" has cropped up in his conversation on multiple occasions. Most Washington media types scoffed at this wondering "what the hell did he expect?" but the new president has a point. He wanted to be a leader not a governor. Leaders are accountable to their followers but governors are accountable to everyone within their sphere of governance—and to institutions as well.

When events moved quickly in the ancient world, it was more likely to do so in the palace, out of view of the citizenry, with periods in which brothers and associates assassinated monarchs on a regular basis in Assyria, Israel,

Judea and Egypt. The average citizens of these empires were scarcely aware of changes unless the monarch was determined to rouse them from their stupor by committing sacrilege, executing the wrong people or raising taxes. There were always those on the fringes of these societies that were willing to take advantage of these situations—Gutians, Medes, frontier people, nomads and harbingers of new religions. The Grand Narratives of Ancient Near Eastern history in fact depended upon these people whether or not they came to rule a kingdom or empire.

Their modern-day avatars, Kurds, Bedouin, Palestinians, militant settlers, Huthis and Berbers, have already created their own collective grand narrative that Western powers have denigrated as terrorist. The hope embedded in every Western counter-terrorism strategy is that, eventually, extremist groups can eventually be persuaded or pushed toward moderation but this very much depends on what, in fact, drove them to immoderation. Is extremism in defense of one's culture, religion or land a virtue? Perhaps it would not be to Barry Goldwater, whose idea of liberty was freedom from taxation and regulation. The medieval philosopher John of Salisbury characterized the practice of living a free person's way of life, as defined by the particulars of their culture, as the habitus of liberty. In his view, this consists of rights that the government has no moral authority to give or take away and any attempts to do so could justify violent resistance (Nederman 1988). The concept in Islamic thought of opposition to unjust rule, stemming from the belief that a tyrant is in opposition to God's perfect will, posits a similar precept (van Gorder 2014).

Thus, it is hard not to conclude that the narratives of extremism that build and sustain resistance movements are necessary—and that these movements, themselves, are, in fact, essential for the moral evolution of humanity. On a global level, extremism is the painful punctuation in our equilibrium—it exposes the unraveling seams of corrupt government and the underbelly of liberal democracy. It is extremism that has laid bare the fact that no empire of the ancient world treated its subjects with fairness and that continues to remind us that no modern nation has consistently excelled in its dealings with its minorities within or weaker nations without.

But the anguish inflicted by extremists on individuals is not to be dismissed so easily. There really isn't a good answer to the question posed by Voltaire, "What can be said to a man who says he will rather obey God than men, and who consequently feels certain of meriting heaven by cutting your throat?" (Voltaire, trans. Fleming 1901: 18). Such a man is not to be reasoned with, either by propagating an insipid counter-narrative, threatening drone attacks and big bombs or excessive border control. Passion will always find a way—and rulers will continue to fall into the trap set for those whose concern for their popularity exceeds their interest in governing and who feel it necessary to obliterate bitter memories of the past. "Be it thy course to busy giddy minds with foreign quarrels; that action, hence borne out, may waste the memory of the former days" is advice that Donald Trump will, no doubt, take to heart—as did Shalmaneser III whose commemorative obelisk reads "[a]t the beginning

of my reign, when I solemnly took my seat upon the royal throne, I mobi-
lized my chariots and troops; I entered the passes of the land of Simesi [the
Zagros and Taurus Mountains]; I captured Aridu, the stronghold of Ninni"
(Luckenbill 1926: 200).

Regardless of elite fears about populism, we should be grateful that in many
countries, there is a regular system of turning over regimes when citizens tire of
them. This is an idea that Western nations have been exporting to the developing world for many years and they were finally successful in reaching young
people in the Middle East. Rather suddenly, they began to realize that they
were "mad as hell and not going to take it anymore," to paraphrase the words
of the insane Howard Beale in the 1970s movie *Network*. Unfortunately, it got
them just about as far as it did Howard. The collective impatience of young
people during the Arab Spring brought down governments and clamored for
the installation of new ones—resulting only in leadership that was just as bad,
if not worse, than what they had experienced before.

The nation-state, a not particularly commendable product of the late nineteenth century that the West "sold" to the Middle East after the First World
War, has hit the same wall of irony that contributed to its creation. As a structure in "which falsehood is presented as the truth" (White 1973: 10), irony
supports the emplotment of satire, which "[l]ike philosophy itself paints its
'gray on gray' in the awareness of its own inadequacy as an image of reality.
It therefore prepares consciousness for its repudiation of all sophisticated con-
ceptualizations of the world." Irony also does not enable cultures to cope with
the existential "terror" instilled by its inherent futility (Moses 2005). Irony and
satire often characterize what the well-known Chinese curse would designate
as "interesting times," which may account for the fact that more people in
Western nations are now living in fear than they have at any time since the end
of the Second World War.

Before White took on what became the defining project of his life, he wrote
that we "require a history that will educate us to discontinuity more than ever
before; for discontinuity, disruption, and chaos is our lot" (White 1966: 134).
Whether this was more reflective of his permanent views or the times in which
he was living is difficult to say—perhaps he would say that history is a combination of both. One theme has become increasing clear, however, and that is
as Western liberal democracies increasingly abandon their core narratives, they
become more inured to political mythmaking, demagoguery and "alternative
facts." This may become the way in which our past is characterized or it may
be a mere episode in what will be our *longue duree*. To examine the question
of what the future will make of our past, I ask my students to go through the
exercise of looking at what the archaeology of the future could determine
about their values and beliefs from the material culture in the places where
they live and work.

Most of them, of course, live for the better part of the year in temporary spaces
surrounded by various combinations of pop culture and higher education—posters of contemporary people, places or movements side by side with textbooks

on economics, business, information technology and, increasingly rarely these days, literature, history and philosophy. But they choose instead to describe the homes where they grew up and the various religious objects (representing beliefs that many of them no longer have), the furniture or decor that represents their parents (or their grandparents) country of origin or the souvenirs picked up from travels. It never fails that everyone in my classes report having at least one parent or grandparent who was an immigrant and they describe their homes as being in suburban middle-class neighborhoods, but there are always a few urbanites in the group. The cultural remnants they describe clearly imply that they are what Will Durant would describe as people on "the banks" (page 29, this volume).

Yet, despite many efforts to turn archaeology into a postmortem examination of normal lives, there is little doubt that if the field is still with us several hundred years from now, we will continue to be distracted by the fast-moving stream. The texts of our time, the elaborate residences of the wealthy, the excess, the power, the inequality and the egotism will speak loudest. American artifacts and sites will be compared to the archaeological record of Western Europe if that is still considered to be our "cultural complex" and the United States will be judged as morally lacking. I have every expectation that morality will continue to be a basis upon which civilization will be assessed because, cultural relativism aside, there is a universal morality that governs the balance in human nature between self-interest and the group interest that is necessary to maintain life on the planet.

If modern Western history can be characterized as ironically structured and satirically emplotted, we may be seeing a harbinger of what traditional historians liked to characterize as "decline" or "collapse." I often follow up my question about what my students believe to be their most identifying artifacts with a query as to what they thought violent upheaval would do to their material culture. Most of them are at a loss as to how to do this despite the fact that they are confronted daily with images of the effects of civil war and insurgency on other people's lives. They are unfamiliar with the discourse of revolution so prevalent in the 1960s and have yet to be affected by the violent reactionary ideology now sweeping the United States and Europe. I have a problem in understanding why they, my daughter's generation, do not feel oppressed by their seemingly gloomy prospects but it is becoming increasingly clear that the defining conflicts of our time are covertly planned, sporadically implemented and not affected by alliances or disaffections between governments. This is not a world in which resistance and consciousness of injustice will effect change. It is not to be wondered at that the earnest tragic and romantic emplotments of "extremist narratives" pose a great threat to this world because, in spite of the violence of their means, those who believe in these narratives also believe in the pursuit of good triumphing over evil, while the governments they live under do not.

The Romantic poets were, not surprisingly, taken with the idea of overthrowing oppression, particularly in their beloved Greece, the source of all art and wisdom as they perceived it. Shelley was no different in this respect, but he also displayed a great interest in the orient—the setting for much of his literary production. *Ozymandias*, purportedly written about a statue of Ramesses the Great, is one of the most famous poems ever written about the Ancient Near East. Shelley wrote it in 1818, while he was working assiduously to bring forth his lesser known 4,000-line epic called *The Revolt of Islam*, which could easily have been subtitled "An Orientalist fantasy" and speaks volumes about European ideas about the orient that unfortunately persist to this day. That the 14 lines that comprise *Ozymandias* would be, by far, the most memorable composition he produced that year would, almost certainly, have distressed him, but it is by far the better work (Haddad 2017).

Its obvious message is that even the great must pass away and their achievements come to ruin. It also suggests that the passion and arrogance that characterizes the ruler, both as it is stamped in stone and reverberates throughout history, survives any temporal accomplishments he might have had. Above all, I believe the poem is a narrative of a glorious past ostensibly told by a person whose history is represented by the ruin. Shelley might have seen only the ultimate irony of the inscription but, even as the fictitious Egyptian is telling the supercilious poet about this monument, the sun was beginning to set on the British Empire. Less than a century after *Ozymandias* was written, the British occupied Egypt and remained there for many decades—one of their last disastrous enterprises in the East. It took decades of sporadic bloody revolution to finally extract the Empire, only to replace imperial domination with local autocracy.

This is perhaps the oldest and most recurring narrative in Middle East history, both ancient and modern. In many ways representing both the romance and the tragedy of the narratives of insurgency, terror and empire in the region, *Ozymandias* is a fitting coda to these stories:

> I met a traveller from an antique land
> Who said: Two vast and trunkless legs of stone
> Stand in the desert. Near them, on the sand,
> Half sunk, a shattered visage lies, whose frown,
> And wrinkled lip, and sneer of cold command,
> Tell that its sculptor well those passions read
> Which yet survive, stamped on these lifeless things,
> The hand that mocked them and the heart that fed:
> And on the pedestal these words appear:
> 'My name is Ozymandias, king of kings:
> Look on my works, ye Mighty, and despair!'
> Nothing beside remains. Round the decay
> Of that colossal wreck, boundless and bare
> The lone and level sands stretch far away.

(Shelley 1993: 5)

Note

1   Brooks (2017).

Bibliography

Al-Rawi, F 1985. Nabopolassar's Restoration Work on the Wall Imgur-Enlil at Babylon. *Iraq* 47: 1–13.

Brooks, D. 2017. The Coming Incompetence Crisis. *The New York Times*, April 7, 2017. Retrieved from: www.nytimes.com/2017/04/07/opinion/the-coming-incompetence-crisis.html.

Haddad, E. 2017. *Orientalist Poetics: The Islamic Middle East in Nineteenth-Century.* London: Routledge.

Halbertal, M. and S. Holmes 2017. *The Beginning of Politics: Power in the Biblical Book of Samuel.* Princeton, NJ: Princeton University Press.

Khalidi, R. 2010. Under Obama "There Has Been No Real Change in the Fatally Flawed Policies of the U.S. in the Region." *Israel/Palestine Institute for Middle East Understanding*, April 22, 2010. Retrieved from: http://mondoweiss.net/2010/04/rashid-khalidi-under-obama-there-has-been-no-real-change-in-the-fatally-flawed-policies-of-the-u-s-in-the-region/#sthash.aK1MeNvy.dpuf.

Liverani, M. 1996. 2084: Ancient Propaganda and Historical Criticism in *Study of the Ancient Near East in the Twenty-First Century: The William Foxwell Albright Centennial Conference* (J. Cooper and G. Schwartz, eds.), pp. 283–289. Winona Lake IN: Eisenbrauns.

Luckenbill, D. 1926. *Ancient Records of Assyria and Babylonia.* Oriental Institute Chicago, IL: University of Chicago Press.

Moses, D. 2005. Hayden White, Traumatic Nationalism, and the Public Role of History. *History and Theory* 44/3: 311–332.

Nederman, C. 1988. A Duty to Kill: John of Salisbury's Theory of Tyrannicide. *The Review of Politics* 50/3: 365–389.

Rodenbeck, J. 2004. Travelers from an Antique Land: Shelley's Inspiration for "Ozymandias." *Alif: Journal of Comparative Poetics* 24: 121–148.

Romano, C. 2009. Obama, Philosopher in Chief. The Chronicle Review. *The Chronicle of Higher Education*, June 16, 2009. Retrieved from: www.chronicle.com/article/Obama-Philosopher-in-Chief/44524/.

Shelley, P. 1993. *Selected Poems.* New York: Dover Publications. (Originally published in 1905).

Trump, D. 2014–2016. Donald J Trump @realDonaldTrump. Retrieved from: www.trumptwitterarchive.com.

Van Gorder, A. 2014. *Islam, Peace and Social Justice: A Christian Perspective.* Cambridge: James Clarke and Co.

Voltaire. 1901. *The Works of Voltaire. A Contemporary Version.*,. critique and biography by John Morley, notes by Tobias Smollett, Trans. by W .F. Fleming. New York: E.R. DuMont.

White, H. 1966. The Burden of History. *History and Theory* 5/2: 111–134.

White, H. 1973. *Metahistory: The Historical Imagination in Nineteenth-Century Europe.* Baltimore, MD: Johns Hopkins University Press.

Index